A FORGOTTEN MIGRATION

**THE JOHN HOPE FRANKLIN SERIES
IN AFRICAN AMERICAN HISTORY AND CULTURE**

Waldo E. Martin Jr. and Patricia Sullivan, editors

A complete list of books published in the John Hope Franklin Series in African American History and Culture is available at https://uncpress.org/series/john-hope-franklin-series-african-american-history-culture.

A Forgotten Migration

BLACK SOUTHERNERS,

SEGREGATION SCHOLARSHIPS,

AND THE DEBT OWED

TO PUBLIC HBCUs

Crystal R. Sanders

The University of North Carolina Press

Chapel Hill

© 2024 The University of North Carolina Press
All rights reserved

Designed by April Leidig
Set in Garamond by Copperline Book Services

Manufactured in the United States of America

Cover art designed by Martyn Schmoll
using art generated by Adobe Firefly.

Library of Congress Cataloging-in-Publication Data
Names: Sanders, Crystal, author.
Title: A forgotten migration : Black southerners, segregation scholarships, and the debt owed to public HBCUs / Crystal R. Sanders.
Description: Chapel Hill : University of North Carolina Press, [2024] | Includes bibliographical references and index.
Identifiers: LCCN 2024021628 | ISBN 9781469679792 (cloth ; alk. paper) | ISBN 9781469679808 (paperback ; alk. paper) | ISBN 9781469679815 (epub) | ISBN 9781469679822 (pdf)
Subjects: LCSH: Segregation in higher education—Southern States—History—20th century. | Segregation in higher education—Government policy—Southern States. | African American graduate students—Scholarships, fellowships, etc.—Southern States. | Out-of-state students—Scholarships, fellowships, etc.—United States. | Historically Black colleges and universities—Finance—History—20th century. | Public universities and colleges—Southern States—Finance—History—20th century. | Racism against Black people—Southern States—History—20th century. | BISAC: HISTORY / African American & Black | LAW / Legal History
Classification: LCC LC212.722.S68 S36 2024 | DDC 378.3/408997073075—dc23/eng/20240619
LC record available at https://lccn.loc.gov/2024021628

*For Uwemedimo "Eazy" Umoumoh
and our children, Victoria and Alexander*

CONTENTS

List of Illustrations ix

Acknowledgments xi

Abbreviations xv

Introduction 1

CHAPTER ONE
A Gold Brick:
The Creation of Segregation
Scholarship Programs 17

CHAPTER TWO
Chipping Away at Segregation:
The First Legal Challenges to Desegregate
Graduate and Professional Schools 43

CHAPTER THREE
(In)adequate Compensation for Loss of Civil Rights:
Lloyd Gaines and the Constitutionality
of Segregation Scholarships 71

CHAPTER FOUR
Shall We Rejoice or Grieve?
Black Graduate Study at Public Black Colleges
in Tandem with Segregation Scholarships 101

CHAPTER FIVE
Don't Shout Too Soon:
The Ebbs and Flows of the Fight for
Educational Equality 127

Conclusion 167

Notes 179

Bibliography 209

Index 223

ILLUSTRATIONS

FIGURES

Missouri representative Walthall M. Moore 21

Thurgood Marshall, Donald Murray, and
Charles Hamilton Houston in court 58

Lincoln University School of Law 81

John W. Davis, president of West Virginia State College 89

Dr. Eliza Atkins Gleason 113

Willarena Lamar with classmates 133

Willarena Lamar and unidentified classmate on graduation day 133

Segregated bus terminal in Durham, North Carolina 144

Ada Sipuel with J. E. Fellows, Thurgood Marshall,
and Amos T. Hall 151

George McLaurin seated in the classroom vestibule 155

Gwendolyn Harrison's housing card 168

MAP

Southern and border states with segregation
scholarship programs 4

ACKNOWLEDGMENTS

In a show of support while I was completing this book, my husband would often jokingly ask, "How's *our* book coming along?" Even though I am the sole author of this project, I was only able to complete the herculean task of writing a monograph because of the support, encouragement, and assistance of many people named below. Thank you for answering my questions, for putting me in touch with individuals who had information relevant to the project, for letting me share my work, for providing childcare so that I was able to write, and for offering an encouraging word that helped me get to the finish line. In many ways, this is truly *our* book. It is not possible to convey the extent of my gratitude in words.

Historical work grounded in primary sources is not possible without the expertise and knowledge of dedicated archivists and librarians. Even during a pandemic, these resourceful individuals found ways to help scholars stay on track and access valuable materials. I am in debt to Sharon McGee at Kentucky State University, Andre Vann at North Carolina Central University, A'Llyn Ettien at Boston University Alumni Medical Library, Deborah Dandridge at the University of Kansas, Mark Schleer at Lincoln University of Missouri, Cheryl Ferguson at Tuskegee University, Deborah Hibbard at the Kentucky Department for Libraries and Archives, Edward Lomax at West Virginia State University, Alyssa Vaughn at the State Archives Division of the Oklahoma Department of Libraries, and the countless other unnamed library and archival staff who pulled materials, answered questions, and made helpful suggestions,

I would be remiss if I did not acknowledge the individuals who did not hesitate to speak with me about their experiences and stories of their parents. Thank you for returning my phone calls and talking with me for hours about Black commitment to education. A few people that I must call by name are Guion Bluford Jr., Fred D. Gray, Karen Lathen Sabur, Louis Sullivan, Serena Williams, and John L. Withers II. Thank you to those who answered my queries about their loved ones, including Isaac Farris Jr., Joy Gleason Carew, John Whittington Franklin, Jay Prestage, Vanessa Siddle Walker, and Angela Farris Watkins.

I am also grateful for the institutions that provided financial support, including Pennsylvania State University, Emory University, the University of Kansas, the National Academy of Education / Spencer Foundation, and the National Humanities Center. Through these institutions, I have been fortunate to collaborate with and learn from colleagues who have become friends. These individuals have never hesitated to show enthusiasm for the project. I am especially indebted to Carol Anderson, William A. Blair, Amira Rose Davis, Pearl Ford Dowe, Erica Frankenberg, Marla Frederick, Andra Gillespie, Amy Greenberg, Kali Gross, Tikia Hamilton, Maurice Hobson, Michael Kulikowski, Walter Rucker, Kathryn Salzer, Dianne Stewart, Ellen Stroud, Paul C. Taylor, and Nan Woodruff. I also extend gratitude to my editor, Debbie Gershenowitz, who believed in this project from the beginning, and to all of the other UNC Press staff who helped bring this book to fruition.

A great many fellow scholars did not count it robbery to make suggestions and share information, offer an encouraging word, or give me an opportunity to share my work. Among them are Derrick Aldridge, James Anderson, Kathlene Baldanza, Keisha Blain, Stefan M. Bradley, Brandi Brimmer, Alfred Brophy, Katherine Mellen Charron, Rachel Devlin, Erica Armstrong Dunbar, Reginald Ellis, Ansley Erickson, Marybeth Gasman, Jerry Gershenhorn, Jarvis Givens, Leah Gordon, Hilary Green, Ari Kelman, Lionel Kimble, Sheri Randolph, Melissa Stuckey, Carl Suddler, Keeanga-Yamahtta Taylor, Jeanne Theoharis, Cally Waite, and Khaliff Watkins. Thank you for your acts of kindness.

A large community of friends, including Reena Goldthree, Brandi Hinnant-Crawford, Marva Hinton Gibson, Kellie Carter Jackson, Irene Morvey, Ashley Patterson, Leah Wright Riguer, and Dominic Harris Vines, kept me sane with their phone calls and encouraging texts.

And last but certainly not least, I am thankful to my family for their love, encouragement, and support. Thank you to my parents-in-love, Uwemedimo and Eduwem Umoumoh, for cheering me on. Thank you especially to my mother-in-love for helping me with childcare. Thank you to Aunt Renée and Uncle Bill for always believing in me and showing up to support me. Thank you to my only sister and sibling, Natalie, for modeling academic excellence and being my first friend. Thank you to my parents, Nathaniel L. Sanders Jr. and Velvaline Sanders, for your limitless support. Thank you for ensuring that I had quality educational opportunities throughout my entire life. Mama, thank you for helping me navigate motherhood for the first time during a pandemic. To my husband, Eazy, there really are no words to express my appreciation for who you are and the ways you support me. Thank you for believing in *our* book and for doing whatever possible to see that I finished it. Thank you for being a true partner in the rearing of our children. You've made being a working and writing mother much easier. I dedicate this book to you and to our beautiful children. Victoria and Alexander, I will always love you, and I will always be in awe that I am your mother.

This book is also dedicated to the loving memory of my paternal grandmother, Ida Sanders, who taught me that no one could ever take from me what I put in my head. I stand on her shoulders and the shoulders of all striving African Americans I write about in the following pages.

ABBREVIATIONS

A&M	Agricultural and Mechanical
A&T	Agricultural and Technical
ABA	American Bar Association
AU	Atlanta University
BUSM	Boston University School of Medicine
HBCUs	Historically Black colleges and universities
HEW	US Department of Health, Education, and Welfare
IFCWC	Iowa Federation of Colored Women's Clubs
KNEA	Kentucky Negro Educational Association
KSC	Kentucky State College
KU	University of Kansas
LMC	Louisville Municipal College
MCG	Medical College of Georgia
NAACP	National Association for the Advancement of Colored People
NASA	National Aeronautics and Space Administration
NCC	North Carolina College for Negroes
NYU	New York University
OSU	Ohio State University
OU	University of Oklahoma
ROTC	Reserve Officers' Training Corps
SACS	Southern Association of Colleges and Schools
SREB	Southern Regional Education Board
UF	University of Florida
UGA	University of Georgia
UK	University of Kentucky
UL	University of Louisville
UNC	University of North Carolina at Chapel Hill
USAID	US Agency for International Development
USC	University of Southern California
UT	University of Texas
UVA	University of Virginia
WKIC	Western Kentucky Industrial College
WVSC	West Virginia State College
WVU	West Virginia University

A FORGOTTEN MIGRATION

Introduction

In July 2022, just days after Americans celebrated Independence Day, President Joseph Biden presented the Presidential Medal of Freedom to seventeen men and women for their selfless contributions to the United States and the world. Among the honorees was civil rights attorney Fred Gray. President Biden remarked, "When Dr. King, Rosa Parks, and Claudette Colvin, and John Lewis, and other giants of our history needed a lawyer for their fight for freedom, you know who they called? They called a guy named Fred Gray. That's who they called. One of the most important civil rights lawyers in our history, Fred's legal brilliance and strategy desegregated schools and secured the right to vote."[1]

While Fred Gray certainly played an integral role in some of the most important court battles in American history, segregation made obtaining legal training anything but easy for him. Gray was born in Montgomery, Alabama, the cradle of the Confederacy, in 1930. He wanted to attend law school after graduating from Alabama State College for Negroes in 1951, but there was one problem: Alabama did not have any law schools that admitted African Americans. The state's sole public law school, at the University of Alabama, admitted white students only. In fact, Alabama did not offer any in-state postbaccalaureate programs to African Americans.

To feign compliance with the legal doctrine of separate but equal, beginning in 1945, the state of Alabama paid for its Black residents to go out of state to pursue postbaccalaureate degree programs that were available in state to white residents. The state paid the difference between the tuition and housing costs at schools where Black Alabamians studied and those at the University of Alabama. There was a catch, however. The state's tuition assistance program operated on a reimbursement basis, so students had to come up with the financial resources for out-of-state study upfront and receive reimbursement later. With the support of family and friends, Gray secured the necessary funds and matriculated at Western Reserve University Law School (present-day Case Western University School of Law) in Cleveland, Ohio, where he studied from 1951 until

1954. Though he and his relatives paid taxes to support graduate and professional school programs at the University of Alabama, segregation compelled him to leave Alabama and study elsewhere.[2]

Recalling his decision to leave the state in pursuit of a legal career, Gray reminisced, "Privately, I pledged that I would return to Montgomery and use the law to destroy everything segregated that I could find. I kept my plans secret. I did not want anything to interfere with my going to law school."[3] After arriving in Cleveland on a segregated train, he kept thinking of Alabama, where he planned to practice law. Gray asked the law librarian to procure for him a copy of Title 7 of the Alabama Code, which was the section on pleadings and practice. He developed a methodical study plan to learn Alabama's statutes. As he later explained,

> Immediately after class, one of the other African American students and I would stop by the dining facility and have lunch. I would return to the house in the afternoon, review and type up my notes. I would ascertain for each point of law that we covered whether Alabama followed or departed from the same principle. If it differed, I found out what the Alabama rule was and committed it to memory. Then I would prepare for my next day's classes. As further preparation for returning to Alabama, whenever we had legal research papers, I would always do my paper on some facet of Alabama law.[4]

The study plan that Gray described is what this book calls *intellectual warfare*. Intellectual warfare during the era of legal segregation was the subversive act of acquiring knowledge to undermine and dismantle segregation. The very presence of African Americans pursuing advanced degrees in the most prestigious institutions in the world was an example of intellectual warfare. Not stopping there, African Americans used the knowledge obtained to challenge the racial status quo. Had Alabama admitted Black students to its law school, Gray would not have had to go out of his way to add Alabama laws to his law school curriculum. Segregation put him at a disadvantage, but he found ways to overcome the professional handicap. Gray would go on to be a nationally known attorney who used his knowledge of the law to overturn Black voter dilution and dismantle racial segregation in various arenas. He represented Rosa Parks when she refused to give up her seat on a Montgomery city bus. He also represented the men and their families involved in the infamous Tuskegee Syphilis Study and filed the lawsuits that integrated all state institutions of higher learning in Alabama and 104 of the then 121 elementary and secondary school systems in the state. Thus, by using the skills and knowledge he acquired with state aid to systematically disrupt racial discrimination in myriad forms, Gray practiced intellectual warfare.

Fred Gray was one of the thousands of Black southerners who took advantage of what I call "segregation scholarships" to pursue postbaccalaureate study in the North, Midwest, or West because their native state flagship institutions denied them admission on the basis of race. I refer to the funds these states appropriated for Black citizens' graduate and professional school training as "segregation scholarships" because the entire point of the tuition assistance was to preserve segregation. Missouri introduced the idea of appropriating money to send Black citizens out of state for graduate training in 1921 and finally allocated funds eight years later. In subsequent years, West Virginia (1927), Maryland (1935), Oklahoma (1935), Kentucky (1936), Virginia (1936), Tennessee (1937), North Carolina (1939), Texas (1939), Arkansas (1943), Georgia (1944), Alabama (1945), Florida (1945), Louisiana (1946), South Carolina (1946), and Mississippi (1948) set up their own systems of providing scholarships to Black students to study out of state to preserve segregation. Many of these states paid for their segregation scholarship programs by taking money from their already underfunded public Black colleges. Most states referred to the tuition assistance as "out-of-state tuition aid," obscuring its true purpose. The states with the largest Black populations were the last to create segregation scholarships for the graduate and professional education of Black citizens. The only southern or border state that made no graduate provision for its Black residents was Delaware.

In most states, the state boards of education administered the segregation scholarships, but in a few cases, officials from public Black colleges had control over the funding. All the states required applicants to complete an application with some states also requesting transcripts and letters of recommendation. No state's process was as cumbersome as Maryland's, which required applicants to submit an application, official transcript, recommendation letters, a health certificate, and a recent photograph as well as participate in an interview. Demand for segregation scholarships always exceeded supply, and usually the scholarship covered the difference between the cost of pursuing a course of study offered at the state's white institution and the cost of pursuing the same program out of state. Some states also paid travel expenses. Maryland, Texas, and Virginia made some provision for living expenses. Initially, South Carolina only provided funds for Black students to pursue medical education, but it later expanded its segregation scholarship program to cover other disciplines and professions. Alabama was the only state that required students to pay for tuition upfront and seek reimbursement. Most students receiving funds studied at midwestern flagships or private universities in the Northeast.[5]

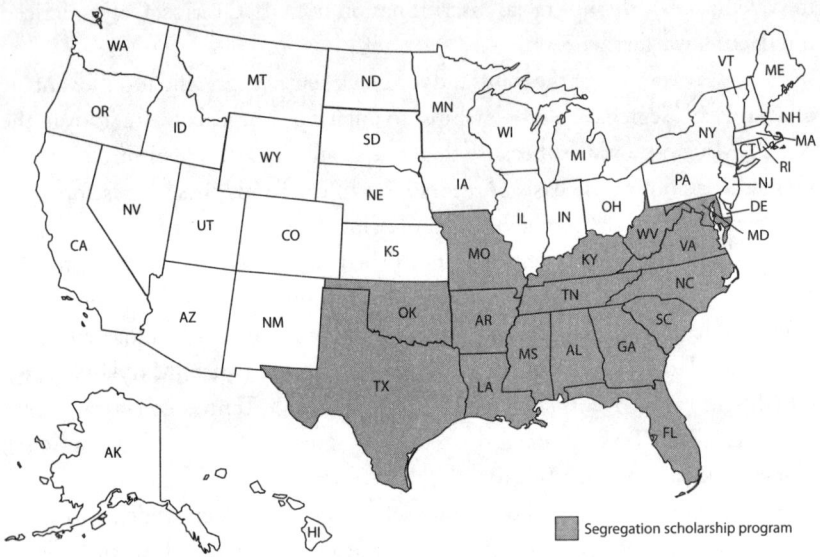

Between 1921 and 1948, sixteen southern and border states established segregation scholarship programs to preserve segregation at their flagship institutions.

Segregation scholarships were inadequate and failed to fulfill states' constitutional obligation to ensure equal protection under the law for all residents. Fred Gray recalled experiencing money crises throughout his law school career. He paid his fees on installment but "still owed money when the time came to take final exams."[6] Thankfully, school officials allowed him to take exams despite his debt. Financial straits were common among segregation scholarship recipients because southern states provided paltry tuition assistance. For example, Texas spent about $1,500 per year for every white student educated at the University of Texas School of Dentistry, but the largest segregation scholarship that a Black Texan could receive to study dentistry out of state was $400. For medical school students, the numbers were $1,900 and $500, respectively.[7]

This book is about the obstacles that Black southerners faced and overcame as they pursued graduate and professional study during the era of legal segregation. While more than 100 public and private Black colleges existed in the South to educate students that white colleges excluded, training beyond the bachelor's degree was almost impossible. Before 1936, there were only 7 schools in the region—all private institutions—where African Americans could pursue graduate or professional school study: Howard University, Hampton Institute,

Fisk University, Meharry Medical College, Gammon Theological Seminary, Atlanta University, and Xavier University. Graduate offerings at these institutions were limited. For example, graduate work at Hampton was only possible in education, and the courses were offered during the summer session only. Even after 1936, postbaccalaureate opportunities at Black institutions, public or private, were rare. No Black institution conferred the PhD until 1955.[8] While non-Black students could pursue master's, doctorate, and professional degrees at state-supported flagship institutions in the South, Black students remained shut out of these schools because of racism.

Charles Hamilton Houston, the National Association for the Advancement of Colored People's (NAACP) special counsel in the midthirties, recognized that "graduate schools were an area where the South was most vulnerable." Given African American southerners' lack of opportunity for study beyond the bachelor's degree, Houston made lawsuits seeking the desegregation of public graduate and professional schools a priority. He envisioned successful suits forcing southern white officials to either admit Black applicants to flagship institutions or establish separate and equal facilities at public Black colleges. Houston did not believe the latter was possible since southern states could not afford equal facilities. While correct that schools that were separate could not be equal, the civil rights attorney did not anticipate region-wide use of segregation scholarship programs.[9]

Houston expected to easily find plaintiffs willing to pursue equality suits to desegregate southern flagship institutions because Black demand for graduate and professional education increased significantly in the 1930s and 1940s. The call for additional training was a natural response to increased Black student college enrollment in the first half of the twentieth century. Black college enrollment jumped from 5,231 in 1922 to 22,609 in 1932. In the six years before World War II, 30,000 African Americans graduated from college and professional school, a figure that "was as many as in the entire previous period of American history."[10]

While several ambitious Black plaintiffs would challenge their exclusion from state universities between 1933 and 1950, thousands of Black southerners secured advanced study with segregation scholarships. By pursuing their highest scholarly potential and obtaining master's, doctorate, and professional degrees, African Americans equipped themselves with the credentials to serve the race as physicians, attorneys, pharmacists, professors, teachers, and principals. They engaged in intellectual warfare by using their education to chip away at notions of white superiority in their respective professions. The additional training and degrees oftentimes led to higher salaries and white-collar jobs, but these benefits came at a cost. Black southerners endured long and tedious commutes, financial hardship, racial discrimination, isolation, and homesickness while studying out of state.

The educational migration of Black scholars is hidden in the shadows of scholarship on the Great Migration that involved 6 million African Americans between 1915 and 1970. Both migrations, the "great" one and the lesser-known education one, stemmed from African Americans' desire for a better life, and both exoduses altered Black life and America's cities north and south. There were, however, key differences between the two. First, those who participated in the Great Migration oftentimes did so under the cover of darkness because southern officials did not support a mass exodus of Black workers out of the region. In contrast, with the little-known educational migration, southern and border state officials encouraged Black students to leave the state for education and subsidized their travel, not only because state-supported graduate programs did not exist but also because educated African Americans were a threat to the racial status quo. Second, the Great Migration and the lesser-known educational migration are different in that most participants in the former movement relocated permanently, while the majority of those in the latter returned to the South after earning their degrees. Thus, this is a narrative not of brain drain but of Black aspiration so resolute that thousands of scholars relocated to unfamiliar terrain and acquired new skills and credentials that they brought back to the very region that denied them educational opportunity.[11]

For certain, African Americans had been leaving home for graduate study long before Fred Gray did. For example, James McCune Smith, a New Yorker and the first Black person to earn a professional degree, studied at the University of Glasgow in Scotland where he earned a medical degree in 1837. Virginia's Carter G. Woodson became the second African American, after W. E. B. Du Bois, to obtain a doctorate degree from Harvard University, doing so in 1912, while educator and North Carolina native Anna Julia Cooper earned her doctorate from the University of Paris in 1925. Economist Milton S. J. Wright, a son of Savannah, Georgia, earned his master's degree from Columbia University in 1928 and his PhD from Germany's University of Heidelberg in 1932. What was new was Black southerners pursuing graduate study with financial assistance from southern state governments.

Before southern states began offering out-of-state aid, the main financial resources available to African Americans pursuing graduate study were fellowships from the Rosenwald Fund, the General Education Board, and the Social Science Research Council.[12] In accepting this new form of assistance, segregation scholarships, recipients appeared to make peace with segregation. In reality, they practiced intellectual warfare and transformed the opportunity for advanced study into state-sponsored opportunities to disprove, negate, and challenge notions of Black inferiority.

Chronicling the efforts of Black women and men to earn advanced degrees during the era of legal segregation advances our understanding of Black resistance to white racism in the educational arena. Even though they paid more for their education at out-of-state institutions, endured long and harrowing ordeals traveling while Black on interstate roads, and entered northern institutions that were anything but welcoming, Black southerners kept matriculating into graduate programs, forcing their home states to provide tuition assistance. These Black scholars knew that the Constitution prohibited discrimination based on race, and that they were entitled to the same public educational opportunities afforded to white citizens, so they did not eschew segregation scholarships. Rather they used them as a vehicle to demonstrate Black intellect, to make segregation more costly for southern state governments, and to lay claim to Black citizenship rights.

I contend that the burdens Black southerners withstood in their quest for advanced study functioned as a double tax levied on account of racism. This double tax was similar to the one that Black communities paid during the era of legal segregation, when on top of contributing their fair share of taxes they had to pool their resources to outfit elementary and secondary schools as white school leaders underfunded Black institutions.[13] With respect to graduate education, while Black students and their families paid taxes to subsidize graduate programs at historically white flagship institutions, they then had to allocate mental, physical, emotional, and financial resources to seek graduate opportunities in unfamiliar regions, arrange housing and transportation with little insider knowledge, and respond to exclusion once on campus. While it is true that Black graduate students self-imposed the double tax, as they voluntarily sought advanced study, it is also true that the additional burden was imposed on them by statutory racial discrimination prescribed by law, which made Black graduate opportunities difficult or nonexistent.

Many states continued to compel Black students to go out of state for the same educational opportunities provided to white students in state until the 1960s, defying the historic 6-to-2 decision in *Missouri ex rel. Gaines v. Canada* (1938). In the first court case with national implications for school desegregation, NAACP general counsel Charles Hamilton Houston convincingly demonstrated that educational facilities for African Americans were not separate but equal and that segregation scholarships did not absolve states of their responsibility to offer white and Black citizens the same education within their borders.[14] The US Supreme Court agreed and gave border and southern states three options to meet this constitutional obligation: discontinue graduate and professional school programs at historically white institutions, desegregate graduate and professional school programs at historically white institutions, or establish separate but equal graduate and professional school programs at Black institutions.

To be clear, this book refers to southern flagship institutions that prohibited Black students as historically white institutions because although white students made up the majority of the student body, most of these institutions also admitted nonwhite students as long as they were not Black. For example, the University of Alabama admitted a student from Japan in 1905. One of the earliest Asian American students at the University of North Carolina attended from 1897 until 1880 and the first Native American student earned his master's degree there in 1929. The first international student hailed from Tokyo, Japan, and studied at UNC during the 1893–94 school year.[15] Thus, southern state legislators did not have a problem with nonwhite students matriculating at southern flagship institutions. They had a problem with Black students doing so.

The *Gaines* decision, which outlawed segregation scholarships, was the first successful legal challenge to the doctrine of separate but equal and paved the way for the 1954 *Brown v. Board of Education* decision. In response to *Gaines*, many states established a few underfunded graduate and professional school programs at public Black colleges. Missouri went so far as to discontinue a storied graduate journalism program at its flagship institution rather than desegregate.[16] And, most egregiously, states maintained, expanded, or established segregation scholarship programs after *Gaines*. Mississippi, for example, inaugurated its tuition assistance program ten years after *Gaines*, with an initial appropriation of $25,000. By 1960, with no end in sight, the state spent $550,000 on segregation scholarships.[17] That amount, adjusted for inflation, is $5.76 million in 2024. Southern recalcitrance in the educational arena proved how hollow court victories could be without enforcement.

By choosing not to invest in public Black colleges, southern state officials underdeveloped the curricular offerings of those institutions and contributed to the pervasive racial inequalities present in the higher education system today. Desegregating historically white institutions or creating segregation scholarship programs were not the only options that state lawmakers had with respect to meeting Black demands for graduate and professional school training. They could have invested in public Black colleges, but by choosing not to, state officials denied Black students access to equitable higher education. Crucial funds needed for laboratories, libraries, and better-trained faculty—the accoutrements of graduate education—were not available at public Black colleges because all-white state legislatures directed funds elsewhere. In state after state, lawmakers diverted part of the appropriation for public Black colleges to fund segregation scholarship programs. Thus, any serious conversation about racial inequality in American higher education must consider this egregious state-implemented and state-sanctioned disinvestment in public Black colleges and repair the harm with meaningful, tangible remedies.

The decision to champion segregation scholarships rather than curricular additions at state-supported Black colleges also harmed Black healthcare. Public medical schools in southern and border states barred Black students, so Meharry Medical College in Nashville, Tennessee, and the Howard University College of Medicine in Washington, DC, the only two Black medical schools in the country after 1918, had the task of educating most Black physicians. These two private institutions graduated more than 80 percent of Black physicians during the Jim Crow era.[18] White northern medical schools admitted only a handful of Black students because of their discriminatory admission practices and quotas, while southern medical schools remained off limits completely.[19] Just how dire the situation was can be seen in the fact that Howard's medical school received 1,300 applications for a class of 70 students in 1947.[20] The first southern and border state public medical schools to admit Black students were the University of Arkansas and the University of Delaware, both in 1948. The damage, however, was already done because of the decades-long Black exclusion from state-supported medical education. In 1949, the ratio of Black physicians to the Black population in the South was 1 Black doctor for every 6,204 Black southerners.[21]

The South also had a critical shortage of Black attorneys. Several Black law schools operated in the nineteenth century and a few severely underfunded Black evening law schools were established at different points in the early twentieth century. These institutions notwithstanding, Howard University School of Law did the yeoman's task of producing Black attorneys. The lack of public Black law schools in the United States resulted in there being one Black lawyer for every 9,667 African Americans in 1934. While the country's Black population was 10 percent, Black lawyers made up 0.007 percent of lawyers.[22] The *Gaines* decision led a few southern states such as North Carolina to establish state-supported law schools for Black students in 1939 or later, but many Black southerners matriculated at law schools in the North or Midwest as Fred Gray did.

All too often, those who learn about segregation scholarships suggest that the arrangement was "not that bad" since recipients studied at some of the best educational institutions in the country, including the University of Wisconsin, the University of Chicago, and Columbia University. Such a view overlooks the emotional and psychological costs of being forced to leave the only land one knew to obtain an education. Moreover, traveling to or from the Jim Crow

South before the construction of President Dwight Eisenhower's interstate highway system was arduous and often an experience in public humiliation for Black passengers, as bus drivers, train conductors, and white passengers degraded African Americans. Along some routes, bathroom facilities did not exist for Black travelers, who were forced to relieve themselves on the side of the road.[23]

Moreover, northern institutions did not roll out the proverbial welcome mat for Black southerners. Nearly forty years before states introduced segregation scholarships, W. E. B. Du Bois matriculated at Harvard after graduating from Fisk. In describing the racism and ostracism that he faced, Du Bois asserted that he was "at but not of Harvard."[24] Oklahoma native and later renowned historian John Hope Franklin followed Du Bois's academic path to a history doctorate, graduating from Fisk in 1935 before also entering Harvard. Franklin was in the first wave of African American southerners to benefit from segregation scholarships. He received a $100 from Oklahoma to offset expenses at Harvard during the 1935–36 academic year.[25] That year Oklahoma appropriated $5,000 toward the tuition of Black students studying out of state. Unwanted at his home state's flagship institution because of racism, he found Harvard to be a socially challenging place for Black students. He later recalled that "a day, and often an hour didn't go by without my feeling the color of my skin—in the reactions of white Cambridge, the behavior of my fellow students, the attitudes real and imagined struck by my professors."[26] Racial slights at the Ivy League institution were not simply perceived. In a class where John Hope Franklin was the only Black student, he endured the professor telling a "darky" joke without shame.[27] Persevering in an anti-Black space, Franklin's form of intellectual warfare led him to master the historian's craft of interpreting the past as evidenced through his seminal work *From Slavery to Freedom*, which exposed the contradictions at the center of the nation's founding.

Franklin's experience at Harvard was not an anomaly. Those who received out-of-state tuition assistance routinely faced racial discrimination and social ostracism while studying at institutions outside of South. After they graduated, these institutions refused to hire them. As scholars have pointed out, "historical narratives of the Great Migration have tended to obscure the entrenched realities of northern racism."[28]

The history of segregation scholarships complicates the idea that massive resistance to school desegregation first erupted in the wake of *Brown v. Board of Education*. After the landmark ruling, Virginia's legislature revised the state's tuition grant law in 1959. Changes to the law allowed officials in Prince Edward County to raise taxes and appropriate the funds to create scholarships to finance white students' attendance at nonsectarian private schools. The arrangement was a form of massive resistance that lasted two years until Black parents won a court order outlawing the use of public funds for segregationist academies.[29] What Virginia's politicians did to circumvent compliance with court-ordered school desegregation was not novel. Lawmakers in Virginia and fifteen other states used tax dollars to preserve segregation beginning in the 1920s. In this earlier instance, the beneficiaries were African Americans, but the goal was the same: the preservation of segregation. Thus, segregation scholarships used to provide graduate study for African Americans offered a model for white resistance to school desegregation during the civil rights era.

A Forgotten Migration builds upon existing literature in Black educational history. At the center of this study are the historically Black colleges and universities (HBCUs) that educated and prepared segregation scholarships recipients to enter graduate programs that were usually at historically white institutions located outside the South. In his book-length study of HBCUs, Jelani Favors asserts that Black colleges offered their students a second curriculum of racial consciousness that prepared them to "launch a full-frontal assault on white supremacy."[30] *A Forgotten Migration* shows how the second curriculum bore fruit in classrooms and laboratories in addition to lunch counters and street demonstrations. Buoyed by encouragement, high expectations, and rigorous training from HBCU professors, Black students achieved remarkable scholarly success in advanced degree programs. These students engaged in intellectual warfare as they entered what were oftentimes anti-Black classrooms in historically white institutions, proving themselves more than capable in terms of academic performance, and departing with the credentials and knowledge to disrupt the status quo in their chosen professions, including education, healthcare, and law.

In telling this history of Black education, I intervene in scholarly conversations about Black student pioneers who desegregated or were in the earliest cohorts of Black students at historically white institutions. Rachel Devlin and Stefan Bradley have explored the experiences and activism of Black student trailblazers, and this book provides a fuller history of the education arm of the Black freedom struggle and the type of choices that African Americans faced.[31] Some declined segregation scholarships, but many more accepted the exportation of their talents and intellect. Many believed that frontal assaults on white supremacy were not yet possible, so they used segregation scholarships to sharpen their skills and make plain the immorality and illogic of keeping African Americans out of historically white universities in the South. Their decision to relocate to unfamiliar settings exposes the myth that Black people do not care about education. Thousands of aspiring Black southerners sacrificed the comforts of familiarity and traveled to obtain the schooling their home states denied them.

Many viewed the educational opportunities and institutions in the North as superior to their southern counterparts. Those seeking postbaccalaureate opportunities pondered a host of questions and uncertainties. *Should I leave or go? Will my family support my leaving? By leaving, am I absolving the state of fulfilling its constitutional obligations? Am I complicit in segregation if I accept a segregation scholarship? Will the North prove to be a "kinder mistress?"*[32] *Could I be my full self in the North in ways not possible in the South? How will the transition from an all-Black college to a historically white one play out? Will I be treated fairly in an institution where I am significantly outnumbered by those of another race?*

College administrators also walked a tightrope regarding segregation scholarships. Until recently, there has been a dearth of studies examining the role and actions of Black and white college presidents in struggles for opportunity and inclusion both within and outside the academy. Scholars such as Joy Ann Williamson-Lott and Eddie Cole have begun to fill that gap in the scholarship, and this book adds to the conversation.[33] Race leaders, especially Black college presidents at public institutions, were divided on the question of out-of-state tuition grants. Their embrace of segregation scholarships could be misconstrued as acceptance of racial discrimination; they knew that not accepting the funds limited educational opportunities for the race. Some Black college leaders had ulterior motives for opposing segregation scholarships. They hoped to establish graduate programs at their institutions. Segregation scholarships forced Black administrators to make difficult decisions as they balanced supporting the race while advocating for their institutions and appeasing all-white legislatures. Race leaders pondered a host of questions and uncertainties: *Should the state create graduate programs at Black colleges? Even if the demand is low? Are undergraduate programs at Black colleges strong enough to begin graduate programs? Is supporting segregation scholarships akin to undergirding Jim Crow? Is calling for the desegregation of historically white institutions a death sentence for Black colleges?*

Although the master's tools can never dismantle the master's house, recipients of segregation scholarships wielded those tools to weaken the house's foundation and undermine white supremacy throughout the United States. Those who received state aid became leaders in the fields of education, law, medicine, and politics. At the elementary and secondary education levels, Black teachers and principals had more academic credentials and advanced training than their white counterparts because of segregation scholarships. They pursued intellectual warfare in their classrooms by offering students a curriculum that affirmed Blackness and prepared impressionable Black students for an anti-Black world.[34]

Segregation scholarships recipients literally remade the academy. Virginia paid for Helen G. Edmonds to study history at Ohio State University, where in 1946 she became the first Black woman to receive a history PhD at the institution and the third Black woman to earn a doctorate there. Edmonds served on the faculty at North Carolina College (present-day North Carolina Central University) from 1941 until 1977 where she rose to the rank of professor and served as chair of the history program and dean of the graduate school. Edmonds's first book, *The Negro and Fusion Politics in North Carolina, 1894–1901*, provides one of the earliest accurate accounts of the 1898 coup d'état in Wilmington, North Carolina. A scholar and an institution builder, she helped to establish the institution's graduate program in history, which today ranks first among historically Black colleges and universities in the number of graduates who go on to earn doctorate degrees in history. Her version of intellectual warfare consisted of creating a pipeline of well-trained Black historians who remade the historical profession by challenging anti-Black ideas in the discipline.

To keep African Americans out of Louisiana State University, lawmakers paid Jewel Limar Prestage $375 per semester to pursue graduate study in political science at the University of Iowa. In 1954, at the age of twenty-two, Prestage became the first African American woman in the United States to earn a PhD in political science. She pioneered scholarship on African American women legislators and mentored nearly fifty Black students who went on to earn doctorate degrees in political science during her tenure on the faculty at Southern University of Baton Rouge and Prairie View A&M University. She also served as a dean at both institutions.[35] Like Edmonds, Prestage used her educational opportunity to create opportunities for successive generations of political scientists and in the process made the academy much more inclusive and diverse.

Segregation scholarship recipients who pursued professional study also wielded their education as a weapon for good as they waged intellectual warfare. U. W. Clemon, a segregation scholarship recipient from Alabama, became that state's first Black federal judge. Before ascending to the bench, he sued renowned University of Alabama head football coach Paul "Bear" Bryant to desegregate the university's football program. Louis Sullivan used a segregation scholarship from Georgia to attend medical school and later founded the Morehouse School of Medicine, whose mission is to improve the health and well-being of communities with an emphasis on people of color. Thus segregation scholarship recipients, through their academic and professional achievements, exploited their state-subsidized educations to dismantle racial segregation and expand opportunity for future generations of African Americans.

Just as the South is diverse, with many different histories, there was great diversity in the origins, policies, and magnitude of segregation scholarship programs. To demonstrate this variety, I have chosen to focus on four states—Missouri, North Carolina, Kentucky, and Alabama—though I include short vignettes from several other states. The four states had archival materials readily available and provide a telling overview of the various rules, procedures, and allowances that governed segregation scholarships. This book also gives in-depth accounts of the experiences of segregation scholarship recipients as they "studied abroad," so that we learn about this educational practice not only through legislative documents and newspaper articles but also through the narratives of students compelled to leave home. Most scholarship recipients attended Black colleges for their undergraduate degrees. Their experiences at northern institutions varied, but a common theme was anxiety about learning alongside white students who had attended better-funded institutions. Time and again, segregation scholarship recipients not only held their own in the classroom but excelled.

Two other demographic characteristics of segregation scholarships recipients revolve around class and gender. The overwhelming majority of students who pursued graduate study were squarely in the Black middle class, as the ability to front tuition, pay for uncovered expenses, and pursue legal remedies demonstrated a privilege that most people in the South did not enjoy. Recipients were often the children of informed and relatively well-off parents who had the knowledge and resources to help their sons and daughters seize the few opportunities available to African Americans. This does not mean that segregation scholarship recipients were wealthy but rather that they had greater means than many of their peers. Moreover, in the earliest years of segregation scholarships, Black men outnumbered Black women as recipients of state aid. In the first half of the twentieth century, historian Linda Perkins has found that many Black women received their undergraduate degrees from teacher training colleges that were unaccredited or did not provide the curriculum necessary for graduate school. Finite time and financial resources made it difficult for these women to take the supplemental courses needed to enter a graduate program, so they were less likely to pursue advanced study. Moreover, as historian Stephanie Evans explained, Black women's scholarly pursuits were often stymied by hostile thesis committees, familial responsibilities, and time-consuming civil rights and social welfare work. In later years, women outpaced men in segregation scholarship programs since many recipients were public school teachers—and there were more female than male teachers in many areas.[36]

This book shows that segregation scholarships were a form of racism just as pernicious and evil as racial violence. Like lynching and disfranchisement, segregation scholarships attempted to maintain white supremacy. It is easy to point to segregationist governors standing in schoolhouse doors or police turning water hoses and dogs on nonviolent protestors and label those actions as racist. We must not, however, ignore the polite forms of racism that were maintained by bureaucracy and designed to preserve the racial status quo of white superiority and Black inferiority. We must not forget the silent bystanders who propped up the racist exportation of Black talent by refusing to speak up and say that the arrangement was unjust, unnecessary, and downright ludicrous. By making their personal peace with segregation scholarships as a middle ground, even the best-meaning white officials embraced the idea that there was something so peculiar, insulting, and wrong with Black people that they had to be educated elsewhere. Thus, white resistance to Black educational advancement came not only in the form of white mobs and segregationist academies but also through the exportation of Black southern intellect. Such an arrangement contributed to the inequity present today in southern states' systems of higher education. This story helps explain how and why.

CHAPTER ONE

A Gold Brick

The Creation of Segregation Scholarship Programs

> There is no doubt that many things can be done by legislation to improve the condition of the [N]egro residents of Missouri.... We have a good state university at Jefferson City, Lincoln Institute, but it needs more funds.... A [N]egro now must go outside Missouri to get any kind of professional training.
> —WALTHALL MOORE, "Negro Explains Idea of Duties as Legislator,"
> *St. Louis Star and Times*, November 5, 1920

On January 5, 1921, a blustery winter day in Jefferson City, the fifty-first session of the Missouri General Assembly was gaveled to order, with white and Black residents from all over the state peering down from the gallery, hoping to catch a glimpse of the first African American to be elected to the state legislature. House officials offered Walthall Moore, a St. Louis Republican, a place of prominence on the right side of the main aisle, in a seat only four rows from the Speaker's platform. The view of many eager onlookers was blocked by the massive floral arrangements, the gift of multiple Black churches and political organizations in St. Louis.[1]

Unbeknownst to the onlookers, Moore's presence in the statehouse would set in motion several important educational changes for African Americans, not only in Missouri but throughout the South. Prior to Moore's election, Missouri rarely provided its Black citizens the same educational opportunities as white citizens, a practice that helped to preserve segregation and the racial caste system that limited African Americans' social, political, and economic trajectories. An Alabama transplant, it would be Moore who introduced out-of-state tuition grants for Black college students and made advanced degrees a more realistic possibility for Black southerners. The grants, the first of their kind in the United States, allowed Black students to study at Black or white institutions that offered graduate programs and served as a forerunner to the equalization strategies that

Black activists pursued to improve Black education at the elementary and secondary school levels.[2] These strategies pressured white state officials to provide African Americans with "equal" educational opportunities or face legal challenges.

As we will see in this chapter, during his first term in office Walthall Moore created the concept of segregation scholarships as a *temporary* response to address Missouri's neglect of its Black citizens' higher education. The state's sole college for African Americans, Lincoln Institute, was a far cry in terms of funding, physical plant, and academic offerings from the well-funded flagship institution for white residents, the University of Missouri. Moore's end goal, though never realized, was an upgraded Lincoln that gave African Americans in Missouri the same opportunities that were available to white residents of the state. Thus, segregation scholarships were not created with nefarious intent. Rather, they were a provisional arrangement to meet Black aspirations for advanced study out of state until the state's Black institution received the public investment necessary to meet Black needs. These scholarships were not offered earlier in other states because of white hostility toward Black education.[3] It took a Black lawmaker to prioritize equal educational opportunity for African Americans.

Segregationists quickly embraced Moore's suggestion of exiling Black students because it allowed them to delay questions about integration. Unlike Moore, who saw segregation scholarships as a temporary measure, they found it more economical to outsource indefinitely the state's responsibility to educate African Americans rather than build up the state's lone public Black college. A Black institution comparable to the all-white University of Missouri required graduate programs and all the usual components of advanced study, including well-equipped laboratories and libraries and faculty with advanced degrees to teach in graduate programs. White lawmakers, however, were unwilling to make such an investment in Lincoln, and segregation scholarships became their halfhearted solution. The long disinterest and hostility to Black education led to the continued underfunding of a Black college.

For their part, African Americans knew all too well that racism limited opportunities and dictated where they could live, sit, eat, and learn. Those desiring postbaccalaureate education in Missouri faced complex decisions that intertwined race, education, civil rights, and exclusion. They could accept a segregation scholarship to better themselves, knowing full well that to do so was to play nice with a racist arrangement that ignored their constitutional right to equal protection under the law. If they chose not to leave home and study elsewhere, they limited their career options and future earnings and, in some ways, cosigned on to the racist idea that Black people did not need or want much education. Whether they stayed or went, they continued paying taxes for academic programs that they could not pursue.

Refusing to be "passive recipients of whites' actions," Black students took advantage of segregation scholarships to receive the education and credentials they desired.[4] They often found that even in so-called open universities in the North and West, the color line still constricted their campus experience. The universities that readily took Black students' tuition dollars did not attempt to make them feel included in campus life. Often, campus housing, dining services, and student organizations excluded Black students, forcing southern transplants to turn inward and toward each other, when possible, for social and academic support.

Walthall Moore was no stranger to moving for better opportunities. Born in Alabama in 1874, Moore was twelve years old when his parents, John and Sarah Moore, left the South and settled in St. Louis, the city with Missouri's largest Black population. The Moores were part of a "great exodus" that began in 1879, when many African Americans from Mississippi, Alabama, Texas, and Tennessee headed for Kansas, where homestead land was available.[5] Moreover, Kansas was a state where slavery had never existed, so Black migrants envisioned better futures there. This migration was a forerunner to the Great Migration of 1915 to 1970, when 6 million Black southerners expressed their discontent with the South's poor economic conditions, Black disfranchisement, and widespread segregation laws by packing their bags and resettling in northern and western cities, including New York City, Chicago, Detroit, and Los Angeles.[6]

During the late nineteenth century exodus to Kansas, many African Americans aborted the journey in Missouri because of lack of finances, and the Moores were among the migrants who cut their journey short. They quickly learned, however, that states such as Missouri and Kansas were no promised land. As was the case throughout the United States, the segregated schools the Moore family attended in St. Louis were grossly unequal. For example, in 1880, white schools in St. Louis received approximately $39,330 per school, while Black schools received $14,600.[7] The city was home to Sumner High School, the first high school for African Americans west of the Mississippi River. The institution opened in 1875 at the demand of the city's Black residents. White school board leaders demonstrated their contempt for Black education by housing Sumner in an abandoned building deemed unsuitable for white students. The school was located across the street from Collier White Lead and Oil Works, so students were exposed daily to small particles of lead in the air and other fine dust. In later years, the all-Black Sumner faculty boasted advanced degrees from some of the best universities in the country. Racism prevented many of these Black professionals from securing faculty positions at colleges and universities, so it was quite common for MAs and PhDs to seek teaching positions in Black elementary and secondary schools like Sumner.[8] Walthall Moore attended Sumner before pursuing higher education at Howard University in Washington, DC, although there is no record that he received a degree at Howard.[9] At some point in the early twentieth century, Moore returned to Missouri and got involved in politics.

When Moore was elected to the Missouri General Assembly in 1920, segregationists made sure that he remembered "his place" as a Black man. While most state lawmakers stayed at the Hotel Governor when the legislature was in session, all hotels in Jefferson City were off limits to Moore and any other Black person. He stayed in private homes or in a dormitory at the nearby all-Black Lincoln Institute when in the capital city for legislative business. He also had his meals on the Black college campus since he could not eat in the capitol building.[10] Moore thus missed informal networking and cajoling with his fellow legislators.

Less than a month after taking office, Moore introduced a bill seeking $1 million to improve higher education for African American residents of his state. The legislature offered Moore half the amount he requested. Nevertheless, in this one instance of political maneuvering, he helped to codify Black Missourians' right to higher education at the state's expense.[11]

Lincoln Institute, Missouri's sole institution of higher education for African Americans, was located in Jefferson City, where Black Civil War veterans had established it as a private institution in 1866. Black Missourians, including many who could not read or write, demonstrated their enthusiasm for the institution by giving money to support it. They desired the education that slavery had denied them. In 1847, the Missouri General Assembly had enacted a law making it a crime to teach people of African descent to read and write. The peculiar institution of slavery and its ban on Black literacy continued during the Civil War, as Missouri was a slave state that did not leave the Union. Financially supporting Lincoln was one way for Missouri's Black residents to distance themselves from their enslaved past and secure their freedom.[12]

The state began funding Lincoln in 1870 to train Black teachers, and the school officially became a state "normal school" in 1879. Lincoln offered both two-year and four-year courses. The two-year course allowed graduates to teach in the state for two years before requiring additional training. The four-year course gave graduates lifetime credentials to teach in Missouri.[13]

WALTHALL M. MOORE

Walthall M. Moore was the first African American to serve in the Missouri General Assembly. In 1921, he successfully introduced legislation creating a temporary segregation scholarship program in the state. Missouri Secretary of State's Office, *Official Manual of the State of Missouri 1921–1922*. In Official Manual of the State of Missouri—The Blue Book Collection, Missouri State Archives, Jefferson City.

The Missouri legislature added industrial and agricultural education to Lincoln's curriculum in 1891 so that the University of Missouri, which was open to white and non-Black students, could continue receiving federal funds under the 1862 Morrill Act. The 1862 Morrill Land-Grant College Act created land-grant colleges in the United States using proceeds from the sale of federal lands. Under the act, each state not in rebellion received 30,000 acres of federal land for each member of Congress the state had during the 1860 census. States had to use the land, or proceeds from its sale, to establish a college that taught military tactics, engineering, and agriculture. The University of Missouri, commonly known as Mizzou, benefited from the 1862 law as Missouri remained loyal to the Union during the Civil War.

The Second Morrill Act of 1890, aimed at former Confederate states, required states to provide educational opportunity in the agricultural and mechanical arts for African Americans to continue receiving federal funds. States had several options under the 1890 act. They could forego the federal money altogether; admit Black students to the historically white land-grant institution; establish a new institution to serve as the Black land-grant college; or adopt an institution for Black students already in operation and designate it as the state's Black land-grant school. The 1890 stipulations meant that the federal government sanctioned racial segregation in higher education even before the United States legalized separate but equal in *Plessy v. Ferguson* (1896). Missouri, which prohibited Black and white students from learning together, chose to make the already-established Lincoln Institute its land-grant college for African Americans in order to continue receiving land-grant funds for the University of Missouri.[14]

Although Lincoln was the only postsecondary school available to African Americans in Missouri, it was not the Black counterpart to the University of Missouri. Lincoln did not offer serious study in the liberal arts and had no offerings for students who wanted to pursue careers in law, medicine, dentistry, or journalism. Mizzou had robust undergraduate and graduate programs in a variety of disciplines. In 1895 and again in 1910, Lincoln supporters unsuccessfully lobbied legislators to make Lincoln a state university for African Americans that was comparable to the University of Missouri.[15]

Walthall Moore set out to rectify the educational disparity. Within weeks of joining the Missouri House of Representatives, he introduced a bill changing the name of Lincoln Institute to Lincoln University. The bill also established an interracial Board of Curators charged with reorganizing the institution as a four-year college that afforded Missouri's Black residents the same educational opportunities as white residents at Mizzou. The bill, which became law in April 1921, also created a segregation scholarship program that used tax dollars to pay the full tuition costs for Black residents to attend universities in states adjacent to Missouri for undergraduate or graduate study that was available at Mizzou and unavailable at Lincoln. While eight states border Missouri, only four of them—Illinois, Iowa, Nebraska, and Kansas—welcomed Black students. Additionally, "pending the full development of Lincoln," the bill allowed Black students to take courses at the University of Missouri that were not available at Lincoln.[16] Nonetheless, Missouri's flagship institution had no intention of admitting Black students and did not.

Even though the 1921 law that Moore authored mandated that Missouri provide its Black residents with the same educational opportunities available to its white residents, that did not happen. Lincoln's reorganization was contingent upon the $500,000 Moore secured from the state legislature, money that was to be appropriated from the state's school fund. The legislature, however, did not have the authority to appropriate money from the school fund. Instead, educational appropriations beyond the secondary level had to be drawn against the general revenue fund for the entire state. The state auditor and superintendent of education maintained, though, that all money in the general revenue fund had already been appropriated, so Moore's groundbreaking bill calling for major upgrades in Black Missourians' higher education opportunities remained an unfunded mandate. According to the Black press, Missouri had given its Black citizens a "gold brick."[17]

In perhaps the first funding lawsuit involving a state-supported Black college, the Lincoln Board of Curators attorney filed suit against the state auditor in the Missouri Supreme Court to compel him to release money from the school fund for the university's benefit. The court sided with the auditor and other state officials, finding that Lincoln's improvement appropriation should have come from the general revenue fund rather than from the school fund, which was not applicable to higher education.[18] The lawsuit was significant despite its lack of success because Black Missourians and their white allies held Missouri accountable for equitable higher education opportunities for African Americans. Also keeping up the pressure was a bill Moore introduced in 1925 to restore Lincoln's $500,000 appropriation. The legislature approved $400,000 for grounds and buildings at Lincoln, but there were still no funds to provide Black residents with graduate training in or out of state.[19]

Missouri gave its Black citizens a promissory note while its white residents enjoyed a bona fide university with many different academic programs. It would be another four years before Missouri funded the segregation scholarship program, in 1929, eight years after Moore first championed the bill in the legislature. Even after the state began exiling striving Black students, Lincoln remained a university in name only. As late as 1938, the institution did not have a single graduate program, leading NAACP attorney Charles Hamilton Houston to refer to the 1921 legislation as nothing but "a legislative fiat."[20]

Missouri's delay in financing its segregation scholarship program allowed West Virginia to become the first state to create and *fund* out-of-state tuition aid for African Americans. The state began exporting Black students in 1927. The practice continued until 1955, when the state's tax-supported universities completely desegregated.[21]

West Virginia became a state in 1863 after breaking away from Virginia, and it remained loyal to the Union during the Civil War. Strong abolitionist sentiment had existed within its borders prior to statehood. John Brown's 1859 raid on Harpers Ferry occurred within the state's present-day boundaries. The 1863 West Virginia Constitution provided for the gradual emancipation of more than

18,000 enslaved people living there, but complete and immediate emancipation did not come until 1865. State lawmakers' anticipation of passage of the Thirteenth Amendment led them to pass a bill ending slavery in West Virginia.[22]

While West Virginia's first Black college, Storer, opened in 1867, the state did not establish a public institution for African Americans until 1891. In that year, the legislature created West Virginia Colored Institute (present-day West Virginia State University) as the state's Black land-grant college. The school was founded in an unincorporated community called Institute near the Kanawha River on land formerly owned by an enslaved woman. Four years after the Colored Institute's founding, the state also established Bluefield Colored Institute (present-day Bluefield State University).[23]

Unlike African Americans in other parts of the South after Reconstruction, Black West Virginians never lost the right to vote. Access to the ballot box meant that from the late nineteenth century until the present, West Virginia's elected officials have included African Americans. What was also unique about Black West Virginians was that agriculture was not their predominant occupation. Most worked in the state's booming coal mining industry, with its "good, steady wages and free housing."[24] Black political power and well-paying jobs, however, could not prevent racial discrimination.

Segregation compelled African American West Virginians who sought post-baccalaureate degrees to pursue them out of state. West Virginia's two public institutions of higher education for African Americans provided vocational training, teacher preparation, and undergraduate studies. Unlike the all-white West Virginia University in Morgantown, the state's Black institutions did not offer graduate curricula.

In 1927, the West Virginia Legislature passed a law setting aside funds to offset the costs of out-of-state study for African Americans. Once again it was an African American legislator, T. Edward Hill of Charleston, who drafted the bill for a segregation scholarship program. Black West Virginians who graduated from a high school in the state or had resided in the state for five years and completed two years of college work in one of the state schools were eligible to receive funds. Moreover, the students had to pursue a course of study available to white residents at WVU but not available at what were then known as West Virginia Colored Institute and Bluefield Colored Institute. West Virginia agreed to pay tuition and fees at universities outside the state in sums equal to the difference in the amounts paid by West Virginia residents and those from other states who attended West Virginia University. Black newspapers throughout the nation celebrated the legislation and pointed out that West Virginia's Black population was only 6 percent, meaning the state was making an important investment in

Black education for a small Black population.[25] While a gesture of goodwill, the fact remained that West Virginia had a constitutional obligation to provide graduate and professional school opportunities for Black citizens if it provided them to white citizens.

Esther Page headed north for postbaccalaureate study in psychiatry in the winter of 1931. The twenty-five-year-old from Kimball, West Virginia, had relocated to the state as a child with her father, who owned a thriving funeral home. In 1929, she graduated third in a class of forty-eight students from West Virginia State College (WVSC). She majored in French and minored in physical education and English. After graduation, she began a career as a teacher in McDowell County, West Virginia, before going to New York for graduate school. Whether she traveled by rail or bus, Page, then twenty-five, disembarked alone in bustling and chilly New York City, where there were no signs saying "For Whites" or "For Colored." Like thousands of migrants before her, she had left behind a "known terror" for an "unknown terror that lay ahead."[26] Even without Jim Crow signs, there were unwritten racial rules that she had to learn in her new home. Unlike most Black migrants of the period, Page had not come north in search of a job. The former high school teacher enrolled at the New York School of Social Work (present-day Columbia University School of Social Work).[27]

Page quickly learned that the North was no promised land. Restaurants in New York City had a color line. The Great Depression–induced poverty meant that one out of every five Black workers in Harlem was unemployed by 1930. Things were so dire that "slave markets" developed on Bronx street corners, where Black women sought work as domestics for meager wages.[28] Page was an anomaly in a society where survival rather than advanced learning was the priority.

While abject poverty was not her lot, Page was not flush with cash either. She encountered problems at the New York School of Social Work when her tuition bill was not paid on time. A few weeks into the quarter, when asked about settling her account, Page explained to the registrar that a West Virginia education official would send a check for eighty-five dollars to pay her tuition since graduate study in West Virginia was unavailable for African Americans. According to Page, the registrar "acted like she thought I had the money then, but didn't want to pay it."[29]

Whether or not the registrar meant to treat the young woman with suspicion and contempt, West Virginia's delay in sending Page's segregation scholarship caused her psychological turmoil and forced her to put her guard up. Her concern for how she was treated was no doubt informed by other encounters she had had or heard about involving white Americans. As a form of self-preservation, she decided to stop attending classes until the tuition check arrived. Believing that it had, Page resumed attending class. To her chagrin, she learned that the school had dropped her from its roll and returned her segregation scholarship to state officials in West Virginia.[30]

It is possible that the registrar questioned every student with a delinquent account. Yet, Page's interactions with white people in New York were informed by her experiences with white people in West Virginia. She and other Black students who traveled north for school consciously and unconsciously reviewed the rules of racial etiquette and policed their own behavior according to what they perceived. Had Page been white, she could have remained near family and attended her native state's flagship institution, WVU, where white and Black taxpayers' funds had established an impressive physical plant with an array of graduate programs. In the end, she left New York and returned home to West Virginia without a graduate degree. She abandoned her dream of becoming a licensed social worker.

Black West Virginia legislator Ebenezer Howard Harper did not support the segregation scholarship program that sent Esther Page to New York. He served three terms in the West Virginia Legislature, including in the legislative session that created out-of-state tuition assistance for African Americans. Born one year before slavery ended, Harper graduated from Virginia Normal and College Institute (present-day Virginia State University) and Howard University School of Law.[31] He opposed the segregation scholarship program on the grounds that it sent large sums of money outside the state.[32] Harper believed that state funds should have been used to enhance course offerings at the state's public Black colleges. His opposition was an important and early harbinger of Black objections to segregation scholarships.

West Virginia originally appropriated $7,000 per year to assist aspiring Black graduate students like Esther Page. The paltry amount was less than the budget for stenographic service at the historically white West Virginia University. Tuition grants typically averaged $150 per student and all funds were exhausted annually, a testament to Black demand for access to advanced education. In 1937, lawmakers increased the appropriation to $8,000 per year. During the first ten years of subsidized out-of-state graduate study, 400 Black West Virginians studied subjects such as education, law, medicine, pharmacy, psychology, and English at institutions including Howard, Meharry, Fisk, Ohio State, Cornell, Northwestern, Wisconsin, and Michigan.[33]

Other Black West Virginia residents who used segregation scholarships to obtain advanced degrees include George W. Williams, Ira James Kohath Wells, and Theodore D. Phillips. Williams graduated from West Virginia State College in 1927 with honors and served as the principal of Riverside High School in Elkins, a mountain community with a significant Black population because of the town's railroad lines. He was also a member of West Virginia's Negro Board of Education, which dispensed segregation scholarships, and he himself received state aid to pursue graduate study at the University of Pennsylvania. During his time at Penn, the school hosted the Eastern Conference on Law, where the Howard University School of Law's student delegation was refused campus housing because of racism.[34] Things were no better for Williams's fellow state board of education member and West Virginia state supervisor of Negro education Ira James Kohath Wells, who studied at Ohio State University in the mid-1930s after earning his bachelor's degree from Lincoln University of Pennsylvania in 1923, where he was classmates with Horace Mann Bond. Wells was at Ohio State during the time when its athletic honor society, Bucket and Dipper, denied admission to track and field standout Jesse Owens, the best athlete in Ohio State's history. While it is unclear why Wells left after just one semester, the white supremacist ethos on campus may have played a role. By 1937, bigotry at Ohio State led white students to establish a student organization called the Anti-Negro Guild that opposed integrated campus facilities.[35]

Even supposedly liberal institutions presented challenges for segregation scholarship recipients. Oberlin College, which had admitted African American students since 1834, was quite discriminatory in the 1930s. The NAACP ran a series of articles in its media publication, *The Crisis*, decrying how the institution and its surrounding town had capitulated to racial intolerance. The local bowling alley refused service to a Black student in Oberlin's graduate school of theology, and a popular eatery only offered service to Black patrons in the kitchen.[36] It was in such a climate that West Virginia resident Theodore Phillips earned his master's degree in music from Oberlin in 1935. Phillips, the music director at WVSC, took a leave of absence from his job to complete his graduate study.[37] Black colleges often granted their faculty leaves of absence to pursue advanced study in the first half of the twentieth century, as the additional training and graduate degrees increased an institution's prestige and helped it win accreditation.

Around the same time that West Virginia began sending Black students out of state for advanced study, a few private Black colleges inaugurated formal master's degree programs, proving a modicum of relief for those who did not want to attend racist northern institutions. Atlanta University (AU) and Fisk created graduate programs in the late 1920s, joining Howard as the only Black institutions in the nation with such offerings. In 1927, Fisk added to its undergraduate program graduate work in history, sociology, English, philosophy, and chemistry.

Atlanta University ceased offering undergraduate courses and became a graduate school to avoid duplicating the course offerings at Morehouse and Spelman, two Black colleges in Atlanta.[38] As multiple southern and border states established segregation scholarship programs, these universities became common destinations for recipients of state aid.

AU was the first and only Black freestanding graduate school in the United States. Georgia native son and Morehouse College president John Hope oversaw AU's transition from an undergraduate to a graduate institution. During the 1929–30 academic year, AU offered master's level and undergraduate courses but did not accept first-year students. The 182 students in their sophomore, junior, and senior years at AU took most of their courses at Morehouse and Spelman. The remaining undergraduate students transferred in the fall of 1930, enabling President Hope to devote his complete attention to building a postbaccalaureate powerhouse in Atlanta. He set out to establish a graduate school of liberal arts, a library school, a business school, and a graduate school of social work, with medical, dental, and law schools planned for the future.[39]

AU's move to offer graduate study exclusively proved successful. In its first year, 10 departments offered 77 graduate courses and 272 students enrolled. The school awarded its first master's degree in 1931 to Joseph Bailey, a student in the History Department who immediately secured a faculty position at Arkansas Agricultural, Mechanical, and Normal College in Pine Bluff (present-day University of Arkansas at Pine Bluff). One year later, AU received an A rating from the Southern Association of Colleges and Schools (SACS), putting its graduate programs on equal footing with those of SACS member institutions such as Vanderbilt and the University of Virginia. President Hope not only secured SACS recognition of AU, but additionally, he assembled a powerhouse faculty of Black scholars in the early 1930s including W. E. B. Du Bois, historian Rayford W. Logan, classicist Frank M. Snowden, and economist William H. Dean. The Atlanta institution was the home of *Phylon*, a peer-reviewed journal about race and culture. By 1950, nearly one-third of all African Americans who earned master's degrees were AU graduates. Most AU alumni worked at Black educational institutions, serving as college presidents, public school teachers and principals, and rural supervisors. AU's School of Library Science, founded in 1941, supplied Black schools and colleges with trained librarians who practiced intellectual warfare by securing library materials that portrayed African Americans in a positive light.[40] While the medical, dental, and law schools never materialized, AU offered African Americans a Black educational center in the Deep South for postbaccalaureate study.

Howard University in Washington, DC, had awarded its first resident graduate degree (master's) in 1922. Its graduate school, formally established in 1934, offered master's degrees in botany, chemistry, economics, education, English, German, history, mathematics, philosophy, physics, political science, psychology, Romance languages, sociology, and zoology. The graduate council at Howard was a who's who of Black intelligentsia. Members included political scientist and future Nobel laureate Ralph J. Bunche, economist and later Guggenheim fellow Abram L. Harris, philosopher and Rhodes Scholar Alain Locke, educational psychologist and *Journal of Negro Education* founder Charles H. Thompson, and historian and Guggenheim fellow Charles H. Wesley. The creation of a stand-alone graduate school at the "capstone of Negro education" was linked to both increased demand created by segregation scholarships and university officials' vision of Howard as the center of Black scholarship in arts and sciences. The number of graduate students increased from 43 in 1926, when no states funded graduate study for African Americans, to 326 in 1937 when seven states did.[41] Private Black colleges filled a void created by the lack of graduate programs at tax-supported Black institutions in the South. Howard conferred its first doctor of philosophy degrees in 1958 to two chemistry students.[42]

In 1929, the same year that AU commenced graduate education, Missouri finally implemented the segregation scholarship program that Walthall Moore had proposed years earlier. Lawmakers set aside $15,000 to pay the full tuition for Black students compelled to study out of state in the fiscal years 1929 and 1930. Black Missourians could then pursue out-of-state undergraduate or graduate education available to non-Black state residents at the University of Missouri. Just two years later, though, lawmakers stipulated that Black Missourians could only receive a segregation scholarship if they pursued courses of study that were not offered at Lincoln and only *after* they completed the first two years of college, since many assumed that the general education courses that students took in those first two years were offered also at Lincoln.[43] In 1935 Missouri decreased the appropriation to $10,000. State lawmakers also changed the scholarship policy so that the state only paid the difference in tuition and fees between the cost to study at an out-of-state institution and the cost charged to study at the University of Missouri, rather than the full tuition.[44] All these changes point to a legislature that funded Black education grudgingly.

The 1935 change may have been an attempt to stretch meager resources during the Depression, but the arrangement was problematic. If Black students studied at schools that charged lower tuition than the University of Missouri, then they were not entitled to any state funding.[45] In addition, Missouri did not appropriate any money for transportation or increased living costs. Black scholars had to arrange travel to and from the out-of-state universities and secure housing on their own. Transportation and higher living costs often impacted their ability to pursue education out of state. If students were lucky enough to raise the money for the initial transportation costs, God forbid that a loved one should fall ill or some other home emergency arise, since scholarship recipients seldom had enough money to return home prior to graduation.

Walthall Moore had envisioned the segregation scholarship program as a temporary arrangement to provide Black students with educational opportunity until Missouri fully developed Lincoln's academic offerings. Missouri's white lawmakers, though, had other plans. Rather than provide the amounts necessary to equalize resources between Lincoln and the University of Missouri, the legislature provided just enough funding to keep Lincoln open. For example, for the biennium of 1935 and 1936, Lincoln's president asked state lawmakers for an appropriation of nearly $950,000. The legislature appropriated just $400,000, making Lincoln's full development impossible.[46]

Missouri's public officials also perverted fair implementation and administration of the segregation scholarship program beginning in 1929. The law stipulated that the Lincoln Board of Curators administer the segregation scholarships, but that rule was not enforced. Instead, Missouri's superintendent of schools doled out tuition checks and did so arbitrarily.[47] He denied support to many worthy applicants.[48] The only positive aspect of state officials' not adhering to the legislative stipulations was that students could matriculate at institutions not adjacent to Missouri. Some recipients attended schools farther away, including Howard University and the University of Michigan. Not limiting Black Missourians to study in adjacent states expanded opportunity at African Americans' expense, since the segregation scholarships did not include travel allowances. Rather than fund Lincoln appropriately, Missouri exported Black citizens seeking the educational opportunities available at the University of Missouri from 1929 until 1950, when the state's flagship university began admitting Black students.

Lincoln's limited academic offerings affected Black Missourians' access to both undergraduate and graduate education. Many Black undergraduates chose not to go to Lincoln because their preferred course of study was not available there. This was the case with sister and brother Lucile and Guion Bluford of Kansas City.[49] The Bluford siblings were born in Salisbury, North Carolina—Lucile in 1911 and Guion in 1915. A second brother, John Henry Bluford Jr., was born in 1913. Their mother, Viola Harris Bluford, was a graduate of Oberlin College, and their father, John Henry Bluford Sr., had degrees from Howard and Cornell. John Sr. taught at the Black Agricultural and Technical College of

North Carolina (present-day North Carolina Agricultural and Technical State University) in Greensboro. Viola Bluford died in 1915, and three years later John Sr. remarried and relocated to Kansas City, Missouri, to teach science at the all-Black Lincoln High School, the only academic secondary school for African Americans in the area until desegregation.[50] Many of the teachers at Lincoln had master's degrees and several had doctorates.

Intellectual curiosity was encouraged in the Bluford home. Lucile recalled being a voracious reader during her childhood: "My neighbors used to say I read all day long. I'd sit out on the swing and read." Her love of books exposed her to the inequality inherent in segregation. She had to visit the library at the local white high school to find reading material unavailable at her school.[51]

At Lincoln High, Lucile Bluford excelled academically and participated in several extracurricular activities. She worked on both the high school newspaper and yearbook staffs. She honed her journalistic talents after school by visiting the office of Kansas City's *The Call*, an African American newspaper founded in 1919 by Chester Franklin. After graduating first in her high school class in 1928, Lucile decided to pursue journalism in college.[52]

Lucile hoped to attend Howard University, but her father wanted her to remain close to home. Given her interest in journalism, the University of Missouri in Bluford's home state was the logical choice because it had the oldest and best-regarded journalism program in the country. The university, however, did not admit African Americans. Lincoln University did not have a journalism program. Thus, in 1928 Lucile matriculated at the University of Kansas (KU) in Lawrence, which was less than fifty miles from Kansas City, Missouri. She majored in journalism. Her brother Guion enrolled at KU in 1932 and studied mechanical engineering. During his last year of undergraduate study, the state of Missouri offset Guion's expenses at KU with a segregation scholarship in the amount of thirty-seven dollars.[53] It is unclear why Lucile never received tuition assistance for her undergraduate study and Guion only in his final year. Perhaps they had not been aware of the available funds, or perhaps the state ran out of money before they received assistance.

The Bluford siblings were fortunate in that they could study closer to home than many of their Black peers. Missouri exported Black students to KU from all over the state, including St. Louis and Jefferson City, locales much farther from Lawrence, making it difficult or impossible for these students to travel home regularly.

Like many Black students studying out of state, the Bluford siblings encountered racial intolerance at the university they attended. During the time Lucile and Guion studied in Lawrence, University of Kansas policy barred Black students from participating in intercollegiate athletics, the ROTC, the debate team, the campus choirs, and the student council. They could not attend campus dances and concerts.[54] University policy mandated that they eat in a special section of the cafeteria because, according to KU chancellor Ernest Lindley, allowing Black students to sit anywhere would cause white students to boycott the cafeteria. The chancellor reasoned that Black students had more to lose from open seating because if the cafeteria closed because of integrated seating, students such as Lucile and Guion Bluford would have no dining options on or off campus.[55] Kansas also barred the Blufords and other Black students from living in campus housing. Even though there was a swimming requirement for KU students, the university waived the requisite for Black students so as not to "contaminate" the pool.[56] Like Du Bois at Harvard, the Blufords were at, not of Kansas. These racist policies meant that Black graduate students compelled to attend the University of Kansas on segregation scholarships faced ostracism.

Joining Black organizations was one way Black students survived racial discrimination at KU. In 1931, twenty-three Black students formed the Paul Robeson Dramatic Club to explore their shared interest in the dramatic arts and playwriting while simultaneously creating community in a hostile environment. Black Greek organizations proved to be a consistent source of support and kinship for segregation scholarship recipients. Lucile Bluford joined the university's chapter of Alpha Kappa Alpha Sorority, the first Black sorority for college-educated women in the United States. Her Guion pledged Alpha Phi Alpha, the first Black intercollegiate Greek-lettered fraternity in the country. Alpha Kappa Alpha established a chapter at KU in 1915, with Alpha Phi Alpha following in 1917. By 1923, Kappa Alpha Psi Fraternity and Delta Sigma Theta Sorority, two other Black Greek organizations, also had campus chapters at KU. Both the Alpha Kappa Alpha and the Alpha Phi Alpha chapters at KU had houses, offering their members affordable off-campus housing. The university's Pan-Hellenic and InterFraternity Councils, however, did not recognize Black Greek organizations or afford them the privileges offered to white Greeks.[57]

Black organizations allowed Black students to form community among themselves while being in a white setting. Lucile Bluford graduated in 1932 as one of 388 class members. Based on an examination of the 1932 KU yearbook, only five members of the senior class were phenotypically African American. Guion's class also lacked racial diversity. He was one of only ten Black students in the class of 1936, which had a student population of 261.

Immediately after graduating from KU, Guion Bluford entered the graduate engineering program at the University of Michigan with a segregation scholarship from Missouri. He received seventy-five dollars for his one-year master's program. The grant covered the difference between one semester of tuition at Mizzou and Michigan, but he also had to pay for housing and transportation. In Ann Arbor, Guion lived at 822 Fuller Street, the home of Albert and Minnie Shaffer, a Black couple who regularly rented to Black students denied campus housing because of racial discrimination. At the time he lived with the Shaffers, there were a few other boarders in the home, including another Black graduate student, Elwood Boone, an alumnus of Virginia State College (present-day Virginia State University), who pursued a master's degree in education with a segregation scholarship from Virginia while Bluford studied engineering.[58]

Guion earned his master's degree in mechanical engineering in 1937.[59] At Michigan, he was the only Black member of the university's chapter of the American Society of Mechanical Engineers.[60] Immediately after graduation, he joined the faculty of Alcorn Agricultural and Mechanical College in Mississippi before relocating in 1942 to Pennsylvania, where he was employed as a mechanical engineer with several engineering and industrial firms during World War II as a result of President Franklin Roosevelt's Executive Order 8802, which required defense industries to hire workers without regard to race, creed, color, or national origin. He died suddenly in 1967, twelve years before his son, Guion Bluford Jr., became the first African American in space.[61] The younger Bluford later recalled that his father was his role model, so he decided to follow in his footsteps and become an engineer. All the obstacles that the elder Bluford endured to secure advanced training in engineering paved the way for his son to serve in several space missions as an astronaut for the National Aeronautics and Space Administration (NASA).

In addition to joining Black affinity groups, Black students who attended KU around the same time as Guion Bluford Sr. fought exclusionary policies on campus by exposing them to the larger world. In 1930, Harry Brown, a KU undergraduate, wrote to the NAACP about the racial discrimination he and other Black students experienced. He detailed how KU barred African Americans from athletics and segregated them to a Black section of the cafeteria. His letter attracted the attention of W. E. B. Du Bois, then the editor of the NAACP's monthly magazine, *The Crisis*. Du Bois responded by writing to KU chancellor Ernest Lindley, seeking clarification about the situation at KU.[62]

Chancellor Lindley, who led the university from 1920 until 1939, blamed Black discontent on the segregation scholarships that increased the number of Black students on campus. He wrote, "We not only admit the colored students of Kansas but also those of Missouri, Oklahoma, and Texas where they are not permitted to enter their own state university. As a result, the attendance of Negroes has rapidly increased."[63] Lindley went on to say that he and other administrators had considered not admitting Black students who were not natives of Kansas, but he did not want to deprive them of the right to a higher education. The rapid increase in the number of Black students that Lindley mentioned amounted to 175 Black students out of a total undergraduate population of 2,604, with the graduate student proportion even smaller. Du Bois asked Lindley if he could reprint his response in the NAACP's magazine to demonstrate how a white administrator blamed Black students for the racial discrimination they experienced. Lindley wisely declined.[64]

Since graduate and professional school students rarely have active roles in campus life, KU's Black graduate students could avoid many of the racial slights that the Blufords experienced, but they were not immune from all discrimination and exclusion. Until 1938, Black students could not complete their last two years of medical school at KU because clinical training was required and white patients in the university's teaching hospital preferred not to be treated by Black students.[65] The university began admitting Black students into its medical school in 1922, but only to complete the first two years of a four-year program.

Geraldine Mowbray was a University of Kansas School of Medicine student forced to leave the institution after her first two years. The Kansas native had attended Howard University for her bachelor's degree before entering KU in 1937. After completing the first two years of medical school at KU, she transferred to Howard's medical school in 1939, and the state of Kansas paid her tuition until she graduated in 1941. Both of Mowbray's parents were also graduates of Howard, and her mother was one of the founders of Alpha Kappa Alpha Sorority. Her family had the financial resources to absorb the hidden fees associated with having to settle in a new area to complete an advanced degree. At Howard, Mowbray lived in a campus dormitory and had the opportunity to participate in the full life of the university.[66] The freedom Geraldine Mowbray found at Howard was impossible for Black students enrolled in historically white institutions.

Universities' discriminatory admission policies meant that Black students often had to travel long distances to achieve their academic goals. It is not clear what mode of transportation Guion Bluford used to commute between Kansas City and Ann Arbor. Whether he drove a private vehicle, took a bus, or rode a train, he had to abide by the unwritten customs of segregation, which included "colored cars" on railways and seating at the back of buses in border states. On trains, he would not have been served in the dining car until all white patrons had been attended to. If Bluford owned an automobile, he still had to learn which establishments had restrooms for African Americans and which motels accepted Black patrons.

Traveling while Black was humiliating and dangerous, so many consulted the *Negro Motorist Green Book*, an annual guidebook for Black travelers that listed services and places throughout the United States that were friendly to African Americans. Victor H. Green, a Black New Yorker who worked as a mail carrier in New Jersey, created the travel directory, whose mission was explained to Black travelers, in bold letters, on the first page: "Just What You Have Been Looking For!! NOW WE CAN TRAVEL WITHOUT EMBARRASSMENT." The *Green Book*, as it was commonly known, was published from 1936 until 1966 except during World War II, and offered road information, travel tips, and listings of hotels, restaurants, service stations, and hair salons that welcomed Black patrons throughout the country. The book's northern roots and its national success, evidenced by a circulation of nearly 2 million by 1962, proved that traveling Black was difficult in all the United States.[67]

Interstate travel, whether by car, rail, or bus, was even more distressing for Black women, who faced both racial and sexual harassment. Many transportation carriers refused to extend the usual courtesies of womanhood to Black women, denying them the accommodations and protections offered to white women. Incidents of poor treatment included the L&N Railroad's refusing meal service to a prominent Black schoolteacher and actress on a train between St. Louis and Atlanta in 1939 and a policeman beating a Black woman, at the train conductor's request, on a train between New York and South Carolina in 1945.[68] Despite the prevalence of such encounters, many Black women found themselves on the road, alone, far from home as they pursued their academic interests with segregation scholarships.

Such was the case for one of Missouri's brightest and most promising young residents, Almeta Virginia Crockett, who grew up in the St. Louis suburb of Websters Grove. Crockett was born in Chicago to upwardly mobile parents who stressed education. Her father, a Chicago attorney and politician, sent his toddler daughter to live in Missouri with an aunt after the child's mother's untimely death. Almeta excelled academically in school, receiving high marks consistently and skipping two grades. Too young to start college, she took classes at Stowe Teachers College (present-day Harris-Stowe State University) for several years before moving away from home. Attending the St. Louis institution gave her a front-row seat to segregation in higher education as she daily disembarked at a bus stop across from Washington University, which did not admit Black students. Crockett matriculated at Lincoln University in 1932 and graduated as valedictorian four years later. During her studies at Lincoln, she was elected homecoming queen and served as president of the campus chapter of Alpha Kappa Alpha Sorority.[69]

As was often the case for Black women with college degrees in the early twentieth century, Crockett found teaching to be the most accessible occupation for her. She taught at a public school in Cape Girardeau after earning her bachelor's degree, but her unquenchable thirst for knowledge led her to pursue graduate study. She wanted to earn a master's degree in home economics to expand her skills in the classroom. Going to Mizzou was out of the question, so she turned her sights northward. New York was an ideal place because she had family members there whom she could stay with to decrease lodging expenses and help her navigate an unfamiliar city.[70]

Almeta Crockett studied at Columbia University for three consecutive summers, making the trip from Missouri by train. Like many Black public school teachers, she completed a master's degree through summer coursework, so that she could continue teaching during the school year. She received a segregation scholarship in the amount of $107 from Missouri in the 1937 summer to offset the costs of her study during her first year. Crockett stayed with her cousins Lillian and Charles Toney, the first Black man elected as a judge in New York. The Toneys resided in Harlem's Sugar Hill, a neighborhood whose residents included some of the wealthiest and most prominent African Americans, including Adam Clayton Powell, Duke Ellington, and Arturo Schomburg. On the rare occasions that she was not boarding in Sugar Hill, Almeta stayed with a great-aunt who lived in the Broadway Theater district. These familial connections played a significant role in Crockett's decision to attend Columbia and made her graduate study more feasible financially.[71]

At Columbia, Crockett met her future husband, John Lathen, while standing in line to register for classes. He, like her, was a graduate student from the South. He was studying Latin at Columbia in preparation for medical school. Crockett socialized with many of the Black graduate students from the South. She recalled years later to her daughter that each southern state had a particular tree on campus under which students from that state regularly gathered. She fraternized with other students from Missouri by frequenting the Missouri tree. Crockett graduated from Columbia in 1939 and accepted a job teaching home economics at all-Black West Virginia State College. She remained on faculty for three years before marrying Lathen in 1942. The couple eventually settled in Teaneck, New Jersey, where she became the first Black teacher in the city's public schools, teaching home economics and later working as a guidance counselor.[72]

Another Black woman Missourian compelled to leave her state for graduate school was Mineola Isabella Briscoe. Briscoe was one year behind Crockett at Lincoln, and the two women participated in many of the same extracurricular activities and both had goals of pursuing graduate study. In 1936, Crockett served as president of Lincoln's chapter of Alpha Kappa Alpha Sorority, while Briscoe served as vice president and dean of pledges. Born in 1911 in Holden, Missouri, and raised in Independence, Briscoe was also president of the Student Council and vice president of the Home Economics Club at Lincoln. After graduating with a bachelor of science degree in home economics in 1936, Briscoe taught for one year in the segregated public schools of Wagoner County, Oklahoma. She then matriculated at the State University of Iowa (present-day University of Iowa), where she pursued her master's degree in home economics.[73]

Briscoe was in good company at Iowa: between 1935 and 1954, Missouri sent more Black students on segregation scholarships to Iowa's flagship university than any other state.[74] Briscoe enrolled in June 1937 and graduated in August 1938. While living in Oklahoma, she had completed fieldwork on the housing and social conditions of Wagoner County's African Americans, and she brought her notes with her. Her master's thesis was titled "A Study of Living Conditions among Negroes in Wagoner County, Oklahoma, as a Basis for Home Economics Instruction." She argued in the thesis that home economics curricula should be tailored to the community served.[75]

Briscoe's studies took her more than 300 miles from home and onto a campus that was not always welcoming of Black students. In 1942, a few years after she graduated from Iowa, a faculty member described the university's racial climate in this way: "The University of Iowa admits colored students, but the student body as a whole does not fraternize with them, and the faculty members do not make protegees [sic] of them; for better or worse what personal recognition that a colored student here receives he has to earn by excellent work and superior traits of personality."[76]

Missouri provided Briscoe with $158 to attend Iowa, an amount that covered her tuition ($98) and the nonresident fee ($40).[77] Yet, she still had to come up with the funds to pay for transportation and off-campus housing because the university barred African Americans from living in campus dormitories until 1946. Rent ranged from ten to twenty dollars per month for a room near the institution.[78] It is likely that Briscoe created community with the few other Black women attending the predominately white campus and the small but close-knit Black population in Iowa City.

Black students studying at large public universities often rented rooms from local Black or white residents since they could not live on campus. Such an arrangement made it harder to socialize with peers after hours since there was not a critical mass of students in one place. Moreover, students often subsidized their expenses by working as domestics in the homes where they lived. Many were too tired to study after completing their chores.[79]

The Iowa Federation of Colored Women's Clubs addressed the poor housing situation at the University of Iowa by purchasing a home for Black women students in 1919. The IFCWC was part of a national network of Black women's clubs organized under the auspices of the National Association for Colored Women. Black women's clubs had been practicing racial uplift and social activism in various ways since 1896. The Federation Home, located at 942 Iowa Avenue, was a twelve-room, two-story residence in a white neighborhood near campus.[80]

During her tenure at Iowa, Briscoe lived at 713 South Capitol Street rather than in the Federation Home. She was a boarder in a house rented by Carl and Frances Culberson. The middle-aged African American couple regularly rented rooms to make ends meet. Carl Culberson worked as a porter, while his wife maintained the home.[81] Briscoe probably learned about the Culbersons' housing availability from local Black residents, who had a habit of meeting Black students at the train station and directing them to one of the six Black boardinghouses in the city.[82] Even after securing housing, Briscoe, like Lucile and Guion Bluford and Harry Brown, had to balance the rigors of school with the realities of segregated campuses.

When Louisiana native Jewel Prestage matriculated at Iowa in 1951 for doctoral study in political science, housing remained an issue for Black students. She recalled decades later that her biggest "dilemma" in Iowa City was lodging. "It was almost impossible to find a house or apartment that would rent to Negros," she said.[83] By that time, the university allowed Black graduate students to live on campus, so she shared a dormitory room with a friend who had graduated two years earlier from what was also Prestage's alma mater, Southern University of Baton Rouge. Prestage later recollected that while she had never lived outside the South and in such a cold climate, having a roommate from home made her adjustment easier. After the friend graduated, things became difficult again. She lived alone for a while and then had another Black roommate. When that roommate left, the university assigned her a Filipino roommate, but only after that student signed a form stating that she agreed to live with a Black student.[84]

The summer before she graduated, Prestage married her husband, James, who was also a segregation scholarship recipient from Louisiana. The couple had trouble finding housing at Iowa, eventually renting an on-campus trailer that lacked toilet facilities and running water. They had met at Southern University, where they had both been undergraduates. James Prestage's educational career was interrupted when he was drafted into the US Navy during World War II. At Iowa, he studied zoology, earning a master's degree in 1955 and his PhD in 1959. He was also inducted into the Sigma Xi Scientific Honor Society because of his academic performance. They would both go on to have storied careers in higher education, with many decades of service at Black colleges.[85]

As was the case with the Prestages, graduate training equipped Mineola Briscoe with the credentials to teach at the collegiate level. By 1944, she was teaching home economics at West Virginia State College.[86] Segregation scholarship recipients chose to teach at Black colleges after earning advanced degrees for a variety of reasons, including their racist exclusion from white college faculties in both the North and South, a desire to return to their undergraduate alma maters, and a commitment to the education of Black students.

Laurence Eugene Boyd overlapped with Briscoe during his time at Iowa, and he too became a Black college faculty member. Born in 1898 in St. Louis, Boyd served in World War I as a lieutenant in the Adjutant General's Department of the Army at Fort Sheridan in Illinois. He remained in the state after the war, earning his bachelor's degree at Knox College in 1919. With tuition assistance from Missouri, Boyd matriculated at the University of Iowa, earning a master's degree in education in 1933 and a doctor of philosophy degree in education with a psychology minor in 1938.[87]

Boyd started his long professional career by returning to Missouri after graduate school. He had stints at two Missouri educational institutions before serving as a teacher, high school principal, and professor in several schools and colleges in North Carolina and Georgia, including Livingstone College, Winston-Salem Teachers College (present-day Winston-Salem State University), and Atlanta University. His last place of employment, Morris Brown College, named him professor emeritus of education after more than thirty years on the faculty.[88]

Some recipients of segregation scholarships avoided the social ostracism and humiliation prevalent at white colleges by pursuing graduate study at Black institutions. Vivian Dreer, a native of St. Louis born in 1916 to educator parents Herman and Clarice Dreer, chose to attend Fisk because it was an institution with prominent Black scholars on the faculty, and she relished the chance to engage with such brilliant Black minds. After graduating from Fisk in 1937, with a bachelor's degree in English, she stayed for graduate study, earning a master's degree in English in 1939. The state of Missouri offset her expenses with a segregation scholarship in the amount of $158.50. Rather than navigating a hostile environment at a historically white institution, Dreer participated in fireside chats at Fisk with guest speakers such as James Weldon Johnson and Aaron Douglass.[89]

John Eric Royston, born in 1914 in Kansas City, Missouri, was another segregation scholarship recipient who chose to pursue advanced study at a Black college. He matriculated at Howard University School of Law in Washington, DC, in the fall of 1937. He had graduated from Tuskegee Institute three years earlier with a bachelor's degree in industrial arts.[90] Missouri gave Royston $139.50 during the 1937–38 academic year to attend Howard. He earned an LLB or bachelor of laws from Howard's three-year program in 1940. Unlike Black Missourians at white schools in the North and Midwest, Royston could live on campus and take part in the social life of his institution. What he did not have, however, was access to the movers and shakers in Missouri's legal scene. He planned to practice law in his home state, so attending Mizzou's law school would have more adequately familiarized him with Missouri law and allowed him to build relationships with the state's other future jurists. The lack of law schools for African Americans in Missouri denied Royston this opportunity.

Whether Black Missourians sought to pursue advanced study at out-of-state Black or white institutions, many had to contend with being denied a segregation scholarship because the state did not provide sufficient funds. Missouri's legislature appropriated segregation scholarship funds biennially, and the funds were regularly exhausted as demand exceeded supply. Ruth Greene and Adell Deboe were two St. Louis public school teachers who studied for their master's degrees at Columbia University during the summers in the early 1940s. It was common for Black teachers to go north, as many institutions there had special programs allowing educators to earn their master's degree after attending for several consecutive summers. In the summer of 1942, Lincoln University president Sherman Scruggs informed Greene and Deboe that only $2.79 remained in the segregation scholarship fund, so the state would not be able to reimburse them for expenses they incurred as graduate students in New York City.[91]

Missouri's failure to adequately fund its tuition assistance program forced Black residents pursuing a graduate degree to bear the entire financial burden of studying in another state. Those who could not afford to do so saw graduate education closed to them. Perhaps Greene and Deboe's outrage about the lack of funds led President Scruggs to ensure that going forward, Black Missourians knew ahead of time that the segregation scholarship fund had been exhausted.[92] Disclosure, however, did not change the fact that Missouri was derelict in its duty to provide Black residents with graduate education opportunities.

No one felt the sting of Missouri's broken educational promises to African Americans more than Walthall Moore. He served four terms in the statehouse and worked tirelessly to upgrade Lincoln, but significant improvements did not come until long after he retired. Missouri did not desegregate its public institutions of higher education until 1955. Moore could not have foreseen that the segregation scholarships he instituted would still be used by other southern states at the time of his death in 1960.[93] Moore lived long enough to see Black students challenge their exclusion from state-supported graduate and professional school programs. Black lawyers educated at Howard University, which bore an unfair burden in providing African Americans with legal education that southern states denied them, led the fight to open these institutions.

CHAPTER TWO

Chipping Away at Segregation
The First Legal Challenges to Desegregate Graduate and Professional Schools

There is little justice in laws which jail a poor man for stealing a loaf of bread and leave at liberty university regents who rob us of our citizenship.
—"There Ought to Be a Jail," *Baltimore Afro-American*, April 27, 1935

On February 7, 1933, NAACP executive secretary Walter White received two letters at his New York office from African Americans in North Carolina. The first letter was from Charles Clinton Spaulding, president of North Carolina Mutual Life Insurance Company in Durham. At the time, North Carolina Mutual was the largest and oldest Black business in the United States, so anything bearing Spaulding's name carried weight. The business executive instructed NAACP staff to expect a letter from "two progressive young attorneys of Durham" about a matter of "vital importance" to African Americans throughout the South.[1]

Even though Spaulding failed to disclose the matter at hand, NAACP staff were not held in suspense, because a letter from Black attorneys Conrad Pearson and Cecil McCoy arrived the same day. Pearson had graduated from Howard University School of Law and McCoy had attended Brooklyn Law School. Pearson and McCoy announced their intent to test the constitutionality of the University of North Carolina's practice of excluding Black students from its professional schools.[2] While the North Carolina Constitution required racial segregation for elementary and secondary school students, it did not mandate segregation of the races in its colleges and universities. Pearson and McCoy planned to have a Black resident of North Carolina apply to the state's pharmacy school. They contacted the national NAACP office seeking permission to use local NAACP funds to support the legal challenge.[3]

NAACP officials in the national office responded enthusiastically, as their staff had been considering legal challenges to educational segregation in the South.

Walter White and other organization leaders understood that separate but equal systems of education were financially impossible and wagered that pursuing taxpayers' suits would quicken the end of segregated schools. Their position, however, was contrary to that of many African Americans who believed that equally funded segregated education was the way to proceed.[4] There were many possible avenues for litigation within education, including suits to equalize the salaries of Black and white teachers and suits challenging the unequal physical facilities of Black and white schools. While the NAACP pursued cases of these sorts, challenging Black access to public graduate and professional schools put the development and leadership of the race at the center of the organization's agenda. Without Black attorneys, physicians, pharmacists, scientists, and other scholars, African Americans were at the mercy of white professionals to provide legal assistance, healthcare, advanced education, and a host of other services.

There were many strategic reasons to litigate graduate and professional school cases. For one thing, it was easy to disprove separate but equal when states made no provision for African Americans to pursue graduate and professional training. Additionally, many of the NAACP's leaders believed graduate education was a less inflammatory arena than elementary and secondary education because there was no chance of adolescent and teenage race mixing with the desegregation of postbaccalaureate programs. Finally, graduate and professional school test cases would not require small children to serve as plaintiffs. Instead, educated, upwardly mobile, and striving plaintiffs stepped into the limelight.

The proposed test case in North Carolina appealed to the NAACP because it had the potential to expand graduate and professional school opportunities for striving African Americans throughout the South. If Pearson and McCoy prevailed, then North Carolina had to either admit Black students to its graduate and professional school programs at historically white UNC or create equal programs for Black students at one of its public Black colleges.[5] The latter option, though financially impossible, offered segregationists a way to preserve the racial status quo. Moreover, if the case went all the way to the US Supreme Court and resulted in a favorable verdict, then the segregation scholarship programs in Missouri and West Virginia would become unconstitutional. Rather than dissuade the lawyers or ask them to delay, White simply inquired about the anticipated costs of the suit and asked if they had found a plaintiff.[6]

This chapter explores the painfully slow desegregation of higher education through an examination of some of the earliest legal battles to secure Black educational equality. Unlike much of the civil rights movement that is illustrated with dramatic marches and speeches, the law was a weapon that did not offer poignant soundbites or a charismatic leader. Thus, the victories won in courtrooms and legal opinions do not usually attract the same attention or celebratory fanfare despite their importance.

Legal challenges gave African Americans access to the courts and the opportunity to right wrongs inflicted on them by racist actors, whether agents of the state or private citizens. Despite the opportunity to wield the Constitution as a weapon, legal challenges required Black plaintiffs to eschew anonymity, a tall order during an era when challenging white supremacy could result in financial ruin or even death. Going into court was also risky in that lack of support from the Black community or from well-known Black leaders often doomed cases from the beginning: the need for money and moral support was constant and without it, uphill battles became much more difficult.

The legal challenges to secure equal educational opportunities for Black southerners exposed southern states' willful neglect of public Black colleges. This chapter also shows that southern state legislatures deliberately withheld equitable funding and curricular programs from Black colleges. If that was not bad enough, white lawmakers robbed Peter to pay Paul by taking money out of Black colleges' budgets to fund segregation scholarships.

Conrad Pearson and Cecil McCoy found their plaintiff, Thomas Raymond Hocutt, after canvassing Black neighborhoods and speaking with Black educators. Many people declined to participate in a test case because the threat of economic reprisal or physical violence was real. Segregationists punished African Americans who challenged the racial status quo with job termination, loan revocation, housing eviction, or bodily harm. Hocutt, a twenty-four-year-old senior at North Carolina College for Negroes (NCC, present-day North Carolina Central University) in Durham, agreed to serve as the litigant despite the possible consequences.[7] The pharmacy school's only requirement for admission was graduation from an accredited high school with fifteen credits. Hocutt had graduated from Durham's Hillside High School with nineteen credits.[8] According to McCoy, Hocutt was a student "possessing the necessary prerequisites for admission [to the University of North Carolina], an average of 'B' for a period of three college years, an excellent record for deportment, and a hue closely approaching ebony."[9] The Durham native had worked at a local drugstore for years before becoming the assistant headwaiter at the Washington Duke Hotel.[10]

While the Durham lawyers laid the groundwork for a test case, segregationists, tipped off by a surprising source, began to stoke the fire of opposition.

Pearson and McCoy had shared their plans with a handful of people including NCC president James Shepard. North Carolina College for Negroes was one of five public Black colleges in North Carolina—three of those institutions offered four years of college training and the other two offered two-year teacher-training programs. None of them offered graduate studies. Shepard relayed what he learned about the impending segregation lawsuit to the white editor of the *Greensboro Daily News*.[11] On February 13, 1933, the newspaper ran an inaccurate article stating that a group of Black students planned to apply to UNC's law school to force the state to pay for African Americans to attend graduate and professional schools out of state. The paper also stated that Black North Carolinians were not united behind the legal challenge, with "the older and less radical members of the race" desiring "adequately equipped and maintained" Black institutions rather than admission into white institutions.[12] The supposed desires of Black elders revealed Shepard's position on the fight to provide African Americans with advanced study.

Shepard's first allegiance was to the all-Black college that he had founded in 1910. The college became public in 1923 and earned the distinction of being the first state-supported liberal arts college for Black students in the nation. Thus, Shepard's institution depended on the goodwill of the all-white state legislature. Moreover, the college's financial health during the Great Depression was in peril. In the spring of 1933, NCC could barely meet its payroll obligations, and the future was not bright as the college contended with declining enrollment the following academic year.[13] Thus, Shepard would not support any political activity that upset the state's all-white legislature and jeopardized NCC's funding. Moreover, to protect his institution's existence, the ambitious educator hoped to see professional schools established at NCC rather than the desegregation of academic programs at white institutions.[14] To thwart Hocutt's case, Shepard refused to release the plaintiff's college transcript, though only a high school diploma was required for admission to UNC's pharmacy school.[15]

Hocutt and his attorneys went ahead with his attempt to enroll at the University of North Carolina without Shepard's support. North Carolina's flagship institution offered students a bachelor's degree in pharmacy (S.B. Pharmacy). In March 1933, Hocutt, accompanied by Pearson and McCoy and Louis Austin, a local Black journalist and activist, made the fifteen-mile drive from Durham to Chapel Hill to register. Standing in the registrar's office at UNC, Hocutt sought admission for the spring quarter. Thomas Wilson, the university registrar, denied the young man's application for admission based on his race.[16]

Having expected an admission rejection, Hocutt and his legal team began preparing their legal challenge. The two attorneys filed a writ of mandamus asking the Durham County Superior Court to compel UNC officials to admit Hocutt on the grounds that he had been rejected on account of his race when the state's constitution did not require racial segregation in higher education. While the Durham NAACP voted against supporting the lawsuit (with Shepard ostensibly playing a role in that decision), the national NAACP office sent William Hastie to assist with the trial given the far-reaching implications of the case. Hastie, a Black graduate of Harvard Law School, taught part time at the Howard University School of Law and was then enrolled at Harvard studying for a doctorate in judicial science. He was also a new member of the NAACP's National Legal Committee, a standing committee of well-trained attorneys who served as an advisory board for the organization. Despite Hastie's legal knowledge, he did not play a significant role in the preparation for Hocutt's case because he did not arrive in North Carolina until the day before the trial.[17]

A Black man taking on the oldest public university in the United States was a blockbuster event. Judges recessed their courts so that lawyers could attend. Professors from both the Duke University and UNC law schools arrived early to secure seating to hear oral arguments. African Americans—taxpayers who had long seen their hard-earned dollars used to provide graduate and professional school study to white students—"packed the courthouse like a sardine box."[18]

Spectators who were lucky enough to secure a seat on the second day of the trial saw Judge M. V. Barnhill deny Hocutt's request for admission to UNC. The judge ruled that Hocutt's attorneys sought the wrong remedy because the court could not compel UNC to admit a student. The most that the court could do was ask the registrar to consider Hocutt's application in good faith without respect to his race. Furthermore, the judge found that Hocutt had not properly applied for admission since his application did not include a transcript of his college credits from NCC (which Shepard had refused to provide). UNC officials maintained that they required an academic record of the last school that an applicant attended. The lack of a college transcript, however, should have been moot since UNC's pharmacy program was an undergraduate program and only required a high school transcript.[19]

Segregation kept Thomas Hocutt from reaching his highest potential. The aspiring pharmacist graduated from NCC in June 1933 with a major in science and resettled in New York soon after. There, he married and had a twenty-nine-year career working for the New York City subway system. He remains the forgotten pioneer who laid the groundwork for *Brown*.[20]

The *Hocutt* case, though usually held up by legal scholars as a failure, signaled that African Americans understood southern states had a legal obligation to provide equal educational opportunities for them. North Carolina lawmakers saw the proverbial writing on the wall and sprang into action to insulate the state from another legal challenge. Weeks after the NAACP's defeat in Durham County Superior Court, white politicians Sumter Brawley and Walter Murphy introduced a segregation scholarship bill in the North Carolina House of Representatives. The bill set aside state funds to offset the tuition costs of Black residents who pursued graduate or professional study out of state that was available to white residents at the University of North Carolina. Lawmakers proposed paying tuition up to the amount that North Carolina spent per white student for graduate study in the state. While the bill passed in the state house, it was defeated in the state senate and Black North Carolinians continued to have neither private nor public options for postbaccalaureate study within the state.[21]

The NAACP chose not to appeal the *Hocutt* decision, instead pursuing another professional school legal challenge in the border state of Maryland. This time the organization had a plaintiff seeking admission to the University of Maryland School of Law, the second-oldest law school in the United States. Donald Gaines Murray, a twenty-one-year-old Black man, had graduated from Amherst College in the spring of 1934 and desired to attend what was the only tax-supported law school in Maryland. Although the University of Maryland was in College Park, the law school was in Murray's hometown of Baltimore. Alpha Phi Alpha Fraternity attorney William Gosnell had first identified Murray as a test plaintiff. The fraternity planned to bring suit since neither Maryland nor the university mandated segregation. NAACP-affiliated attorneys Charles Hamilton Houston and Thurgood Marshall believed that they and the NAACP were better resourced and had more experience than the fraternity counsel, so they took over the case. Houston and Marshall were members of the fraternity.[22]

Houston and Marshall were new additions to the NAACP's legal team who had not been on staff when Thomas Hocutt attempted to enter the University of North Carolina. Houston was the son of a lawyer, a Phi Beta Kappa graduate of Amherst, a World War I veteran, and a two-time graduate of Harvard Law School, where he had served on the prestigious *Harvard Law Review*. After earning his juris doctor, he remained in Cambridge and obtained a doctor of juridical science. Houston joined the NAACP staff as special counsel in May 1934. At the time, he was dean of the Howard University School of Law, where he encouraged law students, including Conrad Pearson, to become social engineers who used the Constitution to improve the lives of the most marginalized citizens. As dean, Houston raised admission standards and discontinued the evening law school. These measures paid off and the American Bar Association accredited Howard's law school in 1931. In June 1935, Houston took a leave of absence from Howard and worked for the NAACP full time.[23]

Marshall was a graduate of the all-Black Lincoln University of Pennsylvania and Howard's law school, where he had been one of Houston's star students. Marshall had wanted to attend the University of Maryland law school, but his mother dissuaded him from applying since the institution did not accept Black applicants.[24] Immediately after graduating from Howard Law in 1933, Marshall opened a law office in his hometown of Baltimore but also did some contract work for the NAACP at Houston's invitation. Marshall would join the NAACP staff full time in October 1936. Murray's lawsuit brought the teacher and student together on a case to challenge unconstitutional inequality in higher education.[25]

Gosnell, like Marshall, was a Baltimore native and Lincoln graduate who had also aspired to attend the University of Maryland law school. Segregation compelled him to attend the University of Chicago Law School instead. Gosnell, who served as counsel for Alpha Phi Alpha Fraternity, first introduced Donald Murray to Marshall.[26]

In fact, two Black students had attended Maryland's law school in the late nineteenth century before it came under state control. Harry Cummings and Charles Johnson enrolled at the law school in 1887 and completed the three-year course in two years, graduating in 1889. Cummings later became Baltimore's first Black city council member. Two more Black students entered the law school in 1889 but the school expelled them in 1890 in response to complaints from white students. The color line remained in place when the law school came under state control in 1920.[27]

Donald Murray had first expressed interest in attending Maryland's law school in December 1934 when he wrote a letter to the president of the university. The president's response to his inquiry showed just how derelict the state had been in providing postsecondary education to African Americans. University of Maryland president Raymond Pearson recommended that Murray apply instead to the state-maintained Princess Anne Academy (present-day University of Maryland Eastern Shore), a "separate institution of higher learning for the education of Negroes," suggesting that the school was the Black counterpart to the University of Maryland, though this was anything but the truth.[28] In reality, as late as 1930, most Princess Anne students received only secondary-level instruction.[29]

In Maryland, state-supported Black higher education was dismal. Historian Martha Putney has found that of the states that practiced racial segregation in education, Maryland was next to the last to provide public facilities for Black higher education.[30] The first public institution was present-day Bowie State University, which began in 1865 as a private preparatory school training teachers before coming under state control in 1908. Coppin State University opened in

1900 as a Black teacher-training school run by the Baltimore City School Board. To continue receiving federal land-grant funds at the University of Maryland, lawmakers affiliated the state with Princess Anne Academy, a privately owned junior college on the Eastern Shore and designated it as its Black land-grant institution in 1890. The state provided Princess Anne with no more than one-fifth of its Morrill Act appropriation, a sign of the state's lack of commitment to Black education.[31]

As higher education scholar Katherine Wheatle has asserted, Princess Anne was a college "in name alone" whose designation as a public Black institution was nothing more than a last-ditch effort to maintain funding for Maryland's white land-grant college, Maryland Agricultural College (present-day University of Maryland, College Park).[32] Princess Anne Academy began in 1886 as a private elementary school for African Americans established by the majority-Black Delaware Conference of the Methodist Episcopal Church. The board of trustees of Morgan College, a Black and private Methodist institution located in Baltimore, oversaw the academy, which was originally called Delaware Conference Academy.[33] Evidence that the institution was far from a full-fledged college included the facts that an annual catalog detailing the academic program was never published and the Maryland Department of Education did not recognize its teacher-training program. The Black school, dependent on the limited resources of Morgan College, offered only secondary education courses in home economics and agriculture with minimal liberal arts instruction, had very few faculty members with bachelor's degrees, and did not have facilities or equipment like what was available to non-Black students at Maryland State College (the name had changed from Maryland Agricultural College in 1916 and would change to the University of Maryland in 1920). Most important with respect to Donald Murray, Princess Anne did not offer any graduate or professional school training.[34]

Advanced degree programs were not possible at Princess Anne because of the state's financial neglect. By 1931, the non-Black Maryland Agricultural College received an *annual* federal appropriation of approximately $250,000. Princess Anne's total federal appropriation from 1890 until 1928 was $284,000.[35] The disparity in funding not only kept Princess Anne from being a bona fide postsecondary institution offering more than preparatory education but also depleted Morgan College (present-day Morgan State University) of financial resources that could have enhanced its own facilities and course offerings.

Princess Anne's drain on Morgan College's finances led the Baltimore institution to seek state takeover of the junior college beginning in the late 1920s. For more than four years, Morgan's president and trustees attempted to sell

Princess Anne to the state, but officials dragged their feet. Instead of purchasing the institution, Maryland's legislature increased funding to the school in 1933 by allocating Morrill Act funds to its two land-grant schools based on population. Princess Anne received a percentage of the funds equal to the percentage of the state's Black residents. The funds supposedly upgraded Princess Anne and achieved the equality stipulated in the 1890 Morrill Act.[36]

At the same time that state officials revised land-grant funding formulas, they also authorized that a portion of Princess Anne's Morrill Act allocation provide Black citizens with segregation scholarships to study at Morgan College or at out-of-state institutions and pursue courses not offered at Princess Anne but offered to non-Black students at the University of Maryland. Because of budget cuts, however, no segregation scholarships were awarded.[37] Even before the scholarship program became law in March 1933, Herman Dennis became the first recipient of a segregation scholarship from the state of Maryland. Dennis, a native of Allen, Maryland, and a graduate of Princess Anne, received state funds to continue his undergraduate education at Virginia State College. He enrolled for the winter quarter that began in January 1933. Dennis walked 250 miles to his new school, a journey that took him four days. He received his scholarship from the University of Maryland, whose president oversaw efforts to give Black students higher educational opportunity. President Pearson maintained that the state provided Dennis with funds for tuition and transportation, so if the young man walked, he did so to save and repurpose his carfare.[38]

Herman Dennis notwithstanding, Maryland's segregation scholarship was nonexistent. It appeared that the state had awarded Dennis a scholarship to maintain the appearance of equality of education when, in reality, higher education for African Americans was a low priority for state leaders. Seven months after Dennis matriculated at Virginia State, Victor Daniel, a resident of St. Mary's County, Maryland, applied to President Pearson for tuition assistance to study engineering at Hampton Institute. Pearson informed Daniel that state law stipulated that a committee meet and award segregation scholarships to eligible applicants. The university president went on to explain that the governor had not yet appointed committee members, so no funds could be disbursed.[39]

It was in this context of separate and unequal education in Maryland that Donald Murray set his sights on the University of Maryland School of Law. Pearson responded to Murray's December 1934 letter by informing him that Maryland maintained Princess Anne Academy for the higher education of African Americans. Moreover, Pearson explained that the legislature had created segregation scholarships in 1933. He asserted that the funds would allow Murray to study out of state and pursue coursework unavailable at Princess Anne.

Pearson neglected to mention that the legislature had not funded its 1933 segregation scholarship law, so the state had not actually awarded any scholarships.[40]

Undeterred, Murray submitted a formal application for admission to the University of Maryland School of Law and paid the application fee in January 1935. The university registrar summarily returned his application and fee, explaining that the university did not admit African American students. Murray then appealed to the university's board of regents for a fair evaluation of his application, precipitating another letter from the university president. This time, Pearson encouraged Murray to attend Howard University's law school. The chief executive of Maryland's flagship institution explained to Murray, a Baltimore resident and a Maryland taxpayer, that Howard's law school, located in Washington, DC, cost $135 per year while Maryland's law school, located in Baltimore, cost $203.[41]

Regardless of higher tuition, Donald Murray desired to attend law school in his native state, so NAACP attorneys prepared a legal challenge in support of his educational dream. Thurgood Marshall and William Gosnell, in counsel with Howard Law dean Charles Hamilton Houston, filed suit in Baltimore Circuit Court for a writ of mandamus to compel the University of Maryland law school to admit him. The NAACP lawyers contended that Donald Murray was a citizen of Maryland, that he was qualified to enter the law school, and that university officials had refused him admission because of race.[42]

Between the time Murray sued to enter the University of Maryland School of Law on April 20, 1935, and the time when the university responded to the suit on May 6, 1935, the state of Maryland purchased Princess Anne Academy from Morgan College.[43] The $100,000 purchase came six years after Morgan College's trustees first approached the University of Maryland about taking control of Princess Anne.[44] The timing of the deal was not coincidental. Pearson, who had corresponded with Murray in December 1934, probably alerted state officials to the possibility of a legal challenge to the state's practice of segregation in higher education. Maryland bought Princess Anne in hopes of convincing the court in its impending trial that it adhered to the doctrine of separate but equal and provided collegiate opportunities to its Black citizens. Princess Anne did not have a law school, however, and was not equal to the University of Maryland. NAACP lawyers planned to argue that the state could either establish a comparable law school for African Americans or admit Murray to the flagship.[45]

Maryland officials' other strategy to comply with the doctrine of separate but equal in the wake of Murray's application to the law school was to finally fund an out-of-state segregation scholarship program for African Americans. Lawmakers set aside $10,000 annually for Black Marylanders desiring undergraduate or graduate programs that were available at the University of Maryland but not at Princess Anne in a desperate attempt to keep the flagship institution free of Black students. The 1935 scholarship law did not include a provision for transportation costs or increased cost-of-living expenses. To legitimate the funding, state officials tapped Carl Murphy, the editor of the Black *Baltimore Afro-American* newspaper, to chair the interracial committee that awarded segregation scholarships. The committee selected recipients based on scholastic ability, financial need, and personality. The latter qualification was assessed through interviews with the awards committee. While committee officials expected to award fifty inaugural scholarships of $200 each, nearly 300 Black residents submitted applications, indicating great Black demand for higher education. Murphy estimated that $35,000 would be needed—a far cry from the $10,000 allocated—to fund all the applicants.[46]

Demand for Maryland's segregation scholarships only increased as Black residents realized the funding could subsidize study at prestigious educational institutions. Carl Murphy's daughter, Frances, who was herself a segregation scholarship recipient, recalled her father telling applicants, "If you're not going to school at home, you might as well go to the best in the country. Let's find the best. They won't let you go to the University of Maryland, so we're going to send you to the best in the country."[47] Making the most out of an unfair system, Black southerners matriculated at graduate programs that ranked higher than the flagship institutions in their home states.

Though *Murray v. Pearson* (1936) would become a landmark legal case on the way to *Brown*, the lower court trial drew little interest in Black circles when it began in June 1935. Unlike the crowded courtroom two years earlier in the Hocutt case, Murray's trial court case was sparsely attended. Houston later said that the reason more African Americans did not take interest in the case was because they thought it was a hopeless cause.[48] Despite limited initial interest, however, the *Baltimore Afro-American* newspaper covered the proceedings in detail and kept its readers informed of the shifting winds in Black higher education.

NAACP attorneys Houston and Marshall got their first unanticipated victory during the opening statements. Charles T. LeViness III, assistant state attorney general and counsel for the university, admitted in his initial remarks that but for Donald Murray's race, he was qualified for admission to the flagship law school. No longer having to prove that Murray was qualified, Houston then set out to establish that the young man genuinely wanted to attend the University of Maryland's law school and was not simply a pawn for the NAACP. One reason why some might have been skeptical of Murray's intentions was because Alpha Phi Alpha Fraternity had actively searched for a plaintiff. Fraternity officials identified nine possible plaintiffs and selected Murray as their best option.

Despite being chosen as the face of a planned legal challenge, Murray genuinely wanted to attend Maryland's law school because he lived in Baltimore and attending the state school would be more convenient than attending any other law school. Additionally, Murray wanted to attend his home state's law school because he planned to practice law in Maryland and wanted the opportunity to become familiar with the state's laws. Houston elucidated these reasons while questioning Murray on the stand.[49]

On cross-examination, the university's counsel mentioned the segregation scholarship program and asked Murray if it was not true that he could commute daily to Howard University using public transportation for approximately fifteen dollars per month. In essence, the defendants' defense was that Howard University had a law school for Black students, so the University of Maryland School of Law did not have to admit Black Marylanders. During the redirect examination, Houston pushed back at the reasoning of opposing counsel by asking Murray to state the expenses he would incur for room and board if he attended Maryland's law school versus room and board if he attended Howard. Murray testified that his living expenses would be zero for the former and an unspecified amount for the latter. In a memorable and strategic end to the questioning of his client, Houston asked Murray how long his family had been Maryland taxpayers, to which Murray responded thirty-three years.[50]

In addition to demonstrating that Maryland taxed all its citizens to benefit white residents, Houston laid bare the racial disparities in the state's educational institutions. The latter strategy was not without problems since it made a claim for equality based on the inferiority of a Black institution. The NAACP lawyer succeeded in getting University of Maryland president Pearson to admit under oath that the two-year academic program at the all-Black Princess Anne was not equivalent to the academic program offered at the University of Maryland. Not only was Princess Anne's biology lab, which consisted of one table, a handful of test tubes, and a butterfly case, significantly inferior to the science labs at the University of Maryland but the former school's faculty did not have the same credentials as faculty at the flagship. He also had the president to concede that the University of Maryland admitted qualified Chinese, Japanese, Indian, Mexican, and Puerto Rican applicants even as it arbitrarily and universally denied admission to Black citizens of the United States.[51]

Houston's ninety-minute questioning of Pearson made it abundantly clear that Maryland failed to provide its Black citizens with equal educational opportunity. First, Pearson conceded that no segregation scholarship funds had been available when he told Murray to apply for such funding in lieu of admission to the University of Maryland law school. According to Houston, all the president offered to Murray was "hope" since actual tuition assistance was not available.[52] Second, the president also admitted that when funding finally became available for segregation scholarships, the state's policy rendered ineligible those Black applicants who attended schools whose tuition was less than the tuition at the University of Maryland. This concession meant that Murray would not have received assistance from the state to attend Howard's law school, since it was less expensive than Maryland's.[53]

Houston also questioned Roger Howell, the dean of the University of Maryland School of Law, under oath. Howell testified that several courses at the law school focused on state law. Thus, anyone who wanted to practice in Maryland but who studied law out of state was at a disadvantage. The state claimed that receiving a segregation scholarship provided Black citizens with the same educational opportunity that was available to white citizens in state, but Howell's testimony demonstrated that this argument did not hold water.[54]

Maryland native son Thurgood Marshall delivered the closing statement in Murray's case. He told the court that the legal precedent in the 1896 US Supreme Court case *Plessy v. Ferguson* required the University of Maryland to admit Murray to its law school. Maryland operating a law school for white residents created a constitutional responsibility for it to offer the same opportunity to its Black residents. Absent a tax-supported law school for Black students, the *Plessy* decision mandated that Maryland's law school admit Black students.[55]

Issuing his ruling from the bench, Judge Eugene O'Dunne sided with the NAACP and ordered the University of Maryland School of Law to admit Donald Murray. The judge recognized that there was no other tax-supported law school in Maryland available for African Americans and therefore, it was Murray's constitutional right to attend the flagship. The ruling was the first victory in the NAACP's effort to desegregate graduate education in the South. The University of Maryland, however, readied its appeal to Maryland's highest court, the Maryland Court of Appeals.

Days after Murray's court win, he received a threatening letter. The letter began, "you damn n——" and promised that nothing good would happen to Murray if he continued to push for admission.[56] The ominous note served as a reminder that white university officials were not the only ones invested in keeping African Americans out of tax-supported graduate and professional schools in the South. White supremacists' intimidation tactics, however, had no effect on Murray.

Murray matriculated in the University of Maryland School of Law in September 1935 as university officials prepared to appeal the lower court's decision. In doing so, he became the first known African American to enter a tax-supported, historically white southern university since the 1890s. Being a Black trailblazer brought a mixture of emotions including excitement, anxiety, and uncertainty. One sign of the import of Murray's enrollment was the action of the law school dean, who initially instructed Murray not to attend classes on the first day. The dean wanted the opportunity to address the study body without Murray being present, but later nixed that plan and the pioneering Black student attended class.[57]

In a segregated society where many assumed that white people were smarter than Black people, Murray could not fail. To that end, Alpha Phi Alpha Fraternity paid for Murray's tuition and books to remove financial barriers to success, and the NAACP arranged for a professor at Howard University's law school to help Murray with his studies. Attorneys Houston and Marshall kept close tabs on Murray's academic progress. Underscoring the gravity of the situation, the Black lawyers told Murray that he could not entertain romantic relationships until he completed his fall exams.[58] The men understood that if Murray did not remain in school and graduate, then segregationists could argue that African Americans did not have the intellectual capabilities for graduate and professional education. The attorneys' reasoning was well-intentioned but also tragic, because it meant that Murray did not have the luxury of being a regular law student who could socialize freely. The cost of racism was so high that Murray had to succeed academically to pave the way for future Black students.

The appellate trial, *Murray v. Pearson* (1936), occurred after Murray had already entered Maryland's law school, so NAACP lawyers had more than Murray's grade point average to ponder. When making oral arguments in November 1935, Assistant State Attorney General LeViness took a different approach from the first trial and attempted to relieve the state of any obligation to provide legal education to African Americans by falsely asserting that the University of Maryland was a private institution since it largely operated from tuition fees. If the school was private, then the state had no constitutional obligation to provide legal training for African Americans because it was not providing it for white residents either—a private institution offered those services. Somewhat ironically, after arguing that Maryland did not operate a public law school for white residents, the assistant attorney general then asserted that if the law school was deemed to be a public institution, then the state had met its Fourteenth Amendment obligation by creating a separate school for African Americans. Additionally, the attorney general claimed that with segregation scholarships, the state provided graduate educational opportunities to African Americans. Without shame, LeViness asserted in court, "if he [Donald Murray] goes to Howard Law School in Washington, the state of Maryland will pay his tuition there. If he desires to go to Columbia, Harvard, or any other law school, the state will pay his tuition."⁵⁹ Donald Murray, however, wanted to go to, and was in fact attending, the University of Maryland School of Law. He had not asked the state to pay for his legal training but rather to afford him the opportunity to study at the flagship.⁶⁰

Charles Hamilton Houston stressed in the second trial that Maryland had no constitutional statute mandating segregation in higher education. He maintained that the board of regents of the University of Maryland law school excluded Donald Murray from his state's law school based on their own prejudices rather than because of a state law.⁶¹ Houston also questioned the availability of Maryland's segregation scholarships and the sacrifices required of recipients. He not only showed that demand for the tuition assistance far exceeded supply but also that the aid did nothing to compensate students for the hours lost commuting to faraway places to study. Moreover, with respect to legal education and the localized nature of law, losing the ability to learn with and from the people who would be future colleagues or opponents in courtrooms was a disadvantage that money could not compensate.⁶²

In *Murray v. Pearson* (1936), the court quickly rejected the state's first argument that the law school was private and focused on whether there were equal facilities for Black and white students. Appellate judges found that segregation scholarships were not an adequate defense in Murray's case because they were not available at the time that he applied to law school. Furthermore, the scholarships only paid tuition differentials rather than the full cost of attending law school in another state.⁶³

Donald Murray and the NAACP won again, and the state of Maryland chose not to take the case to the US Supreme Court. Triumph in one battle, however, did not mean that the war was won. For one thing, Murray's victory did not overturn *Plessy*, since the court did not invalidate the principle of separate but equal. Moreover, the case did not set a national precedent since it did not go to the US Supreme Court. Yet the NAACP had breached what many considered the impenetrable wall of segregation. A former slave state had desegregated its law school. It became clear early on, however, that Maryland officials did not plan to allow for more desegregation. In fact, the University of Maryland's new president, H. C. Byrd, inquired with the state's attorney general about whether Murray could be removed from the law school since the state had established a segregation scholarship program. The attorney general informed Byrd that the scholarship program was not retroactive and since Murray began his studies before it went into effect, he could not be dismissed.⁶⁴

Desegregation of graduate and professional education at the University of Maryland and throughout the South remained an uphill battle. While another

Left to right: Thurgood Marshall, Donald Murray, and Charles Hamilton Houston at the counsel table in the Baltimore City Courthouse during Murray's legal battle to enter the University of Maryland School of Law in 1935. Prints and Photographs Division, Library of Congress, Washington, DC.

Black student entered Maryland's law school during Murray's second year, every other unit of the university remained segregated. The state purchased Morgan College (present-day Morgan State University) in 1939 to increase public educational opportunities for Black students while also continuing its segregation scholarship program. Black Maryland students received tuition assistance to attend a host of universities in the United States and Canada, including Howard University, Hampton Institute, McGill University, the University of Denver, Harvard, Columbia, and Penn. In 1947, for the first time, Black Maryland residents received segregation scholarships to attend Johns Hopkins University in Baltimore.[65]

The University of Maryland finally opened all its academic programs to African Americans in 1950 when Esther McCready, a Black woman undergraduate, desegregated the nursing school and Parren Mitchell, a Black graduate student and future congressman, desegregated the sociology program after a lengthy legal battle. In a full circle moment, Donald Murray was part of the legal team that filed suit on behalf of the pioneering students. Their legal victories outlawed Maryland's use of segregation scholarships. At that time, Maryland spent $150,000 annually to send Black students out of state for advanced study.[66]

As Murray pursued legal redress in Maryland, segregation scholarships came into existence in other states. Oklahoma passed a 1935 segregation scholarship law providing up to $230 in tuition and transportation costs to Black students to go elsewhere to pursue courses of study available to white students at the University of Oklahoma. Oklahoma had just one university for African Americans, Langston University. The public land-grant, established in 1897, was not comparable to the University of Oklahoma, a problem that state officials supposedly addressed with segregation scholarships. Oklahoma's inaugural cohort of segregation scholarship recipients included several who would go on to make history. In addition to renowned historian John Hope Franklin, who received funds for doctoral study at Harvard and later led every major professional organization in the history discipline, there was Wadaran Kennedy, who studied at Pennsylvania State University and in 1936 became the first African American to earn a doctorate degree in dairy husbandry. Kennedy went on to have a thirty-four-year career at North Carolina A&T State University, where he was a professor and the first dean of the graduate school. Another Oklahoma segregation scholarship recipient was Vertna Sneed Jones, one of the first graduates of the master of social work program after the Atlanta School of Social Work, which affiliated with Atlanta University in 1938. Jones became the first licensed social worker hired by the Oklahoma Department of Public Welfare.[67] In 1946, Oklahoma exported 300 Black scholars out of state. Many more would have pursued graduate study had the state's segregation scholarship allotment not run out, again demonstrating great Black demand for advanced study.[68]

Oklahoma was not the only state to act in the wake of the NAACP's attack on separate but equal in graduate and professional schools. Virginia made provision for Black graduate study after Alice Carlotta Jackson, a twenty-two-year-old Black woman from Richmond, applied to the University of Virginia (UVA) in August 1935. Jackson had earned a bachelor's degree in English from the all-Black and private Virginia Union University in her hometown and had done additional study at Smith College in Massachusetts. She sought a master's degree in French, but none of the Black colleges in Virginia, including the public Virginia State College in Petersburg, offered graduate work. UVA not only offered Jackson's desired program but had begun admitting women to graduate and professional school programs in 1920. Thus, she applied to UVA. As expected, university officials refused Jackson admission based on her race.[69]

The threat of a legal challenge based on the inexistence of separate but equal educational facilities led Virginia lawmakers to create master's degree programs in elementary and secondary education at Virginia State College. Next, state lawmakers established a segregation scholarship program like those operating by that time in Missouri, West Virginia, Maryland, and Oklahoma. Virginia's program was unique, though, in that scholarship applicants had to apply to Virginia's historically white universities first and if university officials deemed them eligible for admission, then they could receive a segregation scholarship to study outside the state. Alice Jackson became one of Virginia's first segregation scholarship recipients. She used state funds to earn a master's degree in English from Columbia University in 1937. Among the other 125 inaugural recipients of state aid were ones who used funding to study at elite institutions such as Michigan, Chicago, Penn, Rutgers, Howard, Fisk, and Cornell.[70]

Black communities were divided on how to respond to segregation scholarship programs. In the weeks after its passage, Virginia's program was the subject of intense debate at the annual convention of the Old Dominion Dental Society. The statewide organization of Black dentists went on record supporting the tuition assistance but not before some expressed their opposition. Leon Reed, a Richmond dentist, believed that Black residents should not apply for tuition assistance because "it's just a subterfuge to get around the NAACP court suits." Many other convention attendees took the opposite view. J. M. Tinsley, another Richmond dentist, called on African Americans to flood state authorities with segregation scholarship applications so that Virginia had to spend $100,000 on Black graduate study. Also focusing on finances, the society's president, Fred Morton, argued, "If you had a patient who owed you $20, and offered to pay $2, you would hardly refuse the $2, would you? Then why should you refuse to accept the state's offer on this occasion?"[71] The spirited debate revealed the diversity of thought among African Americans on the best way to secure educational opportunity in the South.

Alice Jackson's experience demonstrated that segregation scholarships in no way made Black graduate study equal to that white students enjoyed. She received $61.48 from Virginia to offset expenses incurred during her summer term at Columbia. The amount covered only 20 percent of her expenses to live and study in New York.[72] Things did not improve during the regular academic term. While Virginia agreed to give Jackson $75 each semester, the difference between tuition at Columbia and the University of Virginia exceeded $150, so Jackson had to spend significantly more than she would have if racism did not prohibit her from studying at her state's flagship. Rather than admit that they were in violation of the segregation scholarship law that required the state to pay the difference in tuition fees, Virginia officials told Jackson to study at a cheaper institution.[73]

Another inaugural recipient of a segregation scholarship from the state of Virginia was Helen Gray Edmonds of Lawrenceville. Edmonds graduated from Morgan College in 1933 with a bachelor's degree in history. She used state funds from Virginia to enter the graduate program in history at Ohio State University in 1936, earning her master's degree in 1938 and her doctorate in 1946. Edmonds was the first Black woman to earn a doctorate in history from the institution. While a student in Columbus, Ohio, Edmonds barely lived above subsistence. She had exactly fifty cents per day for food. She survived the lean times and went on to have an illustrious career at North Carolina Central University, where she was on the faculty from 1941 to 1977. Edmonds's other history-making roles included being the first Black woman to serve as a graduate school dean and being the first Black woman to second the nomination of a US presidential candidate. Her career success demonstrated both what was possible when southern states created educational opportunities for Black scholars and what was undoubtedly lost as many African American southerners, particularly Black women, did not have the luxury of relocating to a different state for graduate study.[74]

Exporting Black scholars was an expensive enterprise. Virginia doled out just under $10,000 during the 1937 fiscal year. The next year, the amount nearly doubled. Scholars receiving funds then included Spottswood William Robinson III, a Richmond native and Virginia Union University alumnus who was a second-year student in Howard's law school. After earning his juris doctor in 1939, Robinson taught at his law school alma mater and later became a civil rights attorney whose numerous cases include one of the five lawsuits consolidated under *Brown v. Board of Education*. In fact, it was Robinson engaging in intellectual warfare that encouraged Thurgood Marshall in 1950 to pursue a direct attack on all school segregation and offered the strategy. In later years, Robinson became the chief judge of the US Court of Appeals for the District of Columbia Circuit.[75]

By 1955, Virginia was spending more than $149,000 annually. Every dollar spent to send Black Virginians elsewhere was a dollar that could have been used to improve and expand academic programs at the all-Black Virginia State College. Great demand and limited resources led Virginia officials in 1937 to stop providing segregation scholarships for residents enrolled in the medical schools at Howard and Meharry because the tuition at both schools was below that of the University of Virginia.[76] These officials failed to realize or simply did not care that having to travel to another state was an expensive endeavor in itself, even if tuition costs were lower. Denying African Americans access to medical education in the commonwealth while also withdrawing financial support to study at the only two Black medical schools in the country severely limited Black Virginians' access to credentialed Black medical providers.

In addition to Oklahoma and Virginia, Kentucky established a segregation scholarship program after the lower court ruled in Donald Murray's favor. Kentucky's tuition assistance program was the brainchild of Black public school teachers and was introduced in the state legislature by a Black man. Throughout the Jim Crow era, Black teachers organized themselves in statewide teachers associations to secure better educational opportunities for Black children, to pursue professional development initiatives for themselves, and to participate collectively in the Black freedom struggle. Kentucky's Black teacher association, known as the Kentucky Negro Educational Association (KNEA), was founded in 1877.

By 1935, more than 90 percent of Kentucky's 1,525 Black teachers were KNEA members. During that year's state meeting, members engaged in a lively debate about the recent change to state law with respect to teacher certification. A new law required teachers to have one year of graduate work to obtain the standard high school teaching certificate. Black teachers pointed out that while they had no option for graduate study within the state, their white counterparts did. Since the standard high school certificate came with a higher salary, the educators assembled passed a resolution calling on the state to make financial provision for them to secure the training out of state that they could not obtain in state because of segregation.[77] The time was not yet ripe for Black educators to engage in a direct assault on Jim Crow, but they could demand that the state expend resources on their behalf.

Within thirty-three days of taking office in January 1936, Charles W. Anderson, the first African American elected to the Kentucky legislature and the first African American southern state legislator since Reconstruction, successfully sponsored legislation to create Kentucky's segregation scholarship program. KNEA's Legislative Committee had organized a strategic lobbying initiative to support the bill. Committee members wrote letters to each state senator backing the bill and encouraged African Americans across the commonwealth to contact the senator from their district.[78]

The Anderson-Mayer State Aid Act set aside $5,000 for Black Kentuckians to seek graduate education out of state since the University of Kentucky did not admit Black students and Kentucky's sole state-sponsored four-year institution for African Americans, Kentucky State College (KSC, present-day Kentucky State University) in Frankfort, did not have graduate programs. Once again, segregation scholarships took money away from a public Black college. The legislature decreased KSC's appropriation by $5,000 to fund its tuition assistance program.[79] KNEA members, many of whom were graduates of Kentucky State, had envisioned the state appropriating more money for Black education rather than taking funds away from an already meager appropriation for the state's sole four-year public Black college.

Charles Anderson, the man who codified segregation scholarships in Kentucky, was born in Louisville to a physician father and a mother who served as the state supervisor of Negro schools and later the dean of women at Kentucky State College. The family moved to Frankfort, Kentucky's capital, soon after his birth, so from a young age Anderson was exposed to a Black intelligentsia associated with the college. There was never a question that he would attend college and earn an advanced degree. He attended KSC and received his bachelor's degree from Wilberforce University in 1927 before earning a law degree at Howard in 1931, two years ahead of Thurgood Marshall. At Howard, Anderson learned from Charles Hamilton Houston, who became the law school's vice dean in 1929.[80]

When Anderson returned to Kentucky after law school, he settled in Louisville, where he opened a thriving law practice serving the city's large and striving Black population. The most populous city in the state, Louisville was also distinctive in that it was a major southern city where African Americans never lost access to the ballot box. From Kentucky's ratification of the Fifteenth Amendment, African Americans participated in the electoral process and wielded significant influence in elections. For example, Black Louisvillians used their voting strength to compel white Republicans to establish a campus of the University of Louisville for Black students in exchange for Black support on a 1925 education bond issue. The quid pro quo resulted in the city's opening Louisville Municipal College in 1931.[81]

As one of a handful of Black attorneys in the state, Anderson's legal services required him to frequently travel to faraway hamlets to assist African Americans seeking a modicum of justice. In 1934 he found himself demanding justice for the family of Rex Scott, a Black miner in the mountains of eastern Kentucky, who was lynched after defending himself against an unprovoked attack by a drunken white man. Scott overpowered and killed his attacker. Understanding that killing a white man was a capital offense, Scott turned himself in to authorities and hoped for his day in court. Before that could happen, though, a jailer welcomed the slain man's friends into the jail. They abducted Scott and took him out of town, where they mutilated his body. Anderson's inquiries into the lynching led the governor to fire the jailer who permitted the mob to remove Scott from his jail cell. Additionally, the Black lawyer's interest in the case led the state's attorneys to gather considerable evidence identifying the lynchers, an unheard-of step when official reports usually stated that lynchings were committed by parties unknown.[82]

In 1933, as a private citizen rather than as a public official, Anderson first called on Kentucky to pay the graduate tuition of Black students compelled to study out of state because of segregation. In a proposal submitted to Governor Ruby Laffoon and education officials, Anderson offered two suggestions to address the dearth of graduate and professional school opportunities for African Americans. He advised that the commonwealth could either admit Black students to the University of Kentucky and the University of Louisville or pay the tuition for Black students to study out of state.[83] Kentucky's white leaders ignored Anderson's recommendations, but his advocacy did not go unnoticed in Black circles.

Anderson's work on behalf of African Americans made him a leading contender in the 1935 legislative race for Kentucky's Fifty-Eighth District, based in Louisville. A Republican, Anderson ran against a Black Democratic attorney and African Methodist Episcopal Zion presiding elder, Charles Ewbank Tucker, and a white Independent, Samuel Spevack, in a district that was 80 percent African American. On the campaign trail, Anderson vowed that if elected, his priority in the legislature would be "the advancement of my own people."[84] Voters in the district responded enthusiastically. The twenty-eight-year-old rising star defeated Tucker by a three-to-one margin. Spevack garnered only sixty-four votes. The victory gave Anderson a decisive mandate to advocate for African American interests in Frankfort.[85]

Expanding higher education opportunities for Black Kentuckians was at the forefront of Anderson's mind when he took his seat in the Kentucky General Assembly. For one thing, Black public school teachers had supported his candidacy so he likely was aware of the KNEA resolution about out-of-state aid. Additionally, Anderson knew about the limited collegiate opportunities available to Black Kentuckians. Western Kentucky Industrial College and Kentucky State College were the only state-supported institutions of higher education for African Americans in the commonwealth, with KSC being the only four-year public college. Located in Paducah, WKIC was established by a Black couple in 1909, and the state took over the institution in 1918. WKIC offered four years of high school and the first two years of college. It became a two-year technical school in 1938. Long before WKIC existed, state officials had chartered KSC in 1886 as the State Normal School for Colored Persons to prepare Black teachers for the public schools. The institution became the state's land-grant institution for African Americans in 1890 and operated as a high school until the 1920s. In 1931,

KSC began offering bachelor's degrees and seven years later, it changed its name to the Kentucky State College for Negroes. KSC had limited undergraduate offerings and nothing beyond the bachelor's degree. Other Black postsecondary institutions such as Louisville Municipal College and Simmons College existed but did not receive state funds.[86]

KSC operated on a shoestring budget from its inception. At no time in the first half of the twentieth century did KSC's funding, in either actual dollars or per student, approximate the funds allocated to the white flagship and land-grant institution, the University of Kentucky in Lexington, or the white regional colleges in Bowling Green and Richmond. The underfunding hindered the Frankfort institution's physical plant and its curricular offerings, which paled in comparison to the myriad of undergraduate, graduate, and professional school programs that UK hosted.[87]

Black Kentuckians did not benefit from UK's extensive taxpayer-supported academic programs because the 1904 Day Law barred Black and white students from learning in the same educational institutions. Kentucky state representative Carl Day sponsored the bill, calling for segregation in education to end the interracial arrangement at Berea College, where Black and white students learned side by side. The US Supreme Court upheld the racial segregation statute in the 1908 case *Berea College v. Kentucky*. The legal decision cemented higher education inequity in Kentucky. Charles Anderson himself had been a victim of this miscarriage of justice. The racist Day Law required him to relocate to Washington, DC, for law school rather than obtain legal training at UK. Studying in the state of his birth, where his family had paid taxes for generations, was not an option.[88]

Attempting to right an educational wrong he knew firsthand, Anderson introduced legislation establishing Kentucky's segregation scholarship program days after being sworn into office. The only nonwhite member of Kentucky's General Assembly, which consisted of 100 representatives and 38 senators, Anderson impressed upon his colleagues the need to provide graduate education for Black Kentuckians. His bill required the state to pay the tuition of qualified Black students who desired professional and graduate training offered at the University of Kentucky or other state-supported institutions that was not available at KSC. Only African Americans who had lived in Kentucky for at least five years were eligible to receive assistance. The maximum amount allotted to any student was $175 per academic year, with an annual appropriation of $5,000 for the segregation scholarship program. Known as the Anderson-Mayer Act after Anderson and Stanley Mayer, the sponsoring legislator in the senate, the segregation scholarship program became law in February 1936.[89]

Kentucky's State Board of Education administered its segregation scholarships. Prospective recipients had to complete an application provided by the Superintendent of Public Instruction and submit their undergraduate transcript with the application. Applications were considered for one quarter or semester at a time, meaning students had to apply for every academic session in which they desired aid. If a student missed an application deadline such as the last Tuesday in July, which was the deadline for the fall semester, then he or she would not receive tuition assistance.[90]

Anderson had served as president of the Louisville NAACP in the years immediately preceding his being elected, so he was likely familiar with the association's educational legal challenges in Maryland when he introduced the segregation scholarship program bill to the legislature. Despite the initiative's being at odds with the national NAACP's campaign, Anderson maintained that his legislation gave African Americans access to better educational opportunities.[91] Since Kentucky barred African Americans from its flagship institution, the Black legislator compelled it to make provision for them elsewhere. Kentucky became the fifth state that exiled Black scholars, joining West Virginia, Missouri, Maryland, and Oklahoma. Virginia followed suit a few months after Kentucky.

National NAACP leaders did not openly oppose Anderson's legislation. Charles Hamilton Houston issued a press release stating that if Anderson's program was an optional measure, giving Black students the choice to study out of state or remain in state to obtain graduate and professional training, then the NAACP did not object to it. Of course, Anderson's bill made no mention of in-state opportunities, so this was an indirect critique of the legislation. Houston's statement went on to describe segregation scholarships as "palliatives" that fail to "cure the inequalities which exist."[92] Privately, Houston was a bit more oppositional, writing to Anderson, his former Howard Law student, that "the Maryland case was won in spite of the existence of the Maryland scholarship law."[93] In other words, segregation scholarships were not constitutionally adequate.

Anderson's response to Houston's letter makes clear that the Louisville attorney and politician did not see his segregation scholarship program as a cure-all. As Anderson explained to Houston, at the very time that his bill sat on the governor's desk awaiting signature, he met with several civic groups to discuss the possibility of suing the University of Louisville, which barred African Americans. The University of Louisville, a municipal institution, had established the Louisville Municipal College for Negroes in 1931 rather than desegregate. Anderson told Houston that he championed a legal challenge involving the University of Louisville because it was not subject to the state's segregation scholarship law. Moreover, the University of Louisville offered law, dentistry, and medicine, while UK only offered law, so a legal challenge to force the former institution to admit Black students would open many more academic opportunities than a challenge at UK.[94] The proposed lawsuit never materialized, however, and the University of Louisville would not desegregate its student body until 1951.

The Anderson-Mayer Act was legislative proof of the unequal educational opportunities afforded to Black residents of Kentucky. The state had severely underfunded KSC throughout its history, so graduate offerings were out of the question, to say nothing of the college's rudimentary undergraduate curriculum. One year before legislators approved the segregation scholarship program, they appropriated $793,000 to UK and $70,000 to KSC. KSC's president had requested $300,000.[95]

Black Kentuckians seeking graduate and professional training began using state funding to leave home and pursue their dreams in the summer of 1936. As in other states, applicants submitted transcripts and proof of admission and then state officials mailed payment directly to the institutions where students enrolled. Kentucky only offset tuition costs, neglecting the travel and housing expenses that students incurred. While successful applicants could receive up to $175 yearly, very few got the maximum amount. Twenty-two inaugural recipients received segregation scholarships during the first summer from the Kentucky Department of Education, at a cost of $1,046.83. Twelve of the recipients majored in education and ten in arts and sciences. These pioneering scholars matriculated at nine institutions: Atlanta University, Columbia University, Indiana University, the University of Michigan, the University of Chicago, the University of Illinois, the University of Pittsburgh, Harvard University, and the Ohio State University.[96]

During the 1936–37 academic year, the demand for state aid increased and Kentucky spent $3,444.28 subsidizing the graduate study of thirty-four students. In that cohort, twenty-four specialized in arts and sciences, seven in education, and one each in law, medicine, and engineering. Black Kentuckians studied at seventeen institutions, among them Fisk, Howard, Meharry Medical College, the Massachusetts Institute of Technology, and the University of Pennsylvania.[97] Among that year's recipients was William Milton Bright.

Bright obtained a segregation scholarship in 1937 to complete his doctoral studies in zoology at the University of Illinois. A native of Washington, DC, he had earned bachelor's and master's degrees at Howard University. He joined the faculty of Louisville Municipal College when the institution opened in 1931. Six years later, he earned a PhD. Bright remained at LMC throughout the life of the school until it closed in 1951, a casualty of desegregation.[98] At Illinois, Bright learned alongside a handful of other Black students. Their presence at the Urbana-Champaign campus was tolerated but not welcomed: Black students could not live on campus and were prohibited from patronizing campus eateries.[99]

Other Black Kentuckians receiving state aid the same year as Bright were librarians Caroline E. Johnson and Bessie T. Russell, both of Louisville. Library science programs provided aspiring librarians with training in cataloging, classification, book selection, library administration, and reference work. College-trained librarians usually secured jobs at public municipal libraries or in public schools. For a significant period in the twentieth century, the only Black library science school was at Virginia's Hampton Institute, which established a library school in 1925. Additionally, a few historically white northern schools with library science programs admitted a handful of Black students. The University of Kentucky began its library science program in 1918 but barred African American students, forcing them to go out of state. Adding insult to the injury of having to leave the state for the same educational opportunities that white students received in state, Black library science students faced stiffer requirements than their white counterparts. Black Kentuckians did not qualify for Anderson-Mayer aid to study library science unless they had already completed four years of college, while white students at UK could pursue the same academic program after two years of college work.[100]

Bessie Russell, the daughter of Harvey C. Russell Sr., dean at KSC and president of both West Kentucky Industrial College and West Kentucky State Industrial School, earned her undergraduate degree from Louisville Municipal College in 1936. The following year, the twenty-two-year-old scholar completed the library science program at Hampton Institute with sixty-two dollars in tuition assistance from the Anderson-Mayer segregation scholarship fund. She was the third Black librarian from Kentucky to graduate from Hampton's program and the first to do so with a segregation scholarship. Russell went on to a lengthy career as a librarian, serving at several institutions in Kentucky and Ohio, including Kentucky State University.[101]

Caroline Johnson also sought specialized training in library science. Born in Tennessee, she spent her formative years in Minnesota and graduated from the University of Minnesota in 1929. Not long after completing her undergraduate studies, she moved to Louisville and secured employment as the librarian at the city's all-Black Central High School. Her Kentucky residency made her eligible for Anderson-Mayer funds, and in 1937 she received $94.50 to finance her study at Columbia University that summer. Columbia's School of Library Science offered a graduate curriculum leading to the bachelor of science degree over four summers, allowing students to complete the degree program by attending summer sessions. Johnson received her degree in 1943, six years after she began the program. One reason for the extended time it took to complete her degree was personal. Between the year she entered Columbia and the year she finished, Johnson married a Louisville native. Her new marriage prevented her from spending successive summers in New York.[102]

Interest in Kentucky's segregation scholarships remained high, and in 1939 demand for the funds far exceeded supply, even though Charles Anderson had won an increase in the annual appropriation for segregation scholarships to $7,500.[103] State officials notified students who had received Anderson-Mayer funds for the 1938 fall semester that they would not receive any assistance for the spring semester because the fund was exhausted. One recipient who did not take the news too kindly was Alfred Carroll, a twenty-seven-year-old native of Louisville who was studying law at Howard University since the University of Kentucky College of Law did not admit African Americans. Carroll reasoned that if the state could no longer offset his tuition out of state, he would save the commonwealth "the humiliation of telling the world she could not take care of her Negro students" and demand entrance to the historically white flagship. He applied for admission to UK and requested a favorable reply before the second semester so that his studies would not be interrupted.[104]

Kentucky's underfunding of a program designed to preserve segregation created the perfect storm for Carroll to demand the desegregation of UK. While Kentucky's Day Law prohibited Black and white students from learning together, the lack of funds for Black students' postbaccalaureate education put the commonwealth in violation of the Constitution since it provided legal studies to white students but not to Black students. In many ways, the Howard Law student was skillfully deploying the NAACP's strategy of demonstrating that southern governments could not afford separate but equal.

Carroll also thought it a strategic time to press for admission to UK because of a NAACP case ongoing in neighboring Missouri. Even before Alice Jackson applied to UVA and before Donald Murray's case reached the Maryland Court of Appeals, NAACP officials pursued additional legal challenges to segregation at the postbaccalaureate level in the border state of Missouri, where a large and vibrant NAACP chapter existed in St. Louis. The work that had begun in North Carolina with Thomas Hocutt in 1933 bore fruit in Maryland and put southern states on the defensive to at least feign compliance with *Plessy*. With momentum on their side, NAACP attorneys sought a court victory that would have national implications for Black students.

CHAPTER THREE

(In)adequate Compensation for Loss of Civil Rights
Lloyd Gaines and the Constitutionality of Segregation Scholarships

> Do you mean to suggest that a pecuniary payment would be adequate compensation for loss of civil rights?
> —US SUPREME COURT JUSTICE HUGO BLACK,
> "U.S. Supreme Court Hears Arguments in University of Missouri Law School Case," *Black Dispatch*, November 19, 1938

> The obligation of the State to give the protection of equal laws can be performed only where its laws operate, that is, within its own jurisdiction.
> —US SUPREME COURT, *Mo. ex rel. Gaines v. Canada*,
> 305 U.S. 337, 59 S. Ct. 232 (1938)

In the 1930s, one of the most vibrant and bustling places in all St. Louis was the People's Finance Building, located on the northwest corner of Jefferson and Market Streets. According to a 1928 *St. Louis Globe-Democrat* article, the five-story brick edifice was the "only modern office building financed, constructed, occupied and managed by Negroes anywhere in the world."[1] As the center of Black political and social life in St. Louis, the People's Finance Building served as the headquarters and office space for Black organizations, physicians, attorneys. Among those renting space there was Sidney Redmond, a Black St. Louis attorney and the grandson of Hiram Revels, the first Black US senator.

It was not unusual for African Americans from all walks of life to pay Redmond unannounced visits seeking legal assistance. A graduate of Harvard College and Harvard Law, Redmond set up his law office in the People's Finance Building in 1929. He mainly handled personal injury and insurance cases, with some equity matters here or there. Legal work that chipped away at de jure segregation was sporadic for Redmond, but one of the biggest civil rights cases of his career came in 1935, when Charles Hamilton Houston, anticipating another test case, tasked him with gathering information on the history of Missouri's segregation scholarship program. The two Black attorneys were familiar with each other because the Black bar was relatively small and because Redmond had served as president of the St. Louis NAACP in 1934. Redmond found that from 1929 until 1935, Missouri appropriated $55,615.91 for segregation scholarships.[2] Adjusted for inflation, that represents $1,732,615.37 in 2024 dollars.

This chapter demonstrates that the NAACP legal strategy to overturn *Plessy v. Ferguson* was grounded in the often underpaid and thankless labor of a corps of predominately Black lawyers located in cities and towns across the United States. While the national office and its legal team received much of the media attention, it was largely unknown local attorneys who conducted the preliminary research, identified potential plaintiffs, and filed initial motions. Their main objective was not civil rights lawyering but "intraracial institution-building" to secure African American citizenship.[3] Nevertheless, legal attacks on segregation occurred periodically.

In addition to investigating Missouri's segregation scholarship program, Redmond identified a potential plaintiff for a test suit to challenge segregation in state-supported graduate and professional school programs. Finding Black residents willing to challenge segregation in Missouri's higher education system was no easy feat, with several students from the Black Lincoln University in Jefferson City backing out at the last minute. The only willing participant proved to be a twenty-four-year-old Black man and St. Louis resident named Lloyd Lionel Gaines, who desired to attend the University of Missouri School of Law.[4] It remains unclear whether Gaines initiated involvement on his own or was drafted by Redmond.

In December 1938, the US Supreme Court ruled in *Missouri ex rel. Gaines v. Canada* that segregation scholarships violated African Americans' Fourteenth Amendment right to equal protection under the law. The pronouncement should have ended the practice of compelling Black students to leave their home states for graduate study, but it did not. Gaines's case demonstrated the limits of the Supreme Court, as that body has no power to enforce its decisions. The court cannot deploy troops or force Congress to act. Because the court cannot enforce its rulings, segregation scholarships continued to exist after it declared them unconstitutional.

The *Gaines* case was the first in which the Supreme Court took up the issue of racial segregation in education. It paved the way for the court to dismantle the separate but equal doctrine in *Brown v. Board of Education*. Despite its significance in civil rights history, *Gaines* is not widely celebrated or commemorated. This is largely because the plaintiff at the center of the case, Lloyd Gaines, disappeared before the case was completely settled. Additionally, only one state, West Virginia, desegregated its graduate and professional school programs in the decision's wake. Most border and southern states thumbed their nose at the Supreme Court by hastily creating underfunded and unequal graduate and professional school programs at public Black colleges. Even worse, most of these states continued or created segregation scholarship programs *after* the court had invalidated them.

West Virginia desegregated its graduate and professional school programs because of the calculated strategy and power brokering of John W. Davis, the president of the all-Black and state-supported West Virginia State College (present-day West Virginia State University). Black college presidents walked a fine line as they attempted to challenge white supremacy while keeping their institutions open and funded. They also played central roles in administering segregation scholarships.

Lloyd Gaines, the seventh son in a family of eleven children, was born in Mississippi in 1911. His father, Henry, was a rural schoolteacher and farmer who died when Lloyd was quite young, leaving behind a wife, Callie, who wanted something better for her children. Callie Gaines thus moved her family to St. Louis in 1926, putting them among the millions of African Americans who fled the South over the course of the first six decades in the twentieth century.[5] The fact that Lloyd Gaines was at the head of his rural school class in Mississippi "was of no concern to St. Louis school authorities," who placed the fifteen year old in the fifth grade because of the poor education he had received in Mississippi. He quickly caught up, however, completing four years of grammar school in two and four years of high school in three. Gaines attended Vashon High School, one of the two all-Black high schools in the city. Despite working long hours after school to support his family, Gaines graduated first in his high school class. He attended Stowe Teachers College in St. Louis for one year before transferring to Lincoln University in Jefferson City. At Lincoln, Gaines majored in history, joined Alpha Phi Alpha Fraternity, served as senior class president, and graduated with honors, all while working for a family to pay for his education.[6]

Gaines applied to the University of Missouri School of Law in August 1935. School officials learned that Gaines was Black when they received his academic transcript from Lincoln. Rather than deciding on Gaines's admission, Mizzou's registrar, Silas Canada, instructed Gaines to contact Lincoln University president Charles Florence. Florence called Gaines's attention to the Missouri statute offering Black residents tuition assistance to attend schools in neighboring states.[7]

Gaines, however, wanted to go to Mizzou, where he was certain to get legal training at a reasonable cost. Travel between his home and Missouri's law school, 146 miles, cost $2.95 one-way. If he attended law school in neighboring Iowa, he would have to travel 299 miles at a cost of $5.98 each way. Likewise, Nebraska's law school in Lincoln admitted Black students, but it would have cost Gaines $9.35 each way to travel the 468 miles between the school and his home. Given Gaines's working-class background, attending law school anywhere but in Missouri was cost-prohibitive, so he chose not to apply for a segregation scholarship.[8]

Working alongside Charles Hamilton Houston and Sidney Redmond on Gaines's case was Henry Espy, another Black attorney in St. Louis. Espy was a graduate of Howard University's law school and had established a law practice in the city with Redmond. He was also president of the St. Louis NAACP at the time of Gaines's legal challenge. Under advisement from Houston, Redmond, and Espy, Lloyd Gaines pressed the stalling University of Missouri School of Law for an admission decision. When such a decision did not come by January 1936, Redmond and Houston filed suit against the university, on Gaines's behalf, asking the court to order Canada to either approve or reject Gaines's application. In March 1936, seven months after Gaines applied to Missouri's sole state-supported law school, the university's board of curators denied him admission on account of his race, maintaining that the Missouri Constitution mandated separate education of the races.[9]

The university board's actions led NAACP lawyers to file a mandamus writ seeking to have Gaines admitted to the law school immediately. Gaines's lawyers contended that their client possessed the moral and scholastic qualifications for admission to Mizzou and that the Board of Curators of the University of Missouri denied him admission solely because he was African American. In lengthy legal proceedings known as *Missouri ex rel. Gaines v. Canada*, which listed the university registrar, Silas Canada, as the main defendant, the key question was whether Missouri provided its Black citizens with the same educational opportunities as its white citizens. Moreover, did Missouri violate African Americans' Fourteenth Amendment rights by sending them to other states for graduate education? Gaines's case differed from Donald Murray's in that Missouri had laws on the books mandating segregation and indicating its good faith effort to make Lincoln the equivalent of Mizzou. Additionally, Missouri had a functioning and funded segregation scholarship program, whereas Maryland only had such an arrangement in theory when Murray applied for admission.

Even before the circuit court trial began, William Hogsett, the chief legal counsel for the University of Missouri, attempted to demonstrate that Lloyd Gaines did not really want to attend law school and was simply part of an elaborate plot orchestrated by the NAACP to challenge segregation. To support this allegation, Hogsett took depositions from three other Black men who had applied to Mizzou around the time that Gaines had submitted his application. Those applicants, Arnett G. Lindsay, John A. Boyd, and Nathaniel A. Sweets, sought to pursue graduate study in law, mathematics, and journalism, respectively.[10] The men not only denied colluding but also gave compelling reasons why the segregation scholarships did not appeal to them. For example, Boyd, of St. Louis, explained that he had relatives in Columbia, Missouri, so if admitted at Mizzou, he could save on housing costs by living with family. The state's segregation scholarship, however, did not include funding for housing costs, so pursuing graduate study elsewhere was cost-prohibitive for Boyd.

In another surprising pretrial action, university officials suggested that Gaines was not eligible for admission to the law school because Lincoln University, his alma mater, was not an accredited institution. This was the first instance when a state institution attempted to block an African American student from admission by casting doubt on the quality of another state institution—a public college for Black students. Not only was the allegation without merit, as Lincoln was an accredited member of the North Central Association of Colleges and Secondary Schools, but it also supported the NAACP's overarching argument that segregated education was not equal. If Mizzou's allegation that Lincoln was inferior were true, then the state of Missouri was not only guilty of denying African Americans graduate education but also derelict in its duty to provide Black Missourians with undergraduate education equal to that offered white Missourians.[11] Tellingly, university counsel did not present this argument during trial. Lincoln was not comparable to its white counterpart in terms of physical plant, course offerings, and expenditures per student. Despite the inequality, Lincoln graduates later enrolled in institutions where they held their own alongside students from well-resourced institutions.

Charles Hamilton Houston arrived in St. Louis from Washington, DC, on July 6, 1936, four days before the *Gaines* case was set to begin. A little more than a week later, Jesse Owens left on the SS *Manhattan* headed to the 1936 Olympic Games in Berlin. Both men were on important missions to advance the race and root out white supremacy. Stateside, Houston worked long hours alongside

Redmond in the People's Finance Building as the two men prepared their witness lists and cross-examinations.[12] On the morning of the trial, they made the 120-mile drive from St. Louis to Columbia, where they found a courtroom filled to capacity with spectators. Very few African Americans were present because two recent lynchings in the area had terrified the county's Black residents.[13]

Perhaps nothing demonstrated the absurd contradictions of segregation more than the unsegregated court room. All the lawyers, Black and white, shared a single table in front of the witness stand in a trial about the separation of the races. Houston recalled that to confer privately with Gaines and Redmond, "we almost had to go into a football huddle."[14] Even more shocking, everyone present in the courtroom shared the same water foundation and used the same bathrooms.[15] The trampling of racial mores in the Boone County courthouse, however, carried no weight in the matter of the University of Missouri School of Law's admitting Gaines.

In court, Mizzou's lawyers argued that Gaines had not gone through the proper channels for relief. A six-person legal team led by William Hogsett contended that Missouri made provision for the education of African Americans at Lincoln and that according to a 1921 statute, Gaines should have petitioned Lincoln University's Board of Curators to establish a law school rather than seek admission to the University of Missouri. Until Gaines gave state officials the opportunity to create a law school for African Americans, university representatives avowed that he could not demand admission into the one maintained for non-Black students.[16]

NAACP attorneys responded to the university's defense by showing that Lincoln University did not have the funds to establish a law school. Paltry state appropriations caused the Jefferson City institution to regularly operate at a deficit, so adding new academic programs was financially impossible. The lawyers maintained that the state violated Gaines's Fourteenth Amendment rights because Missouri offered white residents an in-state educational opportunity that it denied to Black residents. Additionally, Houston argued that Missouri's segregation scholarship program put Gaines at a professional disadvantage because most attorneys received their legal education in the state where they practiced and this option was not available to Gaines. The state's policy of exporting Black scholars denied Gaines the opportunity to study Missouri law in depth.[17]

Judge W. M. Dinwiddie, ignoring the blatant lack of equal opportunity at the center of the case, ruled in favor of the University of Missouri, denying Lloyd Gaines the right to enter the university's law school. Dinwiddie did not even write an opinion. NAACP lawyers immediately appealed the decision to the

Missouri Supreme Court, fully realizing that every day that legal proceedings dragged on was a day that Gaines could not pursue legal education.[18]

At the Missouri Supreme Court, both sides presented the same arguments that they had put forward in the lower court trial, with NAACP attorneys expecting the appeals court to affirm the lower court's ruling. The court considered the issues at hand so important that it took the unusual step of hearing oral arguments en banc, with all seven judges on the bench. Usually, one set of judges heard criminal cases and the other set heard civil cases, but the constitutional question at the center of *Gaines v. Canada* led to a full bench. The justices unanimously ruled in favor of the University of Missouri, setting the stage for an appeal to the US Supreme Court, where the NAACP had the opportunity to set a national precedent. The stakes were clear. As Houston explained to fellow attorney Osmond Fraenkel, who had represented the Scottsboro Boys, whatever the high court decided about Missouri's segregation scholarship "would affect the entire South and 9,000,000 Negroes."[19]

Missouri had won the first two rounds of the educational equity fight, but the state remained in legal trouble if it continued to starve Lincoln University financially and academically. To ward off an expected Supreme Court battle, William Hogsett, the attorney who had represented Mizzou in Gaines's legal challenges, advised Frederick Middlebush, Mizzou's president, that the Missouri General Assembly should appropriate money for new departments at Lincoln.[20] This call to improve Lincoln's curricular offerings came months before the NAACP filed a petition for a writ of certiorari, requesting a hearing at the US Supreme Court. More important, the suggestion to increase Lincoln's funding was a tell-tale sign that state officials understood that the state had indeed violated African Americans' Fourteenth Amendment right to equal protection under the law.

On October 10, 1938, the US Supreme Court agreed to review the Missouri Supreme Court's *Gaines* decision. Thrilled NAACP officials sent out press releases to Black newspapers around the country heralding the impending showdown at the court of last resort.[21] The University of Missouri's representatives, by contrast, were caught off guard, as Mizzou's president wrote in a letter to William Hogsett. He had expected the court to deny the hearing.[22] Hogsett, quite confident in the state's position, reassured Middlebush that the Supreme Court granting certiorari did not "even inferentially suggest that its final decision will be adverse to the university."[23]

Lloyd Gaines did not sit home mindlessly while legal bodies determined his academic fate. He entered the University of Michigan's master's degree program in economics to pass the time while his case was still before the Missouri

Supreme Court. Racism delayed his dream of law school, but it could not extinguish his passion for learning. Because accepting a segregation scholarship from Missouri might weaken Gaines's case, the NAACP paid his tuition.[24]

In November 1938, before eight sitting US Supreme Court justices, lawyers for the NAACP and for the University of Missouri offered a master class in competing interpretations of the law. Both sides drew on *Plessy* to argue their points. Counsel for Gaines presented their case without interruption, while the justices subjected counsel for the University of Missouri to extensive questioning throughout their oral argument. The university's lawyers maintained that Lincoln University was equal in quality to Mizzou and that Gaines pressed for admission in a desire to achieve social equality with white people. According to William Hogsett, if Gaines sincerely wanted to attend law school, then the state's segregation scholarship program enabled him to do so. In fact, according to Hogsett, Black students seeking legal education out of state had a $150 advantage over white students. In response to that assertion, Justice Hugo Black, an Alabama native, asked, "Do you mean to suggest that a pecuniary payment would be adequate compensation for loss of civil rights?"[25] Justice Louis Brandeis asked Hogsett whether state law prohibited Black students from enrolling at Mizzou. Hogsett explained that while there was not a statute mandating segregation, the state supreme court regarded it to be a question of public policy.[26]

Charles Hamilton Houston challenged the university's arguments with surgical precision and humor. As he rose in his seat to address the court, Associate Justice James McReynolds, a conservative southerner known for racism and antisemitism, allegedly turned his chair around and faced the wall in silent protest at having to hear a Black attorney. Undeterred, Houston avowed that the University of Missouri belonged to all the people of Missouri regardless of race, color, or creed.[27]

Houston maintained that the Fourteenth Amendment mandated that no state could deny any person within its jurisdiction the equal protection of its laws and that Missouri's jurisdiction ended at the state border, invalidating the exile of Black residents to other states. Thus, rather than seeking to abrogate *Plessy*, Houston argued for its enforcement. Anything offered to white residents had to be offered to Black residents on a separate but equal basis. Moreover, Houston asserted that Black Missourians were not discriminated against when it came to the levying of taxes to maintain the university, so they did not intend to be discriminated against when it came to the benefit of those taxes. Finally, Houston refused to allow the social equality claim to go unchallenged. Referencing white men's sexual violence against enslaved Black women during the antebellum period, the NAACP attorney proclaimed that it was now too late to raise the issue of social equality and that the descendants of those women did not plan to allow any veiled outrage about social equality of the races to keep them from exercising their constitutional rights.[28]

In December 1938, in a decision with nationwide implications for Black education, the US Supreme Court ruled 6-to-2 that segregation scholarships violated the equal protection clause of the Fourteenth Amendment. "Manifestly," the majority opinion read, "the obligation of the State to give protection of equal laws can be performed only where its laws operate, that is, *within its own jurisdiction*. The provision for the payment of tuition fees in another state does not remove the discrimination."[29] If Missouri offered its white citizens legal education within the state, then it had to also offer its Black citizens legal education within the state. Additionally, the court asserted that limited Black demand for legal education was not an excuse to discriminate against African Americans. The court thus rejected a common argument made by state officials as to why states did not offer Black residents the same graduate and professional education opportunities offered to white residents. "It was as an individual that he was entitled to the equal protection of the laws, and the state was bound to furnish him within its borders facilities for legal education substantially equal to those which the state afforded for persons of the white race, whether or not other negroes sought the same opportunity."[30] In other words, whether 1 African American or 1,000 African Americans desired legal training, the state had an obligation to provide it.

Gaines was the major victory in the campaign for education equality that the NAACP had sought in order to make graduate and professional school education in the South accessible to African Americans. The legal reasoning could also be applied to elementary and secondary education. It could open the door for widespread desegregation of southern universities or, at the very least, major investments in public Black colleges. If those investments proved insufficient, the NAACP would return to court.

The US Supreme Court did not, however, compel the University of Missouri to admit Gaines to its law school. The court gave officials until September 1939 to create a law school for Gaines and other African Americans and asserted that segregation scholarships were a temporary solution until states created separate graduate programs for them.[31] Thus, while the *Gaines* decision was a significant victory in the fight for educational equality, it did not overturn the 1896 *Plessy* doctrine of separate but equal.

The state of Missouri, unlike Maryland with Donald Murray's legal challenge, decided to evade the court order and establish separate graduate and professional schools for African Americans. With a paltry appropriation of $200,000 and a race against the clock, Missouri opened the Lincoln University School of Law for African Americans in September 1939. The new law school was in St. Louis, 132 miles away from Lincoln's campus, and housed in the former Poro Beauty College building. Annie Malone, a Black businesswoman who developed a line of beauty care products and mentored hair care entrepreneur Madame C. J. Walker, had opened the five-story building in 1918 but closed it in 1930.[32]

Lincoln's law school was not on the main Jefferson City campus for several reasons. In addition to the state's inability to quickly procure a building for the law school in Jefferson City, many government officials believed that St. Louis was attractive because of the city's large Black population. Additionally, there were two private, whites-only law schools in St. Louis, so Lincoln students could benefit from the faculty and resources of those institutions. William Taylor, who had served as the acting dean of Howard's law school when Houston resigned in 1934, became dean of Lincoln's law school. Taylor hired a faculty of three, all Howard Law graduates, and commenced instruction.[33]

Black response to the new law school, the first state-supported professional school for African Americans in the United States, was mixed. Twenty-five Black students enrolled. Whether or not they saw their matriculation as a capitulation to segregation, they pursued the legal education that they desired. While instruction occurred inside the law school building, protests occurred outside. More than twenty Black Missourians picketed outside the building decrying the lack of parity between the Lincoln School of Law and the state's historically white school. Moreover, the protestors believed that the state misspent tax dollars by creating a separate school for a few Black students rather than desegregate Mizzou. The *Pittsburgh Courier* maintained that the law school "is just another stall, an example of how so-called courts of justice work to perpetuate the status quo against which Negroes are in revolt." A St. Louis newspaper equated the school with vestiges of slavery.[34] Despite the preservation of segregation being the motivating factor for the law school's existence, all the press surrounding the institution was not negative. A month after classes began, a representative from the American Bar Association examined the school and found it worthy of admission to probationary status among the ABA's approved schools.[35]

Charles Hamilton Houston planned to challenge in court whether Lincoln's law school met the separate but equal doctrine. If Lincoln's law school was not equal to Mizzou's, then the court had to compel the University of Missouri School of Law to admit Lloyd Gaines. Houston deposed Lincoln University School of Law dean William Taylor and all three Lincoln law school faculty members in October 1939 to expose the shortcomings of the school. He

(In)adequate Compensation for Loss of Civil Rights 81

The Lincoln University School of Law opened its doors on September 30, 1939, at 4310 St. Ferdinand Avenue, St. Louis, Missouri. Lincoln University Archives, Inman E. Page Library, Lincoln University, Jefferson City, Missouri.

demonstrated that Lincoln's law school faculty had very little teaching experience and the law school's location deprived the students of access to the state supreme court library in Jefferson City.[36]

Houston felt confident that he could prove Missouri's noncompliance with the Supreme Court's ruling, but he eventually withdrew the case because his plaintiff, Lloyd Gaines, disappeared. In late February 1939, Gaines took up residence at the Alpha Phi Alpha Fraternity house in Chicago and sought employment in the city. Securing a job proved difficult, despite or perhaps because of his notoriety. In a short note to his mother, Gaines expressed frustration with his financial situation and discussed the pressure that came with serving as the face of a campaign to desegregate higher education. He ominously pondered whether he made the "supreme sacrifice."[37] A few days later, Gaines left the Alpha Phi Alpha Fraternity house where he lived to buy postage stamps but never returned.[38] No one ever saw him again. Without their plaintiff challenging the quality of Lincoln's makeshift law school, Houston and the NAACP had to drop the case. The Lincoln University of School of Law remained open until 1955. Mizzou began admitting Black students five years earlier. The Black law school's closure came on the heels of the *Brown* decision banning segregation in public schools.[39]

The circumstances of Gaines's disappearance continue to be debated, with many pondering whether he met a violent end or disappeared of his own volition. What is clear is that white supremacy prohibited Gaines from reaching his full potential. Had Mizzou's law school admitted him in 1935, perhaps he would have become an attorney who defended the constitutional rights of other African Americans. Instead, he remains a mystery and a representative of the thousands of others nameless Black people denied the opportunity to pursue their graduate dreams.

The NAACP was careful not to pin its hopes for graduate desegregation on a single legal challenge. There were always other plaintiffs in the wings. In the spring of 1936, while Lloyd Gaines's legal challenge was on appeal to the Missouri Supreme Court, William Redmond Jr., a twenty-seven-year-old Black man, applied for admission to the University of Tennessee Pharmacy School. In doing so, he became the first known Black applicant to apply to the institution. The university rejected his application based on race and Redmond then sued for admission.[40]

Redmond was an ideal test case plaintiff for the NAACP as he had the family and educational pedigree that the civil rights organization preferred. His maternal grandfather, Allen Williams, was a well-known businessperson and community leader in Franklin, Tennessee, while both of his parents were also entrepreneurs. His mother ran a millinery business in Nashville and his father operated a hotel and grocery store in Franklin and took in boarders at the family farm. The family was financially independent of the local white power structure. Redmond was a 1933 graduate of the tax-supported and all-Black Tennessee Agricultural and Industrial State College (present-day Tennessee State University), where he majored in chemistry. While in college, he was a member of the Sapphires, a campus organization for students who maintained a grade point average between 90 and 94.[41]

In 1935, Redmond applied and was accepted to Meharry Medical College's pharmacy program but when he reported for class, the college president refunded his money and told him that he was the only student who applied to Meharry for pharmacy that year. The school could not offer a program for one person. The lack of student demand led Meharry to discontinue its pharmacy school.[42]

The only pharmacy school in Tennessee in 1936 was the University of Tennessee's program in Memphis. When the school rejected Redmond based on race, he contended that the state of Tennessee had violated his Fourteenth Amendment rights by offering a pharmacy program for white students only. Through his counsel, Charles Hamilton Houston of the NAACP and Black attorney Z. Alexander Looby of Nashville, Redmond filed a mandamus writ to compel the flagship institution to admit him.[43] Looby had earned his undergraduate degree at Howard, his law degree at Columbia, and his doctorate in jurisprudence from New York University.[44] He was among the small cadre of Black lawyers practicing in the South before World War II.

Tennessee officials denied that their flagship university had violated Redmond's constitutional rights by arguing that state law prohibited Black and white students from attending classes together. Moreover, state leaders asserted that it was not economically feasible to create a pharmacy program for Black students given the small demand. A lower court judge agreed with state officials and decreed that Redmond's rights were not violated, but even if they had been, the lower court said that he should have sought remedy by appealing to the state Board of Education or the legislature for provision to study pharmacy elsewhere.[45]

One direct result of Redmond's legal challenge was Tennessee's creation of a segregation scholarship program in 1937. The authorizing legislation for the program detailed that scholarships were "payable out of the state appropriations made for the Agricultural and Industrial College for Negroes."[46] Robbing Peter to pay Paul, legislators placed the burden of financing African American's out-of-state graduate study on an already cash-strapped public Black college. The scholarship offset the expenses Black citizens incurred to pursue instruction offered to white students at the University of Tennessee. Program rules stipulated that Tennessee only paid the difference between expenses at the nearest college admitting African Americans and the cost for similar studies at the University of Tennessee.[47] The NAACP did not consider out-of-state tuition aid as the constitutional equivalent of Black citizens studying at their home state universities but chose not to appeal Redmond's case since the organization was in the middle of Lloyd Gaines's appeal challenging Missouri's segregation scholarship program.

Tennessee's legislature did not set up a graduate school at its tax-supported Black college until 1942. Sixty-six students enrolled in graduate courses during the 1942 summer session. The expansion of curricular programs at Tennessee Agricultural and Industrial State College was precipitated by six Black Tennesseans who tried to pursue graduate and professional study at the University of Tennessee in 1939. Since the college only offered a limited number of postbaccalaureate courses, segregation scholarships continued to be the vehicle by which most Black Tennesseans secured graduate study. Additionally, the state entered into an agreement with the private Meharry Medical College in Nashville to provide medicine, dentistry, and nursing education to Black residents. Admitted students would pay the same tuition charged to students in those programs at the University of Tennessee. Thus, a Black private institution undertook the professional training of Black students on behalf of the state.[48]

Like Gaines's aspiration to practice law, Redmond's dream of becoming a pharmacist did not come true, as he chose not to travel far from home to receive the education denied him locally. He went on to become a successful businessman and farmer in Franklin, Tennessee. His story and that of many other African Americans demonstrated the racialized limitations African Americans faced in reaching their highest potential during the era of legal segregation.[49] Years later, Redmond pensively suggested that he had been "born too early to be a pharmacist in Tennessee."[50] In reality, it was not that he had been born too early but that segregationists refused to respect African Americans' civil rights.

The NAACP remained committed to not allowing an "accident of birth" to stymie one's educational and professional goals. Armed with a court mandate that Missouri had to offer its Black residents equal in-state education, NAACP lawyers once again pursued legal action against the University of Missouri, with Lucile Bluford as their new plaintiff. While the NAACP had not recruited Bluford, her interest in the *Gaines* case led her to apply for admission to the University of Missouri's graduate journalism program in January 1939, one month after the landmark decision. Mizzou's program was the oldest and one of the most revered journalism schools in the United States. Bluford applied after learning that Mizzou's law school did not allow for spring admissions, so Gaines was not able to enter immediately after his landmark victory. The institution's graduate journalism program did, however, admit new students in the spring, so Bluford decided to pick up the proverbial baton and test Mizzou's compliance with admitting students who sought educational opportunities not available at Lincoln.[51]

When Bluford applied to Mizzou's journalism school, she had seven years of experience as a journalist at Black newspapers in Atlanta and Kansas City. The university's registrar, Silas Canada, provisionally admitted her because he did not know that she was African American, since her undergraduate transcript was from the historically white University of Kansas. When she arrived on campus weeks later to register for classes and officials learned that she was Black, the registrar prevented her from registering and explained that the *Gaines* case remained unsettled. The case remained unsettled because the NAACP had not yet had a chance to prove that Missouri had not adequately funded Lincoln, so its law school was not the equivalent of Mizzou.[52]

Bluford applied for admission to Mizzou again in August 1939 and again university officials denied her admission based on her race. This time, university officials instructed her to apply to Lincoln University, which did not have a journalism program. She then secured the legal representation of St. Louis–based NAACP lawyer Sidney Redmond, who asked a Boone County District Court to grant her admission. Redmond also sued the university in federal court for $20,000 in financial damages to compensate Bluford for the lost time in pursuing her studies and to make segregation an even more expensive enterprise for the state. The NAACP welcomed Bluford's case since Lloyd Gaines was still missing.[53]

Lucile Bluford was intimately aware of the University of Missouri's exclusion of African Americans. Although she was a Missouri resident whose parents paid state taxes, she attended the University of Kansas for her undergraduate degree in journalism since Mizzou was off limits and Lincoln did not have a journalism program. One of her brothers had attended graduate school on a segregation scholarship. At the time that she pursued graduate studies, she worked as the managing editor of *The Call*, a Black weekly newspaper in Kansas City, Missouri. She replaced Roy Wilkins, who left the paper to become editor of *The Crisis*, the official magazine of the NAACP.[54]

Bluford's legal challenge once again put NAACP lawyers Houston and Redmond opposite William Hogsett in a Boone County circuit courtroom. Houston argued that Bluford had a right to enter to Mizzou because the US Supreme Court had stipulated in Lloyd Gaines's case that Gaines had a right to enter the University of Missouri's law school in the absence of equal facilities at Lincoln University. Redmond contributed to the effort by showing that Lincoln was severely underfunded and lacked the resources to establish a graduate journalism program. Representing Mizzou, Hogsett claimed that Bluford should have sued Lincoln rather than its white counterpart and that she did not have a sincere interest in graduate study but was merely suing at the behest of the NAACP. In perhaps the first instance of segregationists making the case that an African American was overqualified for an opportunity, Hogsett and one of his witnesses, Frank Martin, the dean of Mizzou's journalism school, alleged that Bluford knew so much about journalism that the state's flagship graduate program would be of no use to her.[55]

Four months after both sides made their arguments in a courtroom packed with spectators, Judge W. M. Dinwiddie ruled against Bluford and the NAACP. The judge maintained that Bluford should have appealed to Lincoln to create a journalism school rather than demand admission to Mizzou. Houston immediately appealed the decision to the Missouri Supreme Court. With another trial looming, Hogsett encouraged Bluford to accept a segregation scholarship and pursue graduate journalism study at the University of Kansas.[56] This unsolicited advice was a sign that Missouri had no intention of complying with the *Gaines* decision.

As Bluford's case dragged on, she made the case for educational equality in the pages of *The Call*. In a column titled "Nothing Will Happen When the Negro Student Is Admitted to M.U.," she detailed her encounters with white students and administrators when she visited Mizzou's campus to register for classes. She found people on campus to be either cordial or indifferent, smiling or paying her no more attention than they did other students. In addition to arguing that her studying at the university would be peaceful, Bluford also exposed the hypocrisy of excluding Black Missourians by pointing out that the University of Missouri admitted people from all over the world. She noted that the student body consisted of people from all the states in the Union and from eleven foreign countries, including Cuba, Mexico, and the Philippines. To add insult to injury, Bluford witnessed a young man from Portugal gain admittance to the very program to which she, a citizen and taxpayer, had applied. Like a skilled attorney making a closing argument, Bluford ended her essay with a sobering assessment of the facts. "They come from everywhere to Missouri U. I live in Missouri."[57]

In 1941, two years after she first applied, the Missouri Supreme Court ruled that Bluford had the right to enter Mizzou's graduate journalism program if no other graduate journalism course was available to her within Missouri's borders. The court stipulated, however, that Bluford had to give Lincoln the opportunity to develop a journalism program. As they had done with Lincoln's makeshift law school, Missouri officials quickly established a graduate journalism program at its tax-supported Black institution, even though the university did not have an undergraduate program in journalism.[58]

The Lincoln School of Journalism's opening date was February 1, 1942. Bluford inspected the nascent Black journalism program soon thereafter and found that there were no buildings, offices, or classrooms. An instructor's bedroom in Science Hall on the campus of the Jefferson City institution doubled as the journalism school dean's office. Two of the journalism school's three professors had less experience in the field than Bluford did. Bluford refused to enroll in the second-rate program and sought an injunction, since Lincoln's journalism program was not equal to the one at the University of Missouri as required by law.[59]

In a jaw-dropping move to preserve segregation, the University of Missouri discontinued its graduate journalism program. The closure happened three days before Lincoln's poorly funded graduate journalism program was to begin. Mizzou officials claimed that World War II and the number of male students who withdrew to enlist in the military necessitated that the university end its most renowned academic offering.[60] Those sympathetic to Lucile Bluford's plight begged to differ because it was clear to all that her case became moot if white students no longer had the option of taking postbaccalaureate journalism classes.

Mizzou had discontinued its graduate journalism program on paper but continued to offer graduate courses. Harold Wilkie, a white minister based in Columbia, Missouri, shared the information with Bluford. He learned that the supposed abandonment of the program was a sham by contacting Mizzou students who belonged to his church. One student admitted that "the whole thing was a move to keep 'the Negro girl' from entering the school."[61] The program's alleged discontinuation prevented Bluford from acquiring additional training in her career field.

As was the case for so many other young Black scholars, white supremacy kept Lucile Bluford from reaching her full intellectual potential. She applied to the graduate journalism program at Mizzou for six consecutive semesters over a period of two and a half years and was repeatedly denied admission because of racism. She became one of an untold number of Black people with deferred dreams told to wait for full citizenship.[62]

Four decades later, the University of Missouri attempted to right its egregious wrong when it awarded Bluford an honor medal for distinguished service in journalism from the School of Journalism in 1984. In 1989, the university awarded her an honorary degree. When she accepted the degree, she said the honor was "not only for myself, but for the thousands of Black students" the university had denied admission.[63] Lloyd Gaines was among the thousands denied the opportunity to study at his state's flagship institution, yet his pioneering and brave example bore fruit.

Lloyd Gaines and Lucile Bluford were courageous pioneers who attempted to improve the educational landscape for African Americans across the South. While neither succeeded in enrolling at the University of Missouri, their legal challenges sent southern states scrambling to implement advanced study at public Black colleges. Their fights also led one southern state to desegregate graduate programs at a historically white public institution.

West Virginia was the only border or southern state to desegregate graduate education at its flagship institution, West Virginia University, in the wake of the *Gaines* decision. John Warren Davis, the Black president of the all-Black West Virginia State College, deserves much of the credit for breaking down the racial barrier to graduate education in his state. Before taking the helm of WVSC in 1919, the Milledgeville, Georgia, native had studied at Morehouse College, where he roomed with future Howard University president Mordecai Johnson. He then embarked on graduate study in physics and chemistry at the University of Chicago before assuming the presidency of WVSC. Under his leadership, WVSC enrollment increased, more faculty earned advanced degrees, and the college's curriculum was strengthened. In 1929, the North Central Association of Colleges and Secondary Schools rewarded Davis's leadership with accreditation of his institution. WVSC became one of the first four Black colleges in the United States and the only public one to be accredited.[64]

In 1937, the West Virginia House of Delegates considered legislation allocating $2 million a year for two years to establish a graduate school at West Virginia State College. Perhaps Gaines's legal challenge, which was regularly covered in national newspapers, led the state's legislators to act. When WVSC president Davis got wind of the proposed bill, he paid a visit to West Virginia governor Homer A. Holt and expressed his opposition. Davis asserted that two major graduate schools were not necessary in West Virginia and that the $4 million promised to WVSC over a two-year period should be used to improve WVU's graduate programs on the condition that those programs accept Black students. As Davis later recalled, he pushed for a stronger undergraduate program in lieu of two graduate programs in the state. "I respectfully suggested to Governor Holt that the appropriate thing to do was to make West Virginia State College the very best possible undergraduate college so that its graduates might enter West Virginia University and other universities to advantage."[65]

The attitudes and political positions of Black college presidents could help or hinder the NAACP's effort in the fight to desegregate higher education. Davis put the interests of the entire race ahead of the prestige that would have come to him and his institution with more funding and graduate programs. He declined a multimillion-dollar state appropriation in the midst of austerity caused by the Great Depression. Such a move was not only risky but also downright unbelievable for a public Black college president given the disparity in state funding between Black and white institutions. A 1937 study found that public

John W. Davis was president of West Virginia State College from 1919 until 1953. He quietly worked to have West Virginia desegregate its graduate programs soon after the *Gaines* decision. Archives and Special Collections Department, Drain-Jordan Library, West Virginia State University, Institute.

Black colleges in six southern states with sizeable Black populations received less than 10 percent of the total state appropriation for public colleges and universities. For example, although African Americans constituted 43 percent of South Carolina's population in 1937, the state's only public Black college received less than 6 percent of the total appropriation for higher education.[66] Davis, however, gambled the additional funds and eschewed the power and prestige attached to leading an institution with graduate offerings to advance the cause of racial justice. Understanding that creating graduate programs equal to those at WVU was cost-prohibitive, he prioritized desegregation of higher education over his own job security or the academic enhancement of WVSC. After West Virginia University's president agreed to Davis's suggestion, WVU became the first tax-supported university in a border or southern state to admit Black students for graduate study.[67] President Davis's actions were the opposite of James

Shepard's actions at North Carolina College. A pragmatist at heart, Shepard knew that North Carolina's governor and legislators would not voluntarily desegregate UNC, so he pursued additional funding for his institution rather than desegregation.

The historic matriculation of African American graduate students at a previously all-white southern or border state university went unnoticed by both the media and the public in 1940. There were no threats of violence or crowds of jeering segregationists. John Davis personally selected three "unusually capable" Black students to desegregate WVU. William Oscar Armstrong and Katherine Johnson, both WVSC graduates, entered WVU in June 1940. Kenneth James, another WVSC alumnus, entered WVU in September 1940. James and Armstrong both pursued master's degrees in education and graduated in 1941 and 1942, respectively. Armstrong was the principal of the all-Black Dunbar High School in Fairmont, West Virginia, serving in this position for forty-seven years until he retired in 1957. Johnson, who had graduated summa cum laude from WVSC in 1937 with bachelor's degrees in mathematics and French, studied math. Johnson left her WVU graduate program early to start a family before embarking on a career with NASA, where she did the calculations for the first US human spaceflight. Her story is featured in the Hollywood blockbuster *Hidden Figures*.[68]

While African American graduate students had enrolled at WVU, the victory was bittersweet. For one thing, the university only admitted Black West Virginians. WVU remained off limits to African Americans from out of state, even though the school admitted out-of-state white students and non-Black foreign students. Also, the Black graduate students admitted to WVU could not eat in the cafeteria, participate in extracurricular activities, or live on campus. Victorine Louistall-Monroe, another WVSU graduate and the first Black women to earn a graduate degree at WVU, recalled staying at a local boardinghouse while enrolled for her master's degree in education. The owner of the house prepared brown bag lunches for her to carry to campus daily. Louistall-Monroe graduated in 1945 and made history again in 1966 when she became WVU's first Black faculty member.[69]

Despite the trailblazing actions of Johnson, James, Armstrong, and Louistall-Monroe, West Virginia continued to export Black students for graduate study. While a small number of Black graduate students matriculated at the flagship institution annually, the state maintained its segregation scholarship program for Black residents. One of the reasons why the scholarships continued was because of the limited housing opportunities for Black students in Morgantown. University policy prohibited Black students from living on campus, and there were not many Black families in the community to rent rooms.[70] West Virginia thus continued to send Black scholars out of state until the close of the 1953–54 academic year, after the *Brown* decision led the state to completely desegregate its public universities.[71]

No other state followed West Virginia's lead in desegregating graduate education after *Gaines*. In fact, most states doubled down on their commitment to segregation. In the weeks after the landmark court decision, Kentucky governor Albert Benjamin Chandler appropriated $1,600 from his discretionary emergency fund to supplement the state's depleted segregation scholarship fund. This action was a direct response to Alfred Carroll's application to the University of Kentucky law school. Carroll, a segregation scholarship recipient, applied to UK Law after Kentucky ran out of money to continue supplementing his studies at Howard Law. In finding emergency financial resources in the middle of the Great Depression that had severely constricted state revenues, Governor Chandler demonstrated that segregation had to be protected at any cost. Anti-Blackness remained UK's admissions policy and Black Kentuckians continued to receive their graduate educations at out-of-state universities.[72]

Even before the emergency funding materialized, however, UK had rejected Alfred Carroll's application because of the Day Law and because his undergraduate alma mater, Wilberforce University, a private Black college in Ohio, was unaccredited. Carroll completed his legal education at Howard in 1940 and became a noted civil rights attorney in Louisville. He became president of the Louisville NAACP in the years following World War II.[73]

Not all Black Kentuckians championed desegregation in the face of a bankrupt segregation scholarship program and the *Gaines* decision. Rufus B. Atwood, the Black president of Kentucky State College, believed that if Black students attended UK, then the state would close KSC. He thus worked with white leaders to keep Carroll at Howard with state funds. Born in southwestern Kentucky in 1897, Atwood earned a bachelor's degree in biology at Fisk in 1920 after pausing his studies to enlist in the US Army during World War I. His valiant service fighting in France earned him the Bronze Star. Atwood went on to obtain a second bachelor's degree in agricultural education from Iowa State and a master's degree from the University of Chicago. In 1929 he accepted the presidency of KSC, a position he held until 1962.[74]

With each succeeding year at the helm of KSC, Atwood became more committed to the success and perpetuity of the institution. He implemented higher admissions standards and closed the college's high school department to improve KSC's standing. He shepherded the college through the accreditation process and in 1939, the Southern Association of Colleges and Secondary Schools classified KSC as a Class A institution. This recognition by an accrediting agency made it easier for KSC graduates to earn admission to graduate programs. Atwood accomplished these improvements without much state support because unlike the segregation scholarship bill that Walthall Moore introduced in Missouri, Charles Anderson's bill in Kentucky made no mention of expanding the curricular offerings at Black public colleges. Atwood therefore had to remain friendly with white politicians for the benefit of his institution. He did this by not calling for the desegregation of the University of Kentucky. He did not support Alfred Carroll's matriculating at UK because if a Black student enrolled at the historically white flagship, then the legislature might be inclined to close KSC.

Perhaps pragmatically, Atwood intervened in the Alfred Carroll affair by telling media outlets that Governor Chandler's appropriation of additional funds for segregation scholarships satisfied Carroll, who would withdraw his application to UK. The college president sought to curry favor with state leaders and protect KSC. The problem was that Carroll had said no such thing and had not even spoken with Atwood. In fact, Charles Anderson, the Kentucky lawmaker who had sponsored the state's segregation scholarship program, had corresponded privately with NAACP lawyer Thurgood Marshall about Carroll serving as a plaintiff to challenge segregation in Kentucky, so Carroll was in no way satisfied with another segregation scholarship. The civil rights attorney advised Anderson not to go forward with the case, however, because Wilberforce was not accredited.[75]

The Black press castigated Atwood for what many saw as a betrayal of the race. In an editorial in the weekly *Louisville Leader* titled "Negro Leaders as Enemies of the Race," newspaper editor I. Willis Cole condemned Atwood without naming him.

> Any Negro who does not wish the members of his race to receive an equal education to the white race, without extra cost and trouble, is short of the blood which makes him a human being.... Negroes who are always willing and ready to barter with whites in a pact which would give the Negro less than that guaranteed him under the Constitution and supported by the Supreme Court ... are not only spineless cowards in the eyes of those whom they serve as puppets, but they are hypocrites and traitors. They are enemies of the race who should be relegated to the past.[76]

In the days after the editorial appeared, Atwood doubled down on his opposition to Black students entering UK. He covertly informed the governor of a meeting convened by Black educational leaders to discuss equality of education in Kentucky and assured him that there was no organized effort to get Alfred Carroll into the flagship.[77] Atwood's actions are best explained by Lewis McMillan, a history professor at South Carolina State College, who opined that "the president stands a surer chance of keeping his job to the extent that he is hostile to the best interests of his own people."[78] Unlike John W. Davis of West Virginia State College, who was willing to forego job security and the coveted "university" title for his institution to get Black students into WVU, Atwood saw a zero-sum game where desegregation in higher education meant KSC's closure and job insecurity.

In addition to continuing the segregation scholarship program, Kentucky officials arranged for both the University of Louisville and the University of Kentucky to offer graduate courses to Black Kentuckians. To keep Black students from learning on historically white campuses, UL faculty agreed to teach their courses at Louisville Municipal College and UK faculty agreed to teach their courses twenty-six miles from Lexington at KSC in Frankfort. The arrangement allowed Kentucky to say that it offered separate but equal graduate education within the commonwealth's borders even though this was anything but equal. In correspondence with NAACP secretary Walter White, KSC president Atwood surmised that the plan to offer graduate courses at the Black colleges would "gradually work Negroes into the two universities inasmuch as it might prove inconvenient and expensive to set up complete equipment, etc. at the Negro institution, but rather the professor would gradually begin to have the students come where the equipment already is."[79]

The graduate extension courses at KSC proved unsuccessful. During the 1939 and 1940 summer sessions, KSC offered graduate courses in agriculture and home economics, but the college discontinued these courses when administrators learned that the offerings could not lead to graduate degrees, which a state education statute gave UK the sole authority to confer.[80] For Black students, leaving home remained their only option, and hundreds of them did just that.

During the 1939 biennium, 306 Black Kentuckians received segregation scholarships. That number increased to 397 in the 1941 biennium. Demand was so high that at one point, the governor provided $3,600 from his emergency fund to make ends meet.[81] The institutions receiving Kentucky residents and funds included the Art Institute of Chicago, Atlanta University, Cornell University, Fisk, Hampton, Howard, Northwestern, and the University of Wisconsin.[82]

Kentucky made significant changes to its segregation scholarship program after 1942, increasing the annual appropriation to $10,000 and transferring administration of the program from the state Department of Education to KSC president Atwood of KSC.[83] Black Kentuckians pursuing graduate study applied for aid to Atwood's office and if the request was approved, a KSC staff member forwarded the approved amount of aid to the out-of-state institution of the recipient's choice. One of the first recipients receiving funds after Atwood took over program administration was Whitney Young Sr., who received assistance to pursue his master's degree at Fisk University. Young was the father of Whitney Young Jr., who would later head the National Urban League.[84]

Public school teachers and administrators made up most segregation scholarship recipients in southern states, including Kentucky. Black educators taught in their communities during the school year and completed their studies away from home during successive summers. The long list of Black school personnel studying in out-of-state summer programs on a Kentucky segregation scholarship included Louisville teachers Mary Macy Spradling and Lucille Madry, who earned degrees in library science from Atlanta University and education from the University of Cincinnati, respectively. Madisonville educator Helen Noel Teague studied at Cornell, while Frankfort teacher Minnie Hitch spent a summer at the University of Chicago.[85] Although regionally, male recipients outnumbered female recipients of segregation scholarships, women outnumbered men in Kentucky's program and most recipients were teachers.

Graduate degrees increased Black educators' salaries, which were less than those of their white counterparts. Graduate training and the higher salaries it made possible propelled Black educators into the middle class. Teachers were valued and respected in Black communities as people who had "made it" and who were to be looked up to because of their educational success.[86]

As was the case throughout the South, perhaps the Kentucky segregation scholarship recipients who left home most disappointed were law school students, since being compelled to leave the state for law school denied aspiring Black attorneys the opportunity to learn in the same classrooms with those they would one day face in court.

Benjamin Shobe was one such example of a scholarship recipient who expressed regret about how out-of-state educational policies stymied professional possibilities. Born in 1920 in Bowling Green, Shobe spent the first few years of his life in Frankfort, where his father served as dean of men at Kentucky State College and his mother worked as an elementary school teacher. In 1927 the family moved to Middlesboro, where Shobe resided until matriculating at KSC for his undergraduate education. He earned a bachelor's degree from Kentucky State in 1941.[87]

At the urging of a KSC professor, Shobe applied and was accepted to the University of Michigan Law School. He received Anderson-Mayer segregation scholarship funds throughout his studies there and earned his degree in 1946. Years later, reflecting upon his educational career, Shobe remarked, "I regretted one thing . . . that I didn't get to go to law school with people who practiced in my state. I believe my practice would have flourished if I had classmates who came into practice with me."[88]

Shobe expressed the very argument and sentiment that Lloyd Gaines had made in the historic *Gaines* case. No amount of money or even access to the best law schools in the nation could make up for racism that denied Black students the opportunity to study law in the state where they wanted to practice. In what can only be considered poetic justice, Benjamin Shobe went on not only to have a stellar career as an attorney and judge in Kentucky but also to engage in intellectual warfare by drawing on the legal knowledge obtained with Kentucky's financial assistance to help desegregate the University of Kentucky's graduate and professional schools in 1949.[89]

Even with a larger appropriation for out-of-state aid, the maximum amount a recipient could receive remained fixed at $175 per academic year, an amount too small to cover the tuition and fees at several of the institutions where Black Kentuckians chose to study. To remedy this, the Kentucky Negro Education Association recommended that the state increase the amount available per school year from $175 to $300. By 1947, the recommendation had become law, although very few students received anything close to the maximum amount allowed.[90]

Months before Rufus Atwood became the administrator of Kentucky's segregation scholarships in 1942, two African Americans sought admission to the University of Kentucky. During the 1941 summer, William Harkins, a recent graduate of Louisville's Central High, applied to both UK and KSC to pursue a bachelor's degree in engineering. While UK offered his desired course of study, KSC did not. Harkins also submitted a segregation scholarship application to study engineering at Hampton, but state officials told him that aid was only available for graduate study.[91] It is unclear whether UK ever decided on Harkins's application, but he never pursued legal action to gain admission. But another young man who also sought to study engineering did.

Charles Eubanks was born into a working-class Louisville family in 1924. Like William Harkins, Eubanks was a graduate of Central High. He excelled in the classroom and served as president of his senior class and vice president of the student council. Eubanks applied to both Louisville Municipal College and KSC to study civil engineering in August 1941. Representatives from both colleges informed him that their schools did not offer engineering, so he applied to the University of Kentucky, which, like the University of Louisville, offered his desired major. UK registrar Leo Chamberlain denied Eubanks admission, citing state law that prevented Black and white people from learning together. Soon thereafter, Louisville attorney Prentice Thomas, a Howard Law school graduate who shared a law practice with Charles Anderson, filed a writ of mandamus in

Fayette Circuit Court to compel UK to admit Eubanks. Because Eubanks was not yet eighteen, his mother, Bodie Henderson, was listed as a proxy plaintiff. Thomas named UK president Herman Lee Donovan, Chamberlain, and the UK Board of Trustees as defendants.[92]

Thomas consulted with NAACP lawyers Leon Ransom, Charles Hamilton Houston, and Thurgood Marshall on the Eubanks case. While the attorneys understood that Kentucky's Day Law prevented integrated classrooms, they believed that the Supreme Court's ruling in the *Gaines* case gave them the upper hand. In that decision, the justices decreed that states had to provide equal educational opportunities within their borders. Thus Kentucky had to create an engineering school for African Americans or admit Eubanks to UK.[93]

The NAACP had more experience and resources than Thomas did, so the civil rights organization took over the Eubanks case. The first thing Marshall did was have Thomas withdraw his circuit court motion and file an injunction in the US Court for the Eastern District in Kentucky arguing that UK violated Eubanks's Fourteenth Amendment right to equal protection of the law. Marshall planned to ask the court to perpetually restrain UK officials from using the Day Law to exclude qualified African Americans from admission. This strategy differed from Thomas's initial one in that Marshall's injunction, if granted, would make it possible for any qualified Black applicant to enter the university. Marshall also sought $3,000 in damages from the registrar for his refusal to admit Eubanks.[94]

Marshall wagered that Kentucky would not be able to replicate Missouri and simply create an engineering school for African Americans as Missouri did with its makeshift law school. The United States was at war and the national emergency program needed every available engineer, so it would be extremely difficult for UK to secure qualified engineers willing to forego defense contract salaries to teach in a fly-by-night engineering school.[95] Marshall underestimated, though, how strongly white commitment to segregation trumped commitment to the war effort.

As the named defendants in the Eubanks case stalled in responding, the Kentucky legislature gave KSC an additional $20,000 to establish a two-year course in general engineering, which began in September 1942. KSC president Rufus Atwood told NAACP officials that the dean of UK's engineering school told him that no equipment was needed for the first two years of engineering study. KSC needed only to secure an additional faculty member. It became clear that Kentucky officials planned to ask the court to dismiss the NAACP's motion on the grounds that the issue was now resolved. According to state officials, KSC had an engineering school, so Eubanks's constitutional rights were not violated. KSC began advertising its new curricular offering in *The Crisis*, the official publication of the NAACP.[96]

In January 1943, approximately one and half years after the NAACP first filed suit against UK on Charles Eubanks's behalf, the university responded. Represented by Kentucky's assistant attorney general, John W. Jones, UK maintained that KSC's engineering program was comparable to the first two years of the program in Lexington. Jones asserted that "there is no material difference and no partiality" between the two programs.[97] In other words, Eubanks's suit was settled because KSC's program was substantially equal to the one at UK.[98]

NAACP lawyers objected to KSC's inferior program in federal court proving that it was unequal in every measure. They found that the Black college's engineering school "has only one teacher, not an engineer, but a Bachelor of Science in industrial education. The school is practically without equipment. The curriculum is not an engineering course but an industrial course which includes [such] subjects as welding."[99] If Kentucky did not want to admit African Americans to its flagship institution, then it needed to invest significant monetary resources into KSC, a move the commonwealth refused to make time and time again.

Delays and continuances on both sides caused the *Eubanks* case to drag on until 1945, when Judge H. Church Ford of the US District Court for the Eastern District of Kentucky dismissed it because no prosecution had taken place for two consecutive terms of the court. The losers in this ordeal were Charles Eubanks and other African Americans seeking professional degrees. Eubanks gave four years of his life to secure an educational opportunity that remained elusive. He never became an engineer and suffered great personal loss for his legal efforts, including a failed marriage while attempting to enroll at UK. The United States had defeated Nazism abroad but could not free itself from the ironclad commitment to white supremacy at home. Specialized courses of study remained out of reach for most Black students as long as white legislators underfunded public Black colleges and prohibited Black students from entering historically white institutions. Eubanks would later pass away in obscurity at the age of forty.[100]

Charles Anderson, the Louisville attorney and politician who created Kentucky's segregation scholarship law, disavowed his own legislation and tried to get African Americans into UK in 1944. While Eubanks's case was still active, Anderson introduced a bill that excluded graduate and professional schools from the 1904 Day Law prohibiting interracial education. His proposal did not upend segregation at the undergraduate level, but it would have opened graduate programs and professional schools to African Americans. Not only would Black students be able to enroll in postbaccalaureate programs at UK, but they also would be eligible for admission to the University of Louisville, which had medical, dental, and nursing schools.[101]

In explaining why he no longer supported the Anderson-Mayer Act, Anderson asserted that he had envisioned the program as a temporary measure until the time became right to demand the admission of Black students to UK. Additionally, he noted that in the previous twenty years, only one Black student from Louisville who left the state to study medicine had returned. He asserted that the same was true of Black pharmacy students. While the brain drain was costly, expanding KSC's academic programs was also expensive. Anderson estimated that Kentucky would have to spend $1 million to make KSC the equivalent of UK.[102]

Fiduciary duty meant nothing to avowed segregationists, who were committed to a lily-white University of Kentucky at all costs. Leading efforts to increase funding for KSC with the intent of making it equivalent to UK and maintaining segregation was J. R. Dorman, a legislator from rural Jessamine County. Dorman sponsored a bill to increase KSC's appropriation. His bill came up for review on the same day as Anderson's.[103] In an above-the-fold editorial, the state's leading newspaper, the *Courier-Journal*, expressed support for Anderson's bill over Dorman's. The editor opined that "it would take no small amount of money to transform the State College for Negroes into an institution equal in all respects to the University of Kentucky. And the wastefulness for a poor state having only 10 percent of Negroes in its population of such duplicated facilities is self-evident."[104] Kentucky did not have the money necessary to make KSC the Black counterpart of UK.

While Dorman's bill was never brought to the floor, Anderson's bill passed the House by a vote of 41 to 40 after lengthy debate and was the first favorable effort in any southern legislature to end segregation in education. The vote signaled that white legislators were not absolutely wedded to the Day Law, which mandated total segregation in education. The bill died, however, in the powerful state senate Rules Committee, which failed to report it out for action before adjournment. Anderson attributed this failure to a group of African Americans, led behind the scenes by Rufus Atwood, who favored improving KSC rather than desegregating UK. According to the sole Black legislator in the Kentucky General Assembly, Black opponents to his bill gave white state senators an excuse not to act by citing Black division.[105]

Four years after a federal court dismissed Charles Eubanks's case and five years after Charles Anderson attempted to amend Kentucky's Day Law, African American students finally entered the University of Kentucky in 1949. The desegregation of the state's premier institution came only after Lyman T. Johnson, a Black teacher at Louisville's Central High School, applied for admission to UK's doctoral history program in 1948. Johnson, a forty-one-year-old Tennessee native, had earned his bachelor's degree from Virginia Union University and his master's degree in history from the University of Michigan. He had also completed some coursework toward a PhD at the University of Wisconsin. When the university denied him admission because of race, he sued in the federal district court at Lexington. Federal court judge H. Church Ford ruled in Johnson's favor and found that Kentucky had not provided him with equal educational opportunity. He ordered UK's graduate school to admit qualified Black applicants until Kentucky created a Black graduate school equal to the one at UK. Johnson and thirty other Black graduate students entered UK in the summer of 1949.[106]

Throughout the 1930s and 1940s, Black interest in advanced study grew exponentially. For example, the number of graduate students at Howard University in Washington, DC, increased from 3 in 1926 to 326 in 1937. In that year, Howard, Atlanta, Fisk, and Hampton conferred a combined 101 master's degrees. This number was more than 20 percent of the total number of master's degrees, 497, conferred by these institutions in all previous years. Prior to 1937, Howard had awarded 246 master's degrees during its sixteen years of offering graduate study; Atlanta had awarded 141 master's degrees in its eight years of offering graduate study; Fisk had awarded 83 master's degrees in its ten years of offering graduate study; Xavier had awarded 9 degrees during its four years of offering graduate study; and Hampton had awarded 18 master's degrees in its ten years of offering graduate study.[107]

Thus, by the time of *Gaines*, southern state lawmakers could not in good faith say that Black southerners were not interested in advanced study. Yet southern states continued to drag their feet on establishing graduate programs at public Black colleges. Instead, these states strengthened their commitment to segregation in higher education by implementing segregation scholarship programs in defiance of the Supreme Court ruling. Such recalcitrance reminded African Americans that court victories meant nothing without vigorous enforcement.

CHAPTER FOUR

Shall We Rejoice or Grieve?

Black Graduate Study at Public Black Colleges in Tandem with Segregation Scholarships

> Indeed the [Black college] president stands a surer chance of keeping his job to the extent that he is hostile to the best interests of his own people.
> —LEWIS K. McMILLAN,
> "Negro Higher Education as I Have Known It," 14.

> I am certain that I am not receiving and cannot receive equal educational advantages at the North Carolina College.
> —HAROLD THOMAS EPPS,
> in letter to UNC Board of Trustees, June 2, 1949

On December 6, 1938, six days before the US Supreme Court ruled in favor of Lloyd Gaines, Pauli Murray sat in her New York City apartment and fired off a letter to North Carolina College for Negroes president James Shepard. The twenty-eight-year-old Black woman (who struggled with gender identity) from North Carolina was known to wield her typewriter as an instrument for social justice. Earlier in the year Murray had applied to the University of North Carolina for graduate school and she wanted to know Shepard's position on her actions. "Do you not think it is high time that we as Negroes and citizens of North Carolina begin to demand that our students be admitted to Duke University and at the University of North Carolina?" she asked. "If such a student can be found who is willing to test the educational law of North Carolina, what support could he or she expect from Negro educators and liberal forces in that State?"[1] Shepard waited weeks before responding to Murray, and in many ways his delay was an answer, just not the one she had hoped for.

Murray was quite familiar with Shepard and his political dealings. Her family was from Durham, which was Shepard's homebase, and her educator aunt who raised her worked closely with Shepard in the state's Black teachers' association.

Moreover, Murray attended high school with Thomas Hocutt, whose efforts to enter UNC five years earlier had been stymied by Shepard.[2]

This chapter considers the precarious situation that Black college presidents at state-supported institutions found themselves in as Black southerners pursued equal education lawsuits. For Shepard, supporting Pauli Murray would mean taking on the wrath of white state officials and jeopardizing the funding and very existence of his institution, NCC. Not supporting Murray would mean enduring name-calling and ridicule from African Americans who believed anything less than a full-fledged assault on racial segregation was betrayal.

Rather than champion desegregation at UNC, Shepard fought for Black access to graduate and professional school programs at tax-supported Black institutions.[3] He envisioned a range of master's and doctorate programs and schools of law, pharmacy, and medicine at NCC. This ambitious vision appeased many, in theory, as it provided postbaccalaureate training to African Americans without upsetting segregationists. Such a plan, however, required financial investments in public Black colleges that southern officials had heretofore refused to make.

In the wake of the *Gaines* decision, southern states did in fact evade the spirit of the order by creating a few graduate programs at public Black colleges. These programs, born out of a desire to preserve segregation rather than out of genuine acknowledgment that African Americans deserved equal educational opportunities, were limited and underfunded. Separate but equal graduate programs were not possible and rather than cosign such a sham, individuals such as Murray sought admission into the well-funded institutions made possible by Black tax dollars.

Pauli Murray was the second Black woman who applied for admission to graduate programs at the historically white University of North Carolina. Edwina Thomas, a native of Winston-Salem, was the first. Standing at the crossroads of race and gender, Thomas and Murray sought advanced education at UNC during a time when Black women's employment prospects continued to be largely limited to teaching, nursing, farming, or domestic work. They were part of a growing demographic of Black women degree holders with even higher academic ambitions. Neither woman sought graduate study at UNC as a political move or at the urging of the NAACP. Their desire was practical and straightforward. Attending graduate school at UNC was a cheaper and safer option. To that latter point, not having to travel long distances alone when their race excluded them from the privileges usually offered to female travelers was an important factor. Many train stations did not have ladies' waiting rooms for Black women.[4] Moreover, having the ability to live near family lessened the chance of sexual assault or other bodily harm.

While Thomas and Murray had no desire to study away from home, hundreds of other Black North Carolinians did and in doing so, incurred all kinds of difficulties. Their experiences demonstrated that even though northern universities were often superior to their southern counterparts in resources and prestige, segregation scholarship recipients attending these institutions often had to battle racism, isolation, and homesickness.

Believing she had just as much right to attend her state's flagship as anyone else, twenty-year-old Edwina Thomas wrote UNC officials in January 1938 requesting an admission application. While extant evidence does not show whether Thomas was influenced by Lloyd Gaines's lawsuit, she undoubtedly knew about the case because Black communities throughout the South followed it closely. Her father was the pastor of Wentz Memorial Congregational Church in Winston-Salem, and it is highly likely that Edwina was home with her parents when she applied to UNC, since university officials sent the application to her North Carolina address. Had she applied from the all-Black Talladega College in Alabama where she was then an undergraduate student and used her school address as her return address, admission officials would have learned her race much earlier and probably would not have sent the application form. As it happened, she received the form, completed and returned it, and then heard nothing. After writing to the dean of the Graduate School twice, she finally received a reply. Dean William Whatley Pierson informed Thomas that the state's public policy (not law) prevented UNC from admitting Black students and that the university trustees would have to reverse course for her to study there.[5]

Thomas refused to take no for an answer since UNC was financed in part with tax dollars from Black families like hers. She appealed to UNC president Frank Porter Graham, explaining that she was "unable financially to cope with the expenses of graduate school outside of my own state." She then told Graham that "I should like very much for you to advise me just as to what I can expect from the state of North Carolina in the way of help financially if I am to be denied admission to the State University because of my race."[6] In no uncertain terms, Thomas made a citizenship claim by asking what financial assistance her home state would provide her in lieu of the citizenship or residency benefits that the state denied her. Responding a little more than a week later, Graham assured Thomas that he had taken her letter directly to the governor and that he believed state provision for African Americans to pursue graduate and professional school study was forthcoming. Graham's conjecture about forthcoming state aid, written six months before the Supreme Court ruled in the *Gaines* case, revealed that southern states were already devising ways to feign equal educational opportunity for African Americans before a court order required them to do so.[7]

Thomas graduated from Talladega College in June 1938 with degrees in psychology and mathematics and waited patiently for news about state aid. When nothing came by August, she again wrote to President Graham and inquired about the possibility of state action during the special session of the legislature that was currently in session. Graham told her that legislators would only take up the issue of Public Works Administration grants during the special session and that it might be 1939 before she received an answer.[8]

Even someone as progressive on race as President Graham expected Thomas and other ambitious Black students to wait indefinitely for the same state-sponsored educational opportunities readily available to non-Black students. Thomas, however, had no plan to wait for the education that she desired and deserved. At great personal expense, she enrolled in Ohio State and earned a master's degree in psychology in June 1939.[9] She returned to North Carolina for a few years after completing her studies, but by the mid-1940s she lived in the North, where she remained for the rest of her life.

While Edwina Thomas settled in at Ohio State, Pauli Murray applied to UNC's Graduate School. She submitted her admission application in November 1938, days after the US Supreme Court heard oral arguments in Lloyd Gaines's legal challenge to enter the University of Missouri School of Law. Born in 1910 in Baltimore, Maryland, Murray moved to Durham, North Carolina, to live with her aunt and namesake after being orphaned at age three. At fifteen, she relocated to New York, where she stayed long enough to earn a bachelor's degree in English from Hunter College in 1933. Five years later, she sought admission to UNC to pursue graduate study in sociology.[10]

Murray's application to UNC placed her family at risk. Her aunt, employed as a public school teacher, feared that segregationists might vandalize the family home or fire her from her job since she reported to a white school board. These very real concerns underscored that no one connected to an individual challenging the racial status quo was immune from reprisal. Making these fears even more credible were the UNC students who vowed to lynch any trailblazing African American who entered the flagship institution. Student opposition to a Black graduate student at UNC was not absolute, however. In a *Daily Tar Heel* poll conducted among graduate students, respondents voted 82 to 38 in favor of admitting Black graduate students.[11]

Murray's biggest supporter in her effort to desegregate UNC was Louis Austin, editor of the Black *Carolina Times* newspaper. Austin, who had accompanied Thomas Hocutt when he attempted to enroll at UNC years earlier, used his pen to defend Murray and make plain the illogic of excluding Black students while admitting other students who were not white. When one North Carolina newspaper questioned why Murray would want to be the lone Black student at UNC, it was Austin who responded. "Is the *Herald* not aware of the fact that there is now a lone Chinese girl attending, as a full-fledged student, the University of North Carolina? Surely a native-born American Negro woman whose parents and foreparents have born their share of tax burden to help maintain the university would feel as much at home as a Chinese girl whose native tongue, habits and customs are different from those with whom she now finds herself in contact?"[12]

Murray never attended UNC because university officials denied her admission based on race two days after the *Gaines* decision. The Supreme Court decreed in the case that states had an obligation to provide Black and white residents with equal educational opportunities within their borders. Murray went on to Howard University School of Law where she graduated first in her class in 1944. In 1965, she became the first African American to earn a doctor of juridical science degree from Yale Law School.[13] No institution in the state of North Carolina offered graduate study to African Americans when UNC rejected Murray's application, but that soon changed.

North Carolina and several other southern states responded to *Gaines* by creating a few graduate programs at public Black colleges and instituting segregation scholarship programs to make up for the limited graduate offerings. The southern states were effectively thumbing their nose at the Supreme Court, which had just ruled segregation scholarships unconstitutional. Legislators in North Carolina voted to provide the state's Black citizens with advanced degree opportunities in March 1939, and classes began in September. Missouri, Texas, and Tennessee also established graduate programs at tax-supported Black colleges that year to demonstrate compliance with the *Gaines* decision. North Carolina lawmakers created limited graduate and professional school opportunities for African Americans at North Carolina College for Negroes in Durham and North Carolina Agricultural and Technical College in Greensboro. NCC offered graduate study in the liberal arts and in law, while North Carolina A&T offered graduate study in agriculture and technology. Thirty students enrolled in master's degree programs at NCC and five at A&T. Faculty from the University of North Carolina and Duke University taught some of the courses.[14] Black North Carolinians desiring graduate study unavailable at the two public Black colleges became eligible for segregation scholarships.

The North Carolina General Assembly had first considered providing segregation scholarships for Black residents to pursue graduate and professional training outside the state in 1933. The bill passed in the state house but failed in the state senate. In 1937, a state senator introduced another bill for segregation scholarships, but the legislation never made it out of committee.[15] What the general assembly did do that year was authorize a commission to study public schools and colleges for African Americans with the purpose of reducing differentials in Black and white education. The question of graduate and professional school opportunities for Black residents was one of the issues that the commission, whose members included state senators J. W. Noell and J. H. McDaniel and Nathan Newbold, the state director of Negro education, took up. The commission recommended that North Carolina provide graduate education for African Americans, noting that the faculties at the state's five tax-supported Black colleges included six with PhDs, nineteen with two years of graduate training, and sixty-four with master's degrees. All the degree holders had secured their postbaccalaureate training outside North Carolina, demonstrating the great demand and lack of opportunity in the state.[16]

North Carolina governor Clyde Hoey supported the commission's recommendation for Black graduate instruction in his January 1939 address to the state legislature. After referencing the *Gaines* decision, Hoey asserted that "North Carolina does not believe in social equality between the races and will not tolerate mixed schools for the races, but we do believe in equality of opportunity."[17] In other words, North Carolina had no plans to desegregate the University of North Carolina.

The obvious problem that state officials refused to acknowledge was that graduate instruction differed from undergraduate instruction in significant ways. A decent graduate program required an adequate library, laboratories, equipment, and faculty with graduate training. North Carolina had already underfunded its Black colleges. Now the state pretended that these financially starved institutions could do even more with meager resources. *Carolina Times* editor Austin sounded the alarm. After pondering whether Black North Carolinians should rejoice or grieve at the creation of graduate programs at Black colleges, he wrote in his weekly, "The measly sum which the state has appropriated for Negro education in the past raises a suspicion in the minds of thinking Negroes. Negroes in this state will not be satisfied with graduate courses that will not meet the standard already set for by the state for its white citizens."[18] Without a sizeable investment of state resources for graduate instruction, North Carolina forced Black colleges to do more with less.

Among the first graduate cohort to enter NCC was Maude J. Yancey, a Black woman from Wilson, North Carolina. Yancey's family embodied Black ambition and the belief in education as a vehicle for social mobility. Her father, D'Arcey Yancey, was among the small Black population that earned bachelor's degrees at the turn of the century, obtaining his undergraduate degree from Biddle University (present-day Johnson C. Smith University) in 1903 before completing the pharmacy program at Shaw University's Leonard School of Pharmacy in 1906. He owned a thriving pharmacy in Wilson. Maude Yancey's mother, the former Leila Beatrice Ireland, studied at Scotia Seminary before becoming one of the first teachers renowned educator Charlotte Hawkins Brown hired to teach at Palmer Memorial Institute near Greensboro.[19]

Given the Yanceys' educational achievements, it was not surprising that their only daughter would make educational strides herself. On June 4, 1940, NCC awarded Maude Yancey its very first graduate degree. She had graduated a year earlier from Knoxville College in Tennessee before earning her master's degree in biology at NCC. Yancey went on to receive a master's degree in public health and a doctorate in health education from the University of Michigan in 1946 and 1952, respectively. She served on the faculties at NCC, Southern University in Baton Rouge, Louisiana, and Elizabeth City State University in Elizabeth City, North Carolina.[20]

North Carolina A&T awarded its first graduate degree in 1941 to Woodland Hall, a native Virginian who had attended the University of Maryland Eastern Shore for his undergraduate study. Hall earned a master's degree in agricultural education from North Carolina's Black land-grant before serving as a principal in several cities throughout the state.[21] Yancey's and Hall's scholarly and professional success demonstrated the Black intellect that the South stifled when state universities excluded Black students based on race.

Makeshift public graduate programs at Black colleges were initially nothing more than an attempt to evade the spirit of the *Gaines* decision. Because the course offerings of these programs were so limited, southern and border states also exported Black scholars with segregation scholarships. In North Carolina, A&T's graduate program was limited to agriculture and technology, and NCC's graduate programs were limited to social science, science, mathematics, education, English and law. This meant that students interested in fields such as medicine, pharmacy, zoology, physical education, and history had to leave the state.

Some Black college presidents colluded with white lawmakers to thwart desegregation and expand their institutions. No one was more adept at this than NCC's James Shepard. He did what he could to maintain an all-white UNC when Thomas Hocutt applied in 1933 and received increased state appropriations in return. After *Gaines*, he once again resisted desegregation by calling for graduate programs at NCC, and legislators rewarded him with a 400 percent increase in funding to his college over the previous year and the establishment of a law school there.[22]

There was no question that African Americans needed access to legal education. The 1930 Census listed 1,230 Black lawyers and 159,735 white lawyers in the United States. According to Charles Hamilton Houston, many of the Black lawyers included in that number had never passed the bar or practiced. In North Carolina, there were only 27 Black lawyers practicing alongside 2,362 white lawyers.[23] African Americans needed access to law schools to begin closing such stark gaps in the profession.

With respect to NCC's law school, access did not mean equality. The *New York Amsterdam News* called NCC's law school nothing more than an effort to avoid the mandate of *Gaines*, and the *Chicago Defender* called it a "Jim Crow law school."[24] NAACP officials certainly saw NCC's new school as a betrayal, as it was in no way the Black equivalent of UNC's law school. Walter White, the civil rights organization's executive secretary, lamented, "Every time the NAACP wins a case against a Southern state, new buildings spring up on the campuses of the colored land-grant colleges."[25] NCC was not a land-grant, but *Gaines* led to the addition of a new and unequal law school at the college.

Though NCC's law school first opened in September 1939, it discontinued classes one week after opening because of low enrollment. Logan Delany, a graduate of Saint Augustine's College and the grandson of Henry Delany, the first elected Black bishop of the Episcopal Church, was the lone registered student, so class discussion was impossible. The state offered to pay for Delany to attend law school elsewhere, but he resolved to wait until NCC's law school reopened in September 1940.[26]

Pauli Murray, who had first applied to UNC in November 1938, took her case to the NAACP rather than enroll at NCC or accept a segregation scholarship to study in exile. The civil rights organization chose not to pursue a legal challenge deeming Murray a problematic litigant. NAACP attorney Thurgood Marshall raised concerns about Murray's residency since she had not lived in North Carolina for several years. The question of residency made a test case too risky.[27] It is likely that Marshall was also troubled by the fact that Murray had been arrested while on a picket line in New York and that she had briefly attended the leftist Brookwood College shortly before applying to UNC. Marshall knew that segregationists would use the information to discredit the young woman. Moreover, Murray had engaged in "confrontation by typewriter," writing critical open letters to college presidents, the Black press, and national figures.[28] Her actions were at odds with the civil rights organization's focus on the law and the courts. Like her childhood friend Thomas Hocutt, who had attempted to enroll at UNC in 1933, Murray came up short in her attack on Jim Crow, but she served as further proof that African American southerners continued to desire graduate and professional study.

In her letters to Shepard, as a matter of goodwill, she had given him advance notice of her intention to apply to UNC. She reached out to the NCC president because he was good friends with her aunt, who also served as her adoptive mother. As expected, Shepard did not support Murray's decision to apply to UNC. He warned that a "court case would be useless."[29]

Unlike John W. Davis of West Virginia State College, James Shepard championed the establishment of separate graduate programs for African Americans. As early as 1933, a UNC representative asked Shepard for his thoughts about the possibility of NCC's affiliating with UNC to offer graduate training but he demurred. Shepard based his preference on Black self-determination explaining, "I believe Negroes should control their own colleges so as to develop self-consciousness and racial leadership."[30] Race pride notwithstanding, Shepard gained a lot from the preservation of segregation in higher education. Not only did graduate offerings increase the prestige of an institution he founded, but he also served as the conduit through which segregation scholarship money flowed.

Shepard was the main administrator of out-of-state tuition grants for Black students in North Carolina, overseeing requests for tuition assistance for all disciplines except for agricultural and technical ones. He awarded forty-nine segregation scholarships during the first academic year that funds were available, while Ferdinand D. Bluford, his counterpart at North Carolina A&T, awarded just three scholarships. Shepard rejected many more applications than he approved. Black citizens of North Carolina who could attest their citizenship by church membership, voter registration, birth certificate, or tax records and provide proof of admission to a university were eligible for tuition assistance. Applicants could receive funding for the entire school year, for a summer session, or for both. The summer session option catered to Black principals and schoolteachers who worked full time during the school year. Shepard and Bluford sent tuition checks, which were paid on a semesterly or quarterly basis, directly to the applicant's institution after receiving proof of enrollment. Students received a check in the amount equal to one roundtrip railroad fare from his or her home to their graduate institution. Pullman fare was provided if night travel was necessary. Since NCC initially only offered master's work in social science, science, mathematics, English, and education and A&T in fields such as animal husbandry, industrial education, and agronomy, hundreds of letters arrived at Shepard's office from students desiring to study other disciplines out of state.[31]

CHAPTER FOUR

Unlike Missouri and Tennessee, North Carolina did not pay for Black students to pursue undergraduate study out of state, even if a student pursued a bachelor's degree program that was offered at UNC but was not offered at the state's five Black public colleges. The exception, however, was pharmacy. UNC offered non-Black students a bachelor's degree in pharmacy (S.B. Pharmacy). North Carolina's attorney general approved segregation scholarships for Black undergraduates studying pharmacy out of state because the state considered the degree program professional work and the bill authorizing the segregation scholarships stipulated that the state award funds to Black students for "graduate and professional courses."[32]

From September 1, 1939, until July 1, 1940, the first academic year segregation scholarship funds were available in North Carolina, James Shepard awarded scholarships totaling $9,772.31. No applicant received the full tuition amount. Scholars attended some of the best institutions in the country, including Radcliffe, Atlanta University, New York University, and the University of Michigan. Eight Black men in that first group of scholarship recipients received funds to pursue medical degrees at Meharry Medical College in Nashville.[33]

The educational backgrounds and achievements of inaugural recipients of out-of-state tuition grants demonstrate the intellectual curiosity of Black North Carolinians compelled to leave home. Many recipients were already on the faculties of Black colleges and pursued advanced study with leaves of absence. For instance, James McRae received a leave of absence from Fayetteville State Teachers College to pursue his master's degree at Columbia. McRae had graduated from Lincoln University of Pennsylvania in 1924 before working as a teacher and principal in North Carolina public schools. In 1931, he joined the faculty at Fayetteville State, where he remained for several years before becoming dean at Lincoln.[34]

Charles Reginald Eason and his wife Sarah received funding to pursue doctorate degrees in mathematics and Romance languages, respectively, at the Ohio State University in 1939. Eason was born in 1905 in Elizabeth, New Jersey. He moved to North Carolina in 1930 to teach mathematics at Shaw University after becoming the first African American to earn a graduate degree in mathematics from Rutgers University.[35] While on faculty at the oldest Black college in the South, Eason met his wife, the former Sarah Martin. Martin, a native of Cleveland, Ohio, had joined Shaw's faculty in 1931, teaching French. She earned her undergraduate degree from OSU, where she was the first Black woman elected to Phi Beta Kappa, and received her master's from Western Reserve University.[36] Shaw University granted the couple leaves of absence to earn terminal degrees.

Ohio State was not a hospitable place for Black students during the Easons' tenure. While the first Black undergraduate student had enrolled in 1888, OSU did not award a doctoral degree to an African American student until 1936. As was the case at nearly all the historically white institutions where segregation scholarship recipients matriculated for graduate study, Ohio State was a racially hostile campus. The university had twice benched its star football player in 1930 to appease institutions that did not want to play against teams with Black players. The following year, when an OSU professor took a group of white students to Wilberforce University, a private Black institution affiliated with the African Methodist Episcopal Church, the university terminated the scholar for promoting racial intermingling. Later in the 1930s, two Black coeds majoring in home economics were refused housing accommodations in the campus house set aside for home economics majors to live together and learn to solve common family and home problems.[37] The Easons lived off campus because, even though OSU provided on-campus graduate student housing, the university barred Black students from living there.

Sarah Martin Eason received her doctorate degree in Romance languages in 1942 and went on to teach at several institutions, including the University of the District of Columbia and Johnson C. Smith University.[38] Charles Eason, for reasons that remain unclear, never completed his degree. After returning to Shaw for several more years on the faculty, he left academia for federal service, working with the US Army at Fort Monmouth. He became a nationally renowned physicist, known for his work in radar reflection research and microwave antennas.[39] The couple, who, together, were among the first to receive funding from North Carolina to earn terminal degrees, divorced shortly after Sarah Eason earned her PhD.

Another Black North Carolina resident who received a segregation scholarship as soon as funds became available was Eliza Atkins Gleason. Born in 1909, she was the ninth and last child of Simon Green Atkins and Oleona Pegram Atkins. In 1892, her father founded Slater Industrial Academy, which became present-day Winston-Salem State University. Her mother served as a teacher and assistant principal at the school. As the daughter of educators, Gleason had an advantage that many Black southerners of the era did not have. Her parents were informed and aware of what educational opportunities existed for African Americans and how to go about seizing them. She also had a name advantage when it came to securing funds. Before his death in 1934, Simon Atkins had moved in the same Black educational circles as James Shepard, so Shepard would have recognized Eliza Atkins Gleason's name when she applied for state assistance.

Gleason was already pursuing graduate study out of state when segregation scholarships became available for North Carolinians. She had earned a bachelor's degree from Fisk University in 1930 and a bachelor's degree in library science from the University of Illinois in 1931. She worked as a librarian for several years in Kentucky before earning her master's degree in library science at the University of California, Berkeley, in 1936. After graduation, she had a one-year stint as an assistant professor and head of the Reference Department at Fisk University's library before matriculating at the University of Chicago, where she pursued a doctorate in library science. In the same year that she started the doctoral program, she married Maurice Gleason, a student at Meharry Medical College in Nashville. The two lived apart as they pursued their studies because segregation prevented them from studying their chosen disciplines in the same place.[40]

In 1940, Gleason became the first African American to earn a doctorate in library science. During her final year of doctoral study, North Carolina paid $122 of Gleason's tuition and fees at the University of Chicago. The state also gave her $31.40 for railroad fare. Rather than return to North Carolina after graduation, she relocated to Georgia, where she established and became the first dean of the School of Library Science at Atlanta University. Between 1941 and 1986, more than 90 percent of all Black librarians in the United States received their training in the program Gleason created.[41]

Stories abound of Black North Carolinians relocating to the North, Midwest, and West to continue their education. John Withers, born in Greensboro in 1916 to a college-educated janitor and a seamstress, did not allow Jim Crow or lack of family support to stymie his ambition. Withers grew up as the penultimate child of four children in the shadow of A&T's campus. He enrolled there at age sixteen after skipping a grade because of stellar academic performance in high school. Withers's father believed that his son's success in the classroom prepared him to be a first-rate minister in the future.[42] Teaching and preaching were high-status jobs for African Americans during the era of legal segregation, so it was no surprise that the elder Withers saw the pulpit as the pinnacle of achievement for his son.

College exposed John Withers to a world quite different from the religious one that dominated his parents' home. He discussed politics and international affairs with fellow students and faculty. He read *The Crisis* and longed to be an intellectual like the magazine's editor, W. E. B. Du Bois. After graduation, Withers got a job in the registrar's office at A&T but graduate school beckoned him. The problem was that he had no funds for additional schooling, and his parents believed that he had had enough education. He needed to earn a living.[43]

Working in the registrar's office made Withers aware that North Carolina had appropriated funds for Black students to pursue graduate study out of state.

Dr. Eliza Atkins Gleason during her 1940 commencement from the University of Chicago. Dr. Gleason was the first African American to earn a PhD in library science. Photo courtesy of Dr. Joy Gleason Carew.

It also helped that he was a mentee of A&T president Ferdinand Bluford, who knew about the segregation scholarships firsthand since he reviewed the scholarship applications from students planning to study science or engineering.[44] Withers applied for state funds and became another inaugural recipient of a segregation scholarship. He used the tuition assistance to pursue a master's degree in economics from the University of Wisconsin. An acquaintance from college had encouraged him to apply there.[45] North Carolina paid $80 of Withers's tuition and fees and gave him $57.32 for railroad fare. The amount was far short of the $255 in tuition and fees that the University of Wisconsin charged nonresidents annually.[46]

As was the case for so many Black migrants before him, Withers sat in a railroad car headed north, leaving his birth state for the first time in his life. The car reserved for Black passengers was usually right behind the locomotive, so fumes and engine noise would have been a part of the journey as the train headed to Wisconsin.[47] With each passing hour the land and the landscape changed, making him acutely aware that he was entering unchartered territory.

Upon disembarking in Madison, John Withers sought out Lucille Miller, a middle-aged Black woman who rented rooms to Black students because the university prohibited them from living on campus. Withers's friend at A&T had recommended Miller for lodging, and luckily she had a vacancy. Miller's orientation for Withers consisted of more than an overview of the house rules. She reminded the southern transplant that he was not in Dixie anymore and that he should carry himself as such. He could sit where he wanted and say what he pleased. In no uncertain terms, she encouraged him to be confident, proud, and assertive.[48]

Lucille Miller's pep talk to John Withers was prescient because when he set foot on the University of Wisconsin campus for the first time, he immediately felt like a fish out of water. The university had more students in its graduate school than in A&T's total student body. A regular classroom on the Madison campus was bigger than the largest auditorium at his alma mater. Perhaps most jarring was the experience of interacting closely with white people. In North Carolina, he worked for white people here and there but never mingled socially. Now he sat with them in class and shared notes during study sessions.[49]

Withers often felt out of place among his classmates at Wisconsin who came from well-to-do families. While they had traveled abroad and had many cosmopolitan experiences, his claim to fame was that he had seen snow for the first time in Madison. On more than one occasion, he was tempted to make up stories about his family and upbringing to fit in. While peers seemed more worldly than him, he found his classmates naive about race and racism. They knew little about how Black people lived "although they assumed they did."[50]

Despite not always feeling as if he belonged, Withers excelled in the classroom. He took classes with the famed economist Milton Friedman, who also sat on his thesis committee. Withers's academic success led him to pondering a doctorate, but first he had to complete the master's.[51]

Like many college students, Withers returned home for the summer and found a job. He hoped to earn enough so that he would not have to work during the next academic year. Complementing his meager earnings that summer was a tuition check from North Carolina. While it was rare for the state to send tuition checks directly to the student, Withers received the check for his upcoming fall semester the preceding summer. He cashed the check and hid the funds in cigar box in his room at his parents' home. Days before heading back to Wisconsin, Withers found the cigar box empty: someone had found and taken his secret stash. Upon further investigation, he learned that his father had taken the money to prevent him from being able to leave home again. Filled with anger and shock, Withers gathered the few dollars that he had placed in a different hiding spot and stormed out of his parents' home. After staying with a friend for a few days, he boarded a train back to Madison unsure of how he would pay his tuition.[52]

By his calculation, Withers had enough to make a partial tuition payment to the University of Wisconsin and hoped to arrange an installment plan for the rest. In the fall of 1940, he nervously entered the bursar's office with every dime that he could spare. He gave his name and turned over the wad of bills bound together with a rubber band. To his surprise, the clerk soon returned the funds and informed him that university policy designated out-of-state students who maintained an A average in their first year of master's programs to be classified as in-state students in the second year. Withers did not have to pay tuition at all.[53]

With his financial concerns now resolved, Withers devoted his time completely to his studies. He earned his master's degree in the spring of 1941. While his parents could not make the trip to Madison to see him graduate, Lucille Miller, his landlord, was in the audience. She stood in for the Black community back in Greensboro, who celebrated his success from afar. Segregation scholarship recipients often received their diplomas with no family present because studying so far from home made it cost-prohibitive for their families to join them.[54]

John Withers did not have a job lined up after graduation, but he was certain that he would not return to the segregated South. Before he could finalize career plans in the North, however, he was drafted into a segregated army as the United States entered World War II. Withers's high marks on the Army General Classification Test led to his enrollment in Officer Candidate School. He served as a lieutenant during the war, leading an all-Black battalion in Germany.[55]

In 1947, armed with a GI Bill educational benefit to pay his tuition, John Withers enrolled at the University of Chicago in pursuit of a doctorate degree. He settled on the University of Chicago in part because Milton Friedman, a professor from his time at Wisconsin, had joined the faculty there. After earning his doctorate in international relations, he became one of the first African Americans to enter the US Foreign Service, working for what became the US Agency for International Development. His career spanned Africa and Asia, including stints in Laos, Thailand, Korea, Ethiopia, and Kenya. Withers retired as the USAID director of mission in India.[56] Having the opportunity to attend graduate school had opened up a much larger world to the Greensboro native.

The list of North Carolina's recipients of segregation scholarships is a record of Black educational aspiration. Another resident who received funds in that first year was Frances Jones, the daughter of David Dallas Jones, president of Bennett College in Greensboro. Like Eliza Atkins Gleason, Jones hailed from one of the better-off Black families in the segregated South. Her family had intimate knowledge of how higher education worked. Jones graduated second in her class from Bennett in 1939 and enrolled in the Boston University School of Medicine in 1940. She requested $475 in tuition assistance from the state of North Carolina, the full tuition amount for the academic year. The state, however, only provided Jones with $280 for tuition.[57] Jones made up the difference every year with family support and graduated from BUSM in December 1943 as part of an accelerated wartime graduating class. She was one of six women in the class of forty-five students and the only African American. While at BUSM, Jones met Charles Bonner, who began medical school the year after her. The two married within days of her graduating from medical school. Frances Jones Bonner went on to become the first African American physician to train and teach at Massachusetts General Hospital. She worked at Massachusetts General for fifty years and was on the faculties of both Harvard Medical School and Boston University.[58] She transgressed racial and gender norms in medicine. Her career was evidence of what was possible when African Americans had the opportunity to be ambitious and scholarly.

Recipients in subsequent years included Ernestine Baylor, a native of Mount Olive, North Carolina, who received her master's degree in education from Boston University in 1955, and Monticello J. Howell, a native of Cabarrus County, North Carolina, who received his doctorate in horticulture from Michigan State University in 1956. Baylor and Howell had distinguished careers on the faculties of Johnson C. Smith and Grambling State Universities, respectively. Another segregation scholarship recipient in the mid-1950s, LeRoy T. Walker, was then head track coach at North Carolina College. College officials gave Walker a one-year leave of absence to pursue his doctorate in exercise physiology and biomechanics at New York University, which he earned in 1957. Walker made history several times over, serving as the first Black coach of the US track team, as chancellor of North Carolina Central University from 1983 to 1986, and as the first Black president of the US Olympic Committee from 1992 to 1996.[59] These recipients demonstrate that segregation scholarships helped create a Black professional class who made strides in their chosen careers.

While the Black professional class included physicians, North Carolina made medical education for African Americans especially difficult. Because the medical school at UNC was a two-year program when segregation scholarships began, North Carolina only provided tuition assistance for the first two years of Black medical students' training. When UNC became a four-year medical school in 1954, Black students received four years of funding. Hubert Eaton of Winston-Salem attended medical school at the University of Michigan with a segregation scholarship. Eaton recalled making twenty-five round trips by bus between Ann Arbor and Winston-Salem between 1938 until 1942 while in medical school. Not only did he have to foot the bill for most of his travel, but he also had to learn the rules of "traveling while Black" to avoid humiliation or physical harm. On trips home, segregation laws required him to move to the back of the bus when he entered the state of Virginia.[60]

Eaton was born in 1916 in Fayetteville, North Carolina, to a father who practiced medicine and a mother who worked as a teacher. The Eaton family later relocated to Winston-Salem, where Hubert excelled at school and in tennis. He won the 1933 national junior championship of the American Tennis Association, an honor that earned him a four-year scholarship to Johnson C. Smith University in Charlotte. After graduating from the Black institution in 1937, he entered the University of Michigan to study for a master's degree in zoology, completing the work in two semesters and a summer. While there, he successfully applied to the medical school and remained in Ann Arbor. His time studying medicine overlapped with that of Maggie Laura Walker, the granddaughter of renowned banker Maggie Lena Walker. Maggie received a fifty-dollar segregation scholarship from Virginia to offset her medical school expenses and when she graduated in 1941, was said to be only the third Black woman to have done so at the medical school.[61]

Immediately after Eaton's 1942 medical school graduation, he established a medical practice in Wilmington, North Carolina. In addition to providing treatment to patients of all races, he pushed back against the racial status quo whenever possible. By initiating a series of lawsuits, he forced the county school board to invest more money in Black schools and later desegregate them, he secured staff privileges for Black doctors at local hospitals, and he integrated the municipal golf course. He exemplified the leadership that Charles Hamilton Houston asserted would come with more African Americans holding advanced degrees.[62]

Eaton traveled to Michigan for medical school because North Carolina, like every state in the South except Tennessee, did not have a public or private medical school for African Americans. From 1882 until 1918, Shaw University in Raleigh, the first Black college in the South, operated the Leonard Medical School. The school was the first four-year medical school in the United States and trained more than 400 Black physicians, including Eaton's father, who provided badly needed healthcare to Black communities.

Leonard Medical School was a casualty of a 1910 report written by Abraham Flexner and commissioned by the Carnegie Foundation that rated all medical schools in the United States and Canada. The Flexner Report proposed closing schools that were poorly financed and equipped, including five of the then seven Black medical schools, without any acknowledgement of the role racism played in underfunding Leonard and other Black medical schools. The only two Black medical schools that Flexner recommended allowing to remain open were at Howard and Meharry. While the report itself did not close Leonard, its findings led philanthropic groups to withhold support, which proved to be a decisive blow. Leonard's closing contributed to a shortage of Black medical doctors throughout the Carolinas and forced Black North Carolinians who desired to study medicine to leave the state for their training, losing access to valuable local contacts who could later help one set up a practice. It would not be until 1951—thirty-three years after Leonard's closing—that the University of North Carolina at Chapel Hill admitted a Black student to its medical school.

In addition to the travel indignities that Hubert Eaton described, segregation scholarship recipients faced numerous other challenges. Raleigh native Elizabeth Young chose to pursue a master of science degree in physical education at Boston University during the 1939–40 academic year. North Carolina gave her $150 for tuition, $20 for fees, and $16.77 for railroad fare.[63] Young, who aspired to teach physical education at the college level, assumed that the state would pay all her tuition since she had no choice but to leave North Carolina to fulfill her career dream. Had she been white, she could have attended the University of North Carolina and received the same degree. Young expressed her disappointment about the funding gap in a letter to North Carolina College president James Shepard. In his response, Shepard reminded Young that Boston University charged $300 per year while the University of North Carolina charged $150 per year for the same course of study.[64] The burden of making up a shortfall caused by segregation fell to Young.

Many scholarship recipients expressed financial hardship. Charles Ray, a Raleigh native, Durham resident, and instructor of English at North Carolina College, matriculated in the University of Southern California's doctoral program in English language and literature. After completing coursework, Ray relocated back to North Carolina to resume teaching and only traveled to California when necessary. He traveled to California for a few days in May 1952 to defend his dissertation before returning home. Once back in North Carolina, he learned that the University of Southern California required candidates for the PhD to appear in person to receive their diplomas. This meant that Ray needed to travel to California again, but North Carolina's segregation scholarship program only provided recipients with one round-trip fare per academic year. The round-trip railroad fare with Pullman accommodations was $285 and a flight for the same route was $317. North Carolina denied Ray's request for assistance to attend his mandatory commencement.[65] Somehow, Ray came up with the necessary funds and became the first African American to receive a doctorate in English from USC. He became a professor of English at North Carolina College, where he remained for the next quarter of a century.[66]

North Carolina officials were aware of the hardship caused by the state's only providing Black students with one round-trip ticket during the academic year and one round-trip ticket during summer school. In fact, two years before Charles Ray asked for additional travel funds, a special committee on policies and procedures for out-of-state aid met to consider revising the travel allowance. The committee acknowledged that most universities closed for an extended period between the fall and winter semesters and recommended that the state revise its policy and provide two round-trip tickets during the regular nine-month academic year.[67] The suggested change was not novel. Maryland provided its Black segregation scholarship recipients with two round-trip tickets each year.[68] Yet Charles Carroll, the state superintendent for public instruction in North Carolina, disallowed more than one round-trip travel allowance, ignoring the tremendous burden that the state placed on its Black citizens.[69]

Another problem faced by Black students seeking graduate study was that the segregation scholarship law made no distinction between the PhD and the EdD degrees. From 1952 until 1962, NCC offered the PhD in education. White officials in North Carolina created the doctoral program to maintain separate and unequal education in the state. Alphonso Elder, Shepard's successor at NCC, said as much recalling, "The initiative that led to the establishment of the Ph.D. degree at North Carolina College originated at the University of North Carolina.... [NCC] was forced to take on the Ph.D. program which we did not want."[70] The program's existence almost prevented one segregation scholarship applicant from receiving aid.

Roger Russell, who worked as a guidance counselor at NCC, applied for a summer session scholarship in 1953 to pursue an EdD at the University of Pennsylvania. The World War II veteran and Virginia native already had degrees from Virginia State College and Columbia University. He had joined NCC's staff in 1948 and his North Carolina residency made him eligible for tuition assistance from the state. NCC officials initially denied Russell's request for funds since NCC offered the PhD degree in education. Russell fought back, insisting that the degree he wanted to pursue was not offered at NCC but was offered at UNC. In fact, UNC did offer both the EdD and the PhD in education. Russell maintained that he was a working professional and sought an EdD because he desired to go into administration rather than into research. After much back and forth with state officials, Russell succeeded in securing out-of-state aid. He earned his doctorate in 1958.[71]

In the rare event that a public Black college offered the same academic program as its white counterpart *or* if school officials asserted that the programs were the same, Black southerners could not receive tuition assistance. Such was the predicament of Myrlie Beasley Evers, who was born and raised in Vicksburg, Mississippi. She finished high school in 1950, two years after Mississippi had established a segregation scholarship program that allowed Black Mississippians to pursue undergraduate or graduate programs offered at the University of Mississippi but not offered at the state's two public Black colleges: Alcorn and Jackson State. Evers planned to attend Fisk University with state aid and study music. The board of trustees of the Mississippi Institutions of Higher Learning required Black residents to confirm that the state's Black colleges did not offer their desired course of study before applying for a segregation scholarship. In what she considered to be a formality, Evers contacted both schools. Alcorn officials stated that they only offered a minor in music. Jacob Reddix, Jackson State's Black president, with no knowledge of Evers's extensive piano training, wrote that "he thought his college offered enough music" for Evers's needs. The state board summarily denied her request for a segregation scholarship even though Jackson State did not offer a music major. Disappointed and feeling cheated, Evers enrolled at Alcorn, where she declared education as her major with a minor in music. It is probable that Reddix, the president of a Black college controlled by white politicians, stymied Evers's efforts because the all-white board wanted to grant as few segregation scholarships as possible. Colluding with them would have been "money in the political bank" for the Black administrator.[72]

Education was one of the most common majors at Black colleges and hundreds of Black educators at the elementary and secondary education levels used segregation scholarships to pursue advanced study in the field. They often learned about the availability of state funds during meetings of their state teachers associations, known as Colored Teachers Associations. Armed with segregation scholarships, Black educators flocked to northern schools of education to study in budding fields of inquiry such as educational administration and rural education, enabling them to provide an even more rigorous and thorough education to their students.[73] Many northern schools of education had summer session programs that allowed Black teachers to earn master's degrees by attending for several consecutive summers. In fact, North Carolina and most other border and southern states received more applications for assistance during the summer than for the regular academic year. For example, North Carolina officials approved eighty-nine segregation scholarship requests for the 1949–50 regular school year and 218 segregation scholarship requests for the 1950 summer.[74]

One of the most popular and prestigious destinations for Black schoolteachers and principals was Teachers College, Columbia University. During the summer of 1947, for example, more than one-fourth of the 18,000 public-school teachers pursuing graduate work at the New York City institution were Black educators from the South.[75] Though no exact figure is available because the school did not keep detailed records, many of those students were segregation scholarship recipients. Teachers College was a mecca for Black educators not only because the school was at the forefront of educational research but also because the faculty included Mabel Carney, a white woman who took an early interest in Black education and developed a course on "Negro Education" in the 1920s, which she continued to teach for decades.[76] Moreover, Teachers College was especially attractive because it was adjacent to Harlem, a popular destination for southern migrants. The list of Black public school teachers and principals from North Carolina who studied at Teachers College in the summers is long and included educators from nearly every school district.

The University of Michigan, Ohio State University, Cornell University, New York University, and Pennsylvania State University were other popular graduate destinations for Black educators. During NYU's June 1950 commencement exercises, for instance, 254 recipients of master's degrees had received their undergraduate degrees from Black colleges in the South.[77] Many of these graduates were Black schoolteachers from southern states who had traveled north for several consecutive summers. N. Longworth Dillard, the longtime principal of the Caswell County Training School, earned his master's degree from the University of Michigan in 1942 with a segregation scholarship from North Carolina. He traveled to Ann Arbor for four consecutive summers, leaving behind a wife and two small children to complete requirements for the degree.[78]

Helen Beasley was one of many teachers who left North Carolina with tuition assistance. Born to a barber father and a homemaker mother in Elizabeth City in 1929, Beasley dreamed of becoming a physician, but her life circumstances made that impossible. Her working-class parents could not afford medical school, but they made sure that their daughter secured more education than they had. She attended Elizabeth City State Teachers College, which was within walking distance of her home. After graduating in 1951, she began teaching at a Rosenwald School in the small town of Milton, North Carolina. Like so many Black educators and parents during the era of legal segregation, Beasley worked hard to give her students the best education possible despite the inequality in resources and facilities.[79]

Beasley's commitment to pedagogical excellence led her to go back to school. Beginning in the summer of 1954, Beasley pursued a master's degree in education at Pennsylvania State University. Penn State, like many other northern institutions, catered to teachers by offering master's programs that the educators could complete in four summers. Beasley received a segregation scholarship from North Carolina to offset her expenses, since she sought a degree that was available to white teachers in state. She packed her suitcase carefully, rolling her clothes to maximize space because she intended to take her hot plate and other cherished belongings with her as she made the trek north. While able to carry her clothes and other personal effects, she had to leave behind a little girl whom she taught and had basically taken into her home as an adopted daughter. The child stayed with Beasley's parents during the summers when she was away. During the summer of 1955, Beasley married Theodore Siddle in North Carolina, but she still managed to travel to Pennsylvania for school. She resumed graduate study at Penn State during the summer of 1956, but as is often the case for graduate students, Beasley's personal life soon interrupted her studies. She missed the 1957 summer session, when she was scheduled to complete her degree, because she was pregnant. She later completed her master's degree at North Carolina A&T. Thirty-odd years later, Helen Beasley Siddle was able to return to the Penn State campus. Her daughter, education historian Vanessa Siddle Walker, then a visiting professor at the University of Pennsylvania, drove her mother back to her old stomping ground.[80]

Not all Black teachers who applied for tuition assistance received it. Mertye Rice, a 1940 graduate of Shaw University and Spanish teacher at the all-Black West Charlotte High School, applied for funding to pursue graduate study in the summers at the University of Havana. State officials denied the request asserting that funds only supported students who pursued graduate or professional study within the continental United States.[81]

Black students whose graduate and professional school programs were available within North Carolina's boundaries also faced challenges. The problems that these scholars faced stemmed from the state's inability and unwillingness to adequately fund a separate graduate school. Even before NCC and A&T began offering graduate programs, the state severely underfunded the two institutions and the other three state-supported Black colleges. For example, during the 1937–38 academic year, North Carolina spent $1,997,477 on its white institutions of higher education and $199,999 on its Black institutions of higher education.[82] Given such great disparities, separate and equal graduate programs were impossible.

NCC's law school opened for the second time in September 1940 with five students enrolled, and it was anything but equal to UNC's law school. The dean, law librarian, and faculty of the UNC School of Law served in these capacities at NCC's School of Law. How these officials could adequately perform their responsibilities on two different campuses was an unstated question that loomed large in the minds of many African Americans. Instead of an on-campus law library, materials in the UNC and Duke law school libraries were shuttled to NCC on an as-needed basis. In its second year of classes, NCC president James Shepard set aside space in the administration building for a law library and hired a full-time, all-Black law faculty.[83]

With each successive year, NCC Law enrolled more students, but the increase in numbers brought tensions to a head. In 1946, the law school had thirteen first-year students, four second-year students, and five third-year students.[84] The rising student population demonstrated Black desire for legal training and exacerbated the law school's cramped quarters. Fed up with the subpar conditions and concerned that NCC's law school remained unaccredited, two of the law school's students, James Walker and Harold Epps, unsuccessfully submitted transfer applications to UNC Law in April 1948. At the same time, Dewey M. Clayton III, a senior at the all-Black Johnson C. Smith University, applied for admission to UNC's medical school and he, too, was denied admission based on race. Clayton reluctantly accepted a segregation scholarship from the state of North Carolina and received his medical degree from Meharry Medical College in 1956.[85]

Determined to expose North Carolina's shortcomings in the educational opportunities it offered its Black citizens, Harold Epps led fourteen other NCC law students in a demonstration at the state capitol in March 1949. Picketing at the statehouse, the students demanded a law school education equal to that non-Black students received at UNC. They noted that their three-year program offered students a bachelor of laws and was housed in two rooms of the college's administration building. One room served as the dean's office and the other as the classroom. Half of the classroom housed law books purchased from the discontinued New York Law School. According to the *Pittsburgh Courier*, the law books were more accessible to termites than to the students. Most important, NCC's law school was not accredited by the American Bar Association, which meant NCC Law graduates could not sit for bar examinations in other states.[86]

Even though Black and white law school students in North Carolina did not have equal educational opportunities, in violation of *Gaines*, the state remained committed to segregation. Since picketing the state capitol had not moved legislators to act, NCC law students filed suit in the US Middle District Court seeking admission to the law school at the University of North Carolina. Their legal action led state officials to take steps to accredit NCC Law. Black students, however, had had enough. A protracted legal battle ensued, eventually desegregating UNC Law in 1951.[87]

North Carolina officials remained committed to segregation scholarships throughout the 1940s and 1950s. Significant changes occurred during the latter years of the tuition assistance program, as state officials attempted to tweak policies in response to changing developments. First, the Servicemen's Readjustment Act of 1944, better known as the GI Bill, provided returning World War II veterans with tuition benefits that could be used at college or trade schools. The act was later extended to include Korean War veterans and all service members serving in war or peacetime. Many Black veterans who already had bachelor's degrees used their military benefit to attend graduate school. In response, North Carolina revised its segregation scholarship application to include a question about veteran status. The state did not grant aid for tuition expenses covered by the government, so tuition assistance was only given if the applicant's tuition fees exceeded the amount allotted by the veterans' benefit. North Carolina required applicants in this category to obtain a statement from an officer of their graduate school confirming that tuition and fees exceeded the amount allowed by the government. Those veterans who did not receive tuition assistance remained eligible to receive one round-trip railroad fare per school year.[88]

Many veterans believed that the segregation scholarship policy concerning them was unfair. For example, Robert Leathers, a native of Durham, decided to pursue a master's degree in business administration at New York University beginning in 1953. He received $110 per month in veterans' assistance, but that amount did not cover all the educational costs he incurred, including room, board, tuition, and books. He appealed to North Carolina for a segregation scholarship to make up the shortfall between his expenses and his military benefit. In pleading his case, Leathers argued that a white student would not only enjoy "the opportunity and pleasure of attending the nearby state university, but also, if a veteran, [would receive] renumerations with very little educational expenditures resulting."[89] In the end, Leathers was successful and North Carolina's state superintendent of public instruction agreed to pay the difference between the costs the veteran incurred attending a northern university and the military benefit he received.

Beginning in 1950, another change state officials made to North Carolina's segregation scholarship program was to provide for students' increased living costs. Scholarship recipients often studied in cities with room and board expenses that were significantly higher than living expenses in Chapel Hill, where UNC was located. To address this unfair burden, representatives from the state Department of Public Instruction asked the business managers of the institutions that scholarship recipients attended to estimate the average cost of living for graduate and professional school students. State officials requested similar information from UNC's business manager. If the relocating student's living costs exceeded the living costs for students at UNC, then the student received the difference.[90]

The final momentous change to North Carolina's segregation scholarship program was a revision to the calculation of travel grants. While the state originally provided one round-trip fare between the student's home and the out-of-state institution where he or she studied, in 1953 the North Carolina General Assembly decided that grants for travel would be computed based on the distance between Chapel Hill, where UNC was located, and the nearest school where the applicant could get the same degree that UNC offered.[91] This revision was remarkably unfair to Black students because the nearest school where they could study might not have been anywhere close to where they enrolled, so they were then responsible for more of the travel costs necessitated by segregation.

At the exact time that North Carolina began making allowances for living expenses, NCC president Alfonso Elder requested compensation for all the administrative bookkeeping and time-consuming correspondence that fell to college staff while carrying out operation of the segregation scholarship program. James Shepard passed away in 1947 and Elder, his successor, refused to ignore the volume of work that his all-Black college performed on the state's behalf. He told state officials that in one year alone, his secretary had fielded 745 letters requesting applications; distributed 620 applications for state aid; returned 165 incomplete applications to students; mailed 306 grant announcement letters to recipients, and disbursed tuition checks to 45 different institutions. The time required to complete these tasks took the secretary away from her normal duties and responsibilities to NCC.[92]

State officials agreed to address the strain on NCC's manpower caused by the segregation scholarship program. They recommended that Elder of NCC and Bluford of A&T select a faculty member at their institutions to serve as executive secretary of the program. The faculty member would teach half time and administer scholarships the other half of the time. Additionally, the two college presidents received permission to designate a staff member as the full-time secretary of the program who completed all necessary correspondence.[93]

The time-intensive administration of segregation scholarships was not the only negative aspect of the program for Black colleges. Many Black college presidents did not like the fact that segregation scholarship funding came out of their institutions' appropriations. Though it is unclear whether the request was ever made, in 1950 the president of the Colored Normal, Industrial, Agricultural and Mechanical College of South Carolina (present-day South Carolina State University) pondered asking the legislature to separate the college's appropriation from the segregation scholarship program's appropriation.[94] While mixing funds was bad enough, the practice of exporting Black students fostered material and curricular denial at these institutions. Every dollar spent to export Black students was a dollar that the state could have used to improve the physical plant and expand the academic offerings of its Black institutions.

North Carolina lawmakers never established a pharmacy school at NCC, even though the state legislature authorized it in 1939. Instead, the state continued to send Black pharmacy students out of state, including fifteen students in the 1949–50 academic year alone.[95] State officials also never added a medical school to NCC, even though President Shepard had lobbied state officials for one until his death.

Rather than expand the academic programs at North Carolina's Black colleges to include ones in health sciences or desegregate, state legislators would engage in a scheme to pool resources with other southern state governments and create a regional medical school for African Americans. Such a move again denied Black students equal educational opportunities and once again required them to shoulder burdens not required of non-Black students. There is no question that establishing pharmacy and medical schools at a Black college in North Carolina would have dramatically improved Black access to professional healthcare in that state and throughout the South.

CHAPTER FIVE

Don't Shout Too Soon

*The Ebbs and Flows of the
Fight for Educational Equality*

> The responsibility of the southern states to educate their Negro
> citizens cannot constitutionally be met by any plan which would force
> a Negro medical student from Texas to attend a regional medical
> school in Tennessee, while his white compatriot attends
> the University of Texas Medical School.
> —THURGOOD MARSHALL,
> NAACP press release, March 15, 1948

> Perhaps it would be expensive to establish a school offering equal
> opportunities to our [Black] people, but separation is a condition established
> by the state and one for which we [Black people] did not ask.
> —AMOS T. HALL

After the NAACP achieved a significant victory in the fight for educational opportunity by getting Donald Murray into the University of Maryland, Charles Hamilton Houston warned African Americans not to "shout too soon."[1] The attorney understood that "white supremacy remodeled itself to meet any challenge," so one breach in the dam of segregation did not mean that the floodgates would open.[2] Houston knew a long fight lay ahead and the effort required money, brave plaintiffs, and widespread Black support. This proved especially true in the years after *Gaines*, since Lloyd Gaines's disappearance underscored the dangers of serving as the face of legal challenges to segregation. Moreover, the lack of federal enforcement of the decision exposed the limits of the Supreme Court's power. This chapter demonstrates that success and setback occurred in tandem for the NAACP in its campaign to achieve educational equality.

The 1940s started on a high as West Virginia University admitted Black graduate students in 1940 and the University of Chicago hired Allison Davis in 1942 as a professor of education. Davis, who held a bachelor's degree from Williams College and a master's from Harvard, became the first African American to hold a regular faculty appointment at a historically white university in the United States. He earned his doctorate in anthropology from the University of Chicago. Many hoped that Davis's feat was the beginning of new trends in higher education, with Black students and faculty receiving a fair shake.[3] That was not to be the case. It would take another two decades before historically white universities in the South hired full-time Black faculty. In 1962, Duke University hired political scientist Samuel DuBois Cook and the University of North Carolina hired social work scholar Hortense McClinton.

Black hopes of racial progress in education quickly dissipated, though, as southern states maintained lily-white graduate education at their flagship public institutions in spite of *Gaines*. While waging a war against fascism abroad, the states that had previously made no efforts to provide their Black residents with public graduate offerings implemented segregation scholarship programs. In 1943, in response to the demands of the all-Black Arkansas Teachers Association, the state legislature allocated a portion of the public Black college's operating budget to send Black students out of state. The next year it was Georgia. In 1945, Alabama and Florida followed suit. In 1946, Louisiana, and South Carolina began providing financial assistance for African American students to secure out of state the same educational opportunities that white and foreign students could pursue in state. While South Carolina's segregation scholarship was initially limited to medical education, it expanded the eligible subjects for advanced study within three years. Finally, in 1948, as the United States began to desegregate its armed forces, Mississippi became the last southern state to launch a segregation scholarship program.[4] The states with the largest Black populations were the slowest in providing postbaccalaureate opportunities to their Black residents.

In addition to the expansion of segregation scholarships in the post–World War II period, the NAACP contended with the advent of regional education. Regional education schemes allowed southern states to feign compliance with the law by subsidizing graduate and professional school programs at Black institutions and claiming those programs as the state-sponsored Black equivalent to the state-sponsored programs offered at historically white flagship public institutions. Thus, a cash-strapped Meharry Medical College became the white South's answer to Black southerners seeking admission to flagship public medical schools in the region. For every one step of progress the NAACP made on the educational front, it faced two steps of regression because of white southern recalcitrance.

All was not lost, though. This chapter chronicles how after World War II the NAACP charged into the court of last resort multiple times, chipping away at educational inequality and setting the stage for a complete ban on de jure segregation in public education, which was achieved with the *Brown* decision in 1954. In a 1948 case involving Oklahoma's law school and 1950 cases involving Oklahoma's graduate school and Texas's law school, the US Supreme Court found that the separate but equal doctrine was virtually impossible. Yet the court did not completely strike down racial segregation. These cases are important because they show that *Brown* was not inevitable "in the nation's steady march toward race relations progress."[5] Brave African American plaintiffs forced public officials to comply with the Fourteenth Amendment.

Georgia implemented its segregation scholarship program in 1944 after the presidents of the three public Black colleges in the state—Horace Mann Bond of Fort Valley State College, Aaron Brown of Albany State College, and Benjamin Hubert of Savannah State College—jointly petitioned the Georgia Board of Regents for out-of-state aid.[6] To feign compliance with separate but equal, Georgia designated the private Atlanta University as its state university representative in graduate work for African Americans, paying four-fifths of the tuition of Black Georgians who studied there. With this arrangement, Georgia lawmakers maintained that they had met their duty to provide in-state graduate opportunities for African Americans. The state's residents also had the option of going out of state. Those seeking assistance applied to the Regents of the University System of Georgia, headquartered in Atlanta. No matter whether Black students stayed in state or left home, graduate and professional school education was a dream of many. In 1946 alone, Georgia supported 678 students at a cost of $25,000. Most funds that year went to Atlanta University as tuition scholarships for teachers seeking master's degrees.[7] In the first three years, Georgia spent $56,941 at nonstate schools to keep African Americans out of the historically white University of Georgia (UGA).[8]

One of the first recipients of Georgia's segregation scholarships was Annie Louise Brown, an Atlanta native and a 1945 graduate of Spelman College. Since UGA's law school did not admit Black students, Brown attended the Howard University School of Law. Georgia paid the difference between the cost of tuition at Howard Law and the cost of tuition at UGA and provided her with two round-trip train tickets. She was one of four women in a class of fifty students. When reflecting years later on being compelled to go out of state for law school, Brown joked, "Maybe the state of Georgia did me a favor."[9] While the comment was made in jest, the fact remains that Brown received a first-rate education at Howard, where she met her husband, Harold Kennedy Jr., who was also in law school. Brown graduated from Howard's law school in 1951, and in 1954 she became just the second Black women licensed to practice law in the state of North Carolina. She and her husband handled the landmark *Simpkins v. City of Greensboro* case, which desegregated golf courses and other recreational facilities throughout the South. She made history again in 1982 when she became the first Black woman to serve in the North Carolina General Assembly.[10]

Christine King, like Annie Louise Brown, was an Atlanta native compelled to go north for graduate school because of segregation. King, the older sister of Martin Luther King Jr., finished Spelman College with a bachelor's degree in economics in the spring of 1948. That fall, she matriculated at Columbia University with state aid. She did not make the journey alone, as one of her best friends and Spelman classmates, Juanita Sellers, also decided to attend Columbia for graduate study.[11]

After receiving instruction from her parents about how to behave and dress in New York City, King, with Sellers by her side, boarded the northbound Silver Comet train headed to unfamiliar territory. The Seaboard Air Line Railroad had launched the train a year earlier in 1947 with daily service from Birmingham to New York, including stops in Atlanta, Raleigh, Richmond, and Washington, DC. The two young women relished the opportunity to relocate to the biggest city in the country but also felt some sadness at leaving their families. They had plenty of time to ponder their futures in a new place as the train ride was nearly twenty-three hours one-way. When King and Sellers finally disembarked at Penn Station, they headed to Harlem. For the next two years, the women lived at the Emma Ransom House YWCA at the corner of 137th Street and Lenox Avenue, a safe housing spot for Black women new to the city.[12]

Although King's parents had forbidden her to explore the city, she found a way to get around the directive. She wrote to her brother, Martin Luther King Jr., who was studying at Crozer Theological Seminary in Pennsylvania, and asked him to come visit. She knew that her parents would not oppose her sightseeing if her brother was with her. Martin King took her up on the invitation several times, and together the siblings visited Times Square and several other New York City landmarks.[13]

Christine King enjoyed the city socially, but she quickly learned that Columbia was no promised land. Years later, she asserted that her first semester there was the worst time of her life. While the library was second to none and the campus was full of manicured lawns and perfectly placed trees, she found the classroom hostile. As a graduate student in economics at Columbia, she was the only Black student and the only woman in her classes. One of her professors, a white male, never acknowledged her raised hand or answered her questions. Despite being made to feel as if she did not belong, King persevered and finished the course. At the semester's end, she changed her major from economics to the social foundations of education. She earned a master's degree in 1950 from Teachers College and became a teacher in the Atlanta public schools. In 1958, after studying over several consecutive summers, she obtained a second master's degree in special education from Teachers College. The state of Georgia paid the tuition differentials for both degrees from Columbia. King went on to teach at Spelman. When she retired after fifty-six years of service in 2014, she was the college's longest-serving faculty member.[14]

In Augusta, nearly 200 miles from Christine King's childhood Atlanta home, Willarena Lamar experienced educational inequality throughout her formative years. White officials closed the public high school for African Americans in her hometown, so her parents double-taxed themselves and sent her to Haines Normal Institute, a private school, so she could continue her education. When she graduated from high school in 1948, she dreamed of studying biology at the University of Georgia, but the state's segregation laws led her to the all-Black Talladega College in Alabama instead, since Georgia's public Black colleges did not offer a biology major. Again, Lamar's parents found themselves paying for white children to receive public education while having to make other arrangements for their daughter. Lamar excelled academically at Talladega and graduated with honors in 1952. She planned to go to medical school but never heard back from any of the institutions to which she applied, so she settled on graduate school. She applied to Western Reserve University (present-day Case Western Reserve) in Cleveland, Ohio, because she had an aunt who lived in the city.[15]

In 1952, Lamar traveled by Greyhound bus from Georgia to Ohio, changing buses in Cincinnati on her way to Cleveland. Although the US Supreme Court had outlawed racial segregation on interstate buses in 1946, southern states ignored the ruling, so Lamar endured segregated seating on the bus and in the bus terminal. When she arrived in Cleveland, she was pleasantly surprised to see that white and Black people sat anywhere there was an open seat on public conveyances. She was in a new region where segregation was not as entrenched.

While Talladega had more than prepared Lamar academically, she was in a very different world socially at Western Reserve. She went from a school of 400 to one of 10,000. She studied with people from all over the world. The two other women in her master's cohort studying biology were from Panama and Poland.[16]

The funds that Georgia provided did not cover all of Lamar's expenses, so she made ends meet through frugal living. When she first arrived in Cleveland, she lived with her aunt before securing a room at the local YWCA. She also worked throughout graduate school. She had a part-time job giftwrapping in a Cleveland department store, and she found work at the Western Reserve medical school inoculating mice as part of a research study to develop a flu vaccine.[17]

Despite having to commute to campus and work, Lamar made good grades. While she did not recount incidents of explicit racism during her graduate career at Western Reserve, she did share the sting of being denied membership in Sigma Xi despite her high marks. Sigma Xi, an honor society for scientists, extended membership by invitation only from other members. None of the faculty at Western Reserve nominated her despite her stellar academic performance. In the little time that she had to socialize, she fellowshipped with other southern transplants also pursuing advanced study there. After graduating in 1954, Lamar taught at Spelman College before marrying and returning to Augusta, where she taught high school science.[18]

Narratives abound of striving African Americans who exploited an arrangement meant to preserve segregation and transformed it into an opportunity to disprove notions of Black inferiority. Louis Sullivan was one such segregation scholarship recipient. Born in Atlanta in 1933, he was the son of activist parents who challenged white supremacy by filing lawsuits and by pursuing the best educational opportunities for their children. In fact, because the local high school for Black students in the county where his parents resided was severely underfunded, his parents arranged for him to live with friends in Atlanta and attend Booker T. Washington High School, the first public high school for Black students in Atlanta. After graduating from Booker T. Washington in 1950, Sullivan matriculated at Morehouse College because of its strong science program and his interest in a career in medicine. There, his professors offered him rigorous premedical training and assured him that he had the mental acuity and work ethic to succeed anywhere. During his senior year, Morehouse faculty and NAACP representatives told him to apply to medical schools widely. The NAACP encouraged students at Black colleges to apply to graduate and professional school programs at historically white institutions to diversify those campuses. His professors encouraged that plan and told him that while Howard and Meharry were good schools, he had the ability to "compete anywhere, so he should apply anywhere." Following that advice, Sullivan applied to both Black medical schools and the medical schools at Boston University, the University of Michigan, and the University of Minnesota. All five schools accepted him and he chose the Boston University School of Medicine.[19]

Georgia gave Sullivan tuition assistance to offset his medical school training since Black students could not attend the state-supported Medical College of

Willarena Lamar (*center*) sitting with the other two women graduate students in biology at Western Reserve University in 1953. Photo courtesy of the children of Willarena Lamar Williams.

Willarena Lamar (*left*) and unidentified classmate on graduation day at Western Reserve University in 1953. Lamar earned a master's degree in biology. Photo courtesy of the children of Willarena Lamar Williams.

Georgia in Augusta. For all four years of medical school, Georgia paid the difference between tuition at Boston University School of Medicine and tuition at MCG. MCG was $200 per year and BUSM was $900 per year. The state also provided a stipend to cover the increase in living expenses and the transportation differentials for travel between Sullivan's parents' hometown of Blakely, Georgia, and Augusta, where MCG is located, and travel between Blakely and Boston.[20]

Sullivan found the educational arrangement designed to preserve segregation attractive because BUSM was ranked higher than MCG and because Boston was a more diverse and cosmopolitan city than Augusta. Moreover, going to the North for graduate school became his first experience living in a nonsegregated environment. He wondered, however, how he would be received at BUSM because he was the only Black student in his class of seventy-six students. There were only two other Black students in the entire medical school. Additionally, his classmates had studied at Amherst, Princeton, and Harvard, so he wondered how he would compare academically. His classmates had never heard of Morehouse. He had a burning desire to do well so that he did not disappoint himself, his parents, Morehouse College, and the African American race, more broadly.[21]

Sullivan's fears about not belonging at BUSM eventually proved unfounded. He did exceptionally well both academically and socially. His peers elected him class president during his second and third years of medical school. He graduated third in his class in 1958. Looking back on his experience, he proudly remarked that "my preparation [at Morehouse College] was just as solid as that of the guys from the Ivy League schools."[22] Sullivan even did well in his personal life. While in Boston, he met and married his wife.[23]

After securing prestigious internships and fellowships and serving on the faculty of several medical schools, Sullivan became the founding dean and director of the Medical Education Program at Morehouse College in 1975. The program became what is present-day Morehouse School of Medicine.[24] In a sweet bit of irony, Sullivan, drawing on the segregation scholarship program, convinced the state of Georgia to make an annual appropriation to Morehouse School of Medicine. Sullivan was president of Morehouse School of Medicine for more than two decades, a tenure only interrupted by his service as secretary of the US Department of Health and Human Services from 1989 to 1993. On July 1, 2002, he retired and became president emeritus. In 2021, BUSM established an endowed professorship in Sullivan's name.[25] Though segregation forced him to leave his native state to pursue his professional aspirations, he endured and used his training and networks to create another medical school in the South to expand opportunity for potential healthcare providers of color.

Don't Shout Too Soon   135

Louis Sullivan's apprehension about how he would perform at a historically white northern institution was common among segregation scholarship recipients. Most of the students grew up in affirming Black communities where adults told them that they were just as smart as white students, but they rarely had a chance to test that assertion until they attended graduate schools with white classmates. Such was the case for Carrie Pittman of Florida.

Pittman was born and raised in Tallahassee during a time when segregation governed every aspect of Black life. She recalled that African Americans were at first prohibited from riding city buses and then when bus companies finally allowed them to do so, they had to sit at the back. When young Carrie went downtown with her family to shop, store policy prohibited African Americans from trying on the merchandise. Whether it was a hat, shoes, or a dress, Black shoppers had to "eye" their desired items to select the correct size. With the support of her family and teachers in the segregated public school system, Pittman did well in school, and in 1942 she matriculated at Florida A&M College for Negroes (present-day Florida A&M University), the only public Black college in the state. She earned bachelor's degrees in biology and physical education in 1946 and left the institution as a standout athlete and star student.[26]

While Florida is not often thought of as Deep South state with a racial history akin to that of Alabama or Mississippi, the state adhered to segregation, and its lawmakers intended to keep African Americans out of the University of Florida. To that end, Florida's state cabinet approved taking $7,000 from Florida A&M's budget to fund a segregation scholarship program in 1945 to send Black residents out of state to study the same courses available to non-Black residents at UF or Florida State College for Women. Under the plan, funds from the only public Black college in the state paid the difference between the tuition and travel costs for a student to attend a Florida institution and one outside the state.[27]

Carrie Pittman was one of the first students to leave Florida with a segregation scholarship. After Florida A&M, Pittman received $150 in tuition assistance and a train ticket from the state of Florida to relocate to Ann Arbor, Michigan, in 1946. She settled on the University of Michigan because one of her favorite teachers had received her education there. Like millions of Black migrants before her, Pittman packed her cherished belongings and food, including a box of chicken and some sweet potatoes, to sustain her during the long journey and boarded a train headed to an unfamiliar destination. It was quite common for Black travelers on trains to pack shoeboxes of chicken to eat en route, as the dining facilities on trains did not always serve Black patrons.[28]

Pittman found the University of Michigan challenging academically, but she was able to compete because of the education that she had received as an undergraduate. Years later she recalled of her graduate experience, "I held my own because of my training from Florida A&M. My teachers there were so good and they were hard on us. I was with students [at the University of Michigan] who had a much better academic background. But because Florida A&M had taught me how to be disciplined, how to study, and how to seek out more knowledge, that's why I made it there."[29] The overwhelming majority of segregation scholarship recipients came from Black colleges, which cultivated Black intellect and sent their graduates out into a world that often did not expect Black brilliance or Black success. These institutions prepared them for intellectual warfare in historically white classrooms.

After graduating from the University of Michigan in 1948 with a master's degree in public health and physical education, Pittman taught at Bethune-Cookman College in Daytona Beach, Florida, and then later at her alma mater, Florida A&M. In 1961 she moved to Miami, where she served as a professor, administrator, and special assistant to the vice president of Miami Dade College, then Miami-Dade Community College. The school desegregated in 1963, and Pittman played a central role in pushing for integration. She later married Harold Meek and became involved in electoral politics. She won election to the Florida House of Representatives and the Florida Senate before being elected to the US House of Representatives from Florida's Seventeenth Congressional District in 1992. She served six terms.

One year after Carrie Pittman graduated from Michigan, six Black students applied to graduate and professional school programs at the University of Florida. The applicants listed chemical engineering, electrical engineering, pharmacy, law, and agricultural engineering as their desired courses of study and rejected the state's offer of segregation scholarships to study out of state.[30] Based on *Gaines*, Florida officials could discontinue graduate programs at UF, establish graduate programs at Florida A&M, or admit Black students to UF. Lawmakers refused to pursue any of those options. William Gray, the president of Florida A&M, requested $3.76 million from the Florida Legislature to establish graduate colleges of law, pharmacy, journalism, social welfare, and library science at his institution. He believed that the addition of the programs would eliminate the need for segregation scholarships. The state provided only $2.49 million and remained committed to sending Black students elsewhere.[31] Once again, a southern state chose not to invest in Black institutions. At the time, Florida spent $75,000 per year sending Black students out of state.[32]

Beginning in the fall of 1951, Florida stopped providing segregation scholarships for students pursuing graduate courses in law, pharmacy, and engineering because Florida A&M established departments in those fields. Some students, however, continued to request segregation scholarships because Florida A&M's programs were not accredited. Until the programs had been in operation for more than a year, they remained ineligible for accreditation. Florida Board of Control oversaw tuition assistance and denied the scholarship applicants' requests for exceptions.[33]

Florida was not alone in establishing a law school at a public Black college to preserve segregation. While Missouri and North Carolina were early adopters of this practice, South Carolina, Texas, Louisiana, and Oklahoma joined Florida in setting up Black law schools in the post–World War II period. The NAACP did not oppose additions to Black colleges' academic offerings, since these were rare occasions when southern states invested in Black education, but the organization wanted to ensure that the new programs were equally funded and did not supplant desegregation of flagship institutions. Believing that equality was not possible because states never allocated the amount of money necessary to achieve parity and that racial segregation prevented students from gaining experience with the peers they would one day face in the practice of law, NAACP officials saw Black law schools as an additional avenue for aspiring attorneys but remained committed to desegregation. These law schools established to preserve the separation of the races ended up training some of the very attorneys who would later dismantle segregation.

The creation of Black law schools exposed how educational inequality made the path to a professional career that much harder for African Americans. Most southern states had a policy known as the "diploma privilege" that exempted individuals who graduated from an in-state law school from taking the state bar exam. Such arrangements did not benefit Black students compelled to go out of state for law school. Moreover, in South Carolina, white officials eliminated the "diploma privilege" soon after the Colored Normal, Industrial, Agricultural and Mechanical College of South Carolina School of Law (present-day South Carolina State University) opened in 1947. Beginning with students who graduated from South Carolina law schools in 1951, all law school graduates had to pass the state bar to practice law in the state.[34]

Charles Hamilton Houston's advice not to shout too soon proved prescient as southern states continued to use all kinds of schemes to prevent the desegregation of graduate and professional school education. With respect to segregation scholarships, perhaps no state's plan was as burdensome and unfair as Alabama's. It approved using tax dollars to send Black students out of state in 1945, but there was a catch. Initially, students had to pay their tuition fees upfront and then submit receipts for reimbursement. Since most institutions in the North charged much more for tuition than the University of Alabama, the reimbursement requirement was an additional obstacle Black Alabamians had to overcome in pursuit of their educational goals. In later years, students did not have to pay tuition out-of-pocket upfront, but the message had already been sent by the state that advanced education would be difficult and expensive for African Americans.

In June 1945, less than a month after Germany surrendered to the Allies, marking the end of World War II in Europe, the Alabama Legislature allocated $25,000 annually to provide out-of-state tuition assistance for Black students. Black men could die overseas fighting Hitler's Nazism, but they could not learn alongside white men in Dixie. The segregation scholarship program, sponsored by state senator Vernon St. John, was Alabama's response to African Americans inquiries about attending the University of Alabama. Alabama State College began offering summer-session-only graduate work in education in 1940 and made those courses available during the regular academic year nine years later. Graduate work began at Tuskegee in 1943 in agriculture and in 1944 in home economics and rural education. Black Alabamians who wanted to attend courses that were available to white students at the University of Alabama or at Auburn but unavailable to Black students at Alabama State Teachers College in Montgomery, Alabama A&M in Huntsville, or Tuskegee Institute were eligible to receive state aid for schooling elsewhere. Interested parties who had lived in Alabama for at least one year submitted applications to the state superintendent of education, and the State Board of Education who, in consultation with the presidents of Alabama State, Alabama A&M, and Tuskegee, selected recipients. Successful applicants received a scholarship amount equal to the difference between tuition at the University of Alabama and tuition at the alternate institution. Alabama also paid the differential in recipients' living expenses and transportation that was not to exceed $50. Approved grants could not exceed $265 per student annually.[35]

Demand for funding soon exceeded supply in Alabama's segregation scholarship programs. When state funds first became available, 66 residents applied. Between 1945 and 1948, the state awarded 235 scholarships with law, medicine, social work, dentistry, and pharmacy being the most popular fields of study. The most commonly attended institutions were Atlanta University, Howard University, Columbia University, Meharry, and New York University. By 1949, state officials turned away applicants because scholarship funds had been exhausted. In that year, a committee appointed by Alabama governor James Folsom to study Black education in the state recommended increasing segregation scholarships from $25,000 to $55,000 annually to meet the need.[36]

One Black Alabamian who turned down tuition assistance was Paul R. Jones.

Born in 1928, Jones grew up in the company steel town of Muscoda in Bessemer, Alabama, because his father worked in the Muscoda Mining Camp of the Tennessee Coal, Iron and Railroad Company of US Steel Corporation. Jones received his earliest education in the mine schools, but he spent his fifth, sixth, and seventh grade years living in New York City with an older brother because his mother believed that he would get a much better education outside Alabama. In New York, he was often teased because of his accent, but he did not let the insults prevent him from doing well in school. After completing eighth grade in Washington, DC, Jones returned to Alabama for high school, where he excelled academically, ran track, and played football.[37]

Though he had dreams of going to the University of Notre Dame, Paul Jones decided to stay close to home after the death of his mother. He earned a scholarship to Alabama State Teachers College, which was ninety miles from Bessemer. Jones did well in college, serving as freshman class president and pledging Alpha Phi Alpha Fraternity. After two years, he transferred to Howard. During his senior year, he set his sights on law school and planned to return to his native state.[38]

When Jones applied to the University of Alabama School of Law in 1949, a school official indirectly denied him admission, explaining "the problem posed by" Jones's application and informing him that the state had provided "machinery" to help Black students study elsewhere. But Jones did not want to attend law school outside Alabama. Like white residents, he wanted the opportunity to go to the public law school in his native state, a school financed in part with Black tax dollars. He did not want Alabama officials choosing his educational options for him. Jones returned to Alabama after earning a bachelor's degree in political science in 1949. He never attended law school because he had no desire to study law in a state other than Alabama. He went on to a long career as a civil servant in the federal government. In 2006, he received an honorary doctorate of humane letters from the University of Alabama, the school that had refused him admission nearly sixty years earlier.[39]

Like Paul Jones, Medgar Evers of Mississippi desired to study law in his native state. He applied to the historically white University of Mississippi School of Law in 1954. Before outright denying him admission because of his race, state officials offered him a segregation scholarship. Evers declined the aid because he wanted legal education in the state where he would practice law.[40]

There is no telling how many Paul Joneses and Medgar Everses have been lost to history. Many Black southerners chose not to leave home, forfeiting opportunities to live out their academic dreams. Many lived in states where demand far exceeded supply and were denied scholarships as state funds dwindled.

Whatever the circumstances, white southerners' antipathy to Black education stunted the academic potential of untold numbers of African Americans.

Despite the unfairness and burdens posed by segregation scholarships, faculty at Black colleges often encouraged students to continue their education at the state's expense. Gwendolyn DuBose Rogers, a native of Fairfield, Alabama, entered Talladega College the same year as Willarena Lamar. At Talladega, Rogers was mentored by white civil rights activists and educators Don and Lore Rasmussen.[41] Rogers studied elementary education at Talladega and planned to teach after graduation, but the Rasmussens encouraged her to continue her education and explained that Alabama subsidized the tuition of Black graduate students. Their prodding was enough to convince Rogers and her mother who was ready for her daughter to "earn her keep."[42]

After finishing Talladega in 1952, Rogers immediately entered the University of Chicago. Her best friend from college also relocated to Chicago and there were many Talladega alumni in the area, so she had a ready-made social life. She studied educational psychology with Allison Davis and received her master's degree in the summer of 1953. She chose not to return to Alabama, building a long educational career in Chicago, with teaching stints at Chicago State and Northwestern.[43] While Rogers did not mention the reimbursement requirement of Alabama's segregation scholarship program in her recollections about her educational journey, the policy caused headaches for many recipients.

Thomas Todd, born in Demopolis, Alabama, in 1938 and raised in Mobile, was also a segregation scholarship recipient. He grew up in a working-poor household where education was stressed, especially because his mother had to discontinue her education after the second grade and his father could not read or write. He looked up to the teachers in his all-Black schools who modeled excellence and a love for learning.[44] His band teacher helped him win a music scholarship to the all-Black Southern University in Baton Rouge, Louisiana.[45] At Southern, he majored in political science and was mentored by Jewel Prestage, the first Black woman in the United States to receive a doctorate in political science. Louisiana had subsidized Prestage's graduate study at the University of Iowa with a segregation scholarship.[46]

Todd graduated from Southern in 1959 at the age of twenty and returned home to Alabama to ponder his future. While volunteering with other young Black professionals at a local church, he learned about Alabama's segregation scholarship program. Deciding on law school, Todd applied to the University of Alabama School of Law and was summarily rejected. He then applied for out-of-state aid. State officials explained that it was a reimbursement program and that he needed to submit receipts after paying his tuition. As Todd recalled years later, "I took the letter from Alabama back to Southern, where people knew me, and on the strength of that, and the affidavit of the dean that I had graduated, until they got my transcript, they admitted me to law school."[47] Louisiana had created a law school at its state-supported Black college, Southern University, in 1947 after an African American sued for admission to Louisiana State University's law school.[48]

Todd waited for his reimbursement check from the state of Alabama throughout his first semester of law school only to be severely disappointed when it arrived. When he finally received the envelope from his home state, it contained a check for $5.45, the train fare from Mobile to Baton Rouge, minus taxes. Southern University officials had allowed Todd to study law on credit with the expectation that he would pay his tuition when Alabama sent him tuition assistance but now, Todd had no tuition check and a significant tuition bill. He immediately called state officials in Montgomery thinking that there had been some mistake only to learn that Alabama would not provide any tuition assistance because Southern Law was cheaper than the University of Alabama law school and Alabama only paid the difference. Unable to pay his bill, Todd prepared to leave school. Southern's administrators, however, took pity on him and awarded him a scholarship. He finished law school summa cum laude in 1963 and was sworn into the Louisiana bar on August 28, the same day as the historic March on Washington.[49]

Thomas Todd went on to establish the first civil rights office in a US attorney's office. He later became the first full-time Black law professor at Northwestern University, where he taught from 1970 to 1974.[50] Todd's professional success showed what was possible when one was given the opportunity to pursue one's intellectual interests.

Another Black Alabamian who received legal training with a segregation scholarship was U. W. Clemon. The son of sharecropping parents, Clemon graduated in 1965 as valedictorian of the all-Black Miles College, located outside Birmingham, and then enrolled at Columbia Law School in New York. His matriculation at Columbia almost did not happen because Miles College had lost its accreditation because its library did not have enough books. Miles's president, Lucius Pitts, however, was determined that his college's star pupil would not be kept out of Columbia, so he reached out to his friend, John W. Davis, the former president of West Virginia State College. Davis in turn reached out to his friend, Columbia law professor Walter Gellhorn, and Clemon's admission was assured.[51]

Like other segregation scholarship recipients, Clemon experienced culture shock at Columbia, but he also excelled academically. After graduation in 1968, he became a civil rights attorney with the NAACP Legal Defense Fund and later opened his own practice in Alabama. One year after graduation, he successfully sued legendary University of Alabama football coach Paul "Bear" Bryant to desegregate his team. In 1974, Clemon was one of the two Black people elected to the Alabama Senate, the first since Reconstruction. In 1980, he became the first Black federal judge in Alabama when President Jimmy Carter appointed him to the US District Court for the Northern District of Alabama. He stayed on the bench for twenty-nine years.[52]

The large proportion of Alabama's segregation scholarship recipients who chose to study law and thus were compelled to study out of state could not take advantage of the "diploma privilege" extended to white residents who studied at the University of Alabama School of Law. For the NAACP, these kinds of unfair policies made law school education one of the easiest avenues to demonstrate the disadvantages of segregation scholarships. In addition to being denied "diploma privilege," law school students with segregation scholarships were at a disadvantage since this denied them the opportunity to learn the statutes of the place where most planned to practice and to develop relationships with future colleagues whom they would meet in the courtroom.

Knowing that their exclusion from "diploma privilege" was no fault of their own, four Black Alabama attorneys who studied at Howard and Lincoln petitioned Alabama's supreme court in 1949 to grant them licenses to practice without taking the bar, since there was no state-supported law school for African Americans in Alabama. The men contended that since the state paid part of their law school tuition, the law schools they attended became agents of the state.[53] At the time of their request, there were only six practicing Black lawyers in the entire state of Alabama.[54] The court ruled that the Black attorneys had gone out of state for law school "as a result of their free will" and had thus forfeited the privilege extended to University of Alabama law school graduates.[55] There was no semblance of free will in a system of segregation that forced African Americans to go out of state for the same training that white people received in state. The Alabama Supreme Court's decision on "diploma privilege" was yet another example of educational inequality that the NAACP had to attack.

Black law school students had more extensive knowledge of the American legal system than lay people and sometimes engaged in intellectual warfare and waged legal challenges even before completing their education. Such was the case for Bruce Carver Boynton, a native of Selma, Alabama, who studied at the Howard University School of Law between 1956 and 1959. Though not a segregation scholarship recipient for reasons that are unclear, Boynton experienced the same travel restrictions that other beneficiaries of state tuition assistance faced. The son of civil rights stalwarts Samuel William Boynton and Amelia Boynton Robinson and the godson of scientist George Washington Carver, Boynton came of age surrounded by Black elders who visibly and vocally resisted white supremacy.[56]

As Boynton traveled home for Christmas break in 1958 on a Trailways bus, he had a forty-minute layover in Richmond, Virginia. Bus stations remained racially segregated despite federal laws banning segregation in interstate travel. Looking for a bite to eat, Boynton found the Black section of the bus terminal restaurant to be "very unsanitary," so he sat down in the white section and ordered a cheeseburger and cup of tea. Rather than take his order, the waitress summoned the bus station manager, who used a racial slur and told Boynton to leave. The third-year law student stood his ground as an interstate passenger. He was summarily arrested and remained in jail for three days. After being released on bond, he prepared for trial in the city court. After losing in the city, circuit, and supreme courts of Virginia, NAACP attorney Thurgood Marshall petitioned the US Supreme Court to grant a writ of certiorari. The court agreed to hear the case on the first day of Boynton's Alabama bar examination.[57]

In another legal victory for the NAACP, the court ruled in *Boynton v. Virginia* (1960) that racial segregation in public transportation violated the Interstate Commerce Act. The 7-to-2 decision outlawed, at least on paper, racial segregation in public facilities related to transportation. As historian Mia Bay asserted, however, Jim Crow continued to be the modus operandi in restaurants at most southern bus stations. Boynton's stand was not in vain, though, as it inspired the 1961 Freedom Rides.[58]

In the years before Boynton's defiant stand, the NAACP sought qualified plaintiffs to enlist in the desegregation campaign to open southern graduate programs to African Americans.[59] The fight for educational equality became more urgent in the postwar period as graduate and professional schools throughout the South remained off limits to returning Black veterans armed with GI Bill educational benefits. Calls for legal action went out to local chapters across the South with little success. In Texas, for example, every qualified plaintiff identified by NAACP leaders withdrew from participation because of fear of personal and professional scrutiny and economic reprisals.[60] Moreover, the fact that Lloyd Gaines had disappeared months after his court victory gave pause to many who did not want to meet a similar fate.

CHAPTER FIVE

A segregated bus terminal in Durham, North Carolina, in 1940. Segregation scholarship recipients experienced racial discrimination and harassment on public conveyances and in stations and terminals. Prints and Photographs Division, Library of Congress, Washington, DC.

Early in 1946, the NAACP caught a break as promising plaintiffs in two strategic states emerged almost simultaneously. In Oklahoma, twenty-two-year-old Ada Lois Sipuel, who had dreamed of being a lawyer since childhood, stepped forward to apply to the University of Oklahoma College of Law. In neighboring Texas, thirty-four-year-old Heman Sweatt, whose involvement with the National Alliance of Postal Employees whetted his appetite for legal education, decided to apply to the University of Texas School of Law. Oklahoma and Texas were perfect battleground states given their dismal records of higher education for African Americans.

Oklahoma segregated its schools in 1897, ten years before statehood in 1907.[61] At the same time that the territorial legislature codified school segregation in elementary and secondary education, it also established the Colored Agricultural and Normal University in the all-Black town of Langston to meet Black demands for higher education. The Oklahoma Legislature renamed the institution Langston University in 1941 after the Black abolitionist, educator, and politician John Mercer Langston.[62] For most of the twentieth century, Langston, the only college available to African Americans in the state, remained poorly funded and far from equal to the University of Oklahoma (OU), the state's all-white flagship public institution in Norman. Langston remained unaccredited until 1948, in large part because of its deficient facilities and poor physical plant. Aging grounds was not Langston's only problem. A university in name only, it had leaky roofs, dilapidated student housing, and a poorly equipped library. An editorial in Oklahoma's largest newspaper lamented the fact that when it rained, Langston's campus turned into a "sea of mud."[63]

Segregated higher education in Oklahoma was far from equal. Langston was the only institution of higher education for African Americans in Oklahoma, though the state had thirty-two publicly supported colleges and universities for white students. These white schools offered study in a total of 96 academic disciplines compared to the 24 fields offered at Langston. In the year that Sipuel applied to OU, the state spent $7.4 million on white schools and $277,088 on its only Black school[64]

While it was clear that Oklahoma did not practice separate but equal, even more troubling was the fact that graduate and professional school opportunities for African Americans were nonexistent. While Black residents had no in-state options for postbaccalaureate study, white residents had more than seventy graduate programs at OU and Oklahoma A&M College (present-day Oklahoma State University) in Stillwater. Oklahoma had adopted a segregation scholarship program in 1935, and by the mid-1940s, the state was spending more than $25,000 annually to send approximately 400 Black residents out of state. In 1947, the state Department of Education requested $50,000 per year to meet Black demand for tuition assistance.[65] NAACP officials throughout the state and in the national office believed that Oklahoma would have no choice but to desegregate its flagship public institution when an African American applicant sought advanced study in state.

Black Oklahomans drew a line in the sand regarding the dismal state of Black higher education when they voted overwhelmingly to pursue court action during the 1945 state NAACP convention in McAlester. Delegates heard from Roscoe Dunjee, editor of the *Black Dispatch* newspaper and the president of the state conference, and from NAACP lawyer Thurgood Marshall, who told the crowd that a test case would be easy to win.[66] The public pronouncement of a head-on challenge to educational inequality caught the attention of multiple newspapers in Oklahoma and beyond, and the media attention in turn alerted OU leaders. OU's board of regents discussed the newspaper reports in the days immediately after the convention and voted unanimously to instruct OU president George

Cross to "refuse to admit anyone of negro blood as a student in the University for the reason that the laws of the State of Oklahoma prohibit the enrollment of such a student in the university."[67] Sipuel disagreed with the regents and decided to contest OU's color line.

Oklahoma NAACP officials had their sights on a member of the Sipuel family to serve as a plaintiff in the case against OU, but it was not Ada they hoped to recruit. W. A. J. Bullock, a Chickasha native, regional director of the NAACP, and the Sipuel family physician, reached out to Ada's parents requesting a meeting. Bishop Travis Sipuel, the family patriarch and an ordained minister in the Church of God in Christ and his wife, Martha Belle, a teacher turned homemaker, had relocated to Chickasha in the wake of the 1921 Tulsa Race Massacre, in which white supremacists destroyed their home. The Sipuels had two daughters, Ada and Helen, but Bullock was interested in their son, Lemuel.[68]

Sitting in the Sipuels' living room, Bullock explained why the Oklahoma NAACP believed that Lemuel Bullock was the perfect candidate for an educational equality test case. Lemuel had earned high marks in high school and had a 4.0 grade point average at Langston University. After his 1942 graduation, the US Army drafted him for World War II, and he served his country admirably in Europe. His scholastic record and patriotic service made him just the type of plaintiff that NAACP officials wanted to take into court. Additionally, Lemuel had a real interest in law school.[69] Since the University of Oklahoma had a law school but Langston did not, a qualified Black Oklahoman in pursuit of legal training could open the university once and for all.

While Bullock's plan was a strong one, he had not considered that Lemuel Sipuel had no interest in participating in what would surely be a protracted legal challenge. Lemuel had planned to enter law school immediately after earning his undergraduate degree, but the war delayed his plans. He did not want to wait any longer to become an attorney, so he declined to participate in the challenge to desegregate OU and matriculated at Howard Law instead.[70] What happened next remains unclear. Whether the Sipuels suggested their daughter Ada to Bullock or Ada volunteered, she became the plaintiff in the NAACP lawsuit to break down segregation at the OU College of Law.

Ada Sipuel was born in Chickasha three years after the Tulsa Race Massacre. A self-proclaimed tomboy, her childhood consisted of piano lessons, basketball, and endless hours roaming the neighborhood with her older brother, Lemuel. In 1941, she graduated as valedictorian of her Lincoln High School class and enrolled at the all-Black Arkansas Agricultural, Mechanical, and Normal College in Pine Bluff, Arkansas, on scholarship. After her freshman year, she transferred to Langston University, where she majored in English and dreamed of a career as an attorney. While still in college, she married Warren Fisher, who soon after their wedding went overseas to fight in World War II. Sipuel graduated from Langston in 1945. Since her father was a minister and her husband was in the military, jobs independent of the local white power structure, Ada was not subject to the types of economic reprisals commonly wielded against those who challenged the racial status quo.[71]

When Ada Sipuel applied to OU's law school in January 1946 rather than accept a segregation scholarship to attend law school in another state like her brother Lemuel, she became the first African American to apply to a historically white graduate school in the United States since the Allies defeated the Nazis. It remained to be seen if the bigotry that her native country fought overseas would continue to have life at home. Accompanying Sipuel to Norman were Bullock and *Black Dispatch* editor Roscoe Dunjee. Once on campus, the three made their way to the office of OU president George Cross.[72]

Dunjee took the lead once the group settled in the president's office. He told President Cross that Ada Sipuel was there to apply for admission to the OU law school. He then recounted many of her academic achievements and presented the president with a copy of her college transcript. The transcript listed Sipuel's maiden name, and that name rather than her married name became the one used throughout the subsequent legal challenge. After the dean of admissions verified that Sipuel had the scholastic qualifications for admission, President Cross had a decision to make.[73]

Cross removed a prepared statement from his desk and read it to the assembled group. The dictated letter, prepared by the OU Board of Regents in the wake of the NAACP state convention announcing a legal challenge to segregation at OU, instructed the president to refuse admission to anyone of Negro blood because the state laws of Oklahoma prohibited their matriculation at the university. When President Cross finished explaining the law, Dunjee informed him that African Americans were well versed in the law and knew that he could not legally admit Sipuel. What Sipuel, Dunjee, Bullock, and the NAACP state and national offices wanted was a letter explicitly stating that Sipuel was denied admission because of her race.[74]

Cross dictated to his secretary a letter stating that he denied Ada Sipuel admission because she was African American and in doing so handed NAACP officials a smoking gun of sorts for their next legal challenge. A senior-level state political figure had advised Cross that if a Langston graduate applied to OU, he should deny admission based on Langston's lacking accreditation, but he did not go that route. Cross ignored the advice because he did not personally believe in racial segregation and because he knew that OU had admitted several white students from unaccredited institutions in the past. The letter he drafted listed Sipuel's race as the only reason for the admission denial by stating that Oklahoma had a state statue prohibiting Black students from attending the University of Oklahoma and making it a misdemeanor for school officials to admit Black students to white schools, or to instruct or attend interracial classes.[75] Having gotten what they came for, Sipuel and her advisors left the president's office and went to lunch with a small group of faculty, students, and community members. They enjoyed box lunches as no eating establishment in the college town served African Americans.[76]

To Sipuel and Dunjee's chagrin, the national NAACP office delayed filing the OU lawsuit that so many Black Oklahomans had believed to be imminent. For one thing, Thurgood Marshall needed local counsel before proceeding. As was the case throughout the country, local civil rights attorneys licensed to practice in the state in question were indispensable to NAACP lawsuits. Dunjee eventually secured the services of Amos T. Hall, a Black attorney from Tulsa, but Marshall still did not file suit. Instead, he advised Hall to write to the OU Board of Regents and inform them of Sipuel's application because he wanted there to be no question of the NAACP's having exhausted administrative remedies before going into court. In early February 1946, Hall wrote to the regents as Marshall instructed him, but the case remained a no-go. Two days before Marshall was to appear in Oklahoma, he cancelled because preparations for what would become the landmark *Morgan v. Virginia* US Supreme Court interstate bus travel case kept him occupied. Marshall dispatched NAACP attorney Robert Carter in his stead. Carter traveled to Oklahoma to prepare the written brief, but mid-February turned into mid-March and with no real movement in the case, Dunjee became desperate. He worried that Ada Sipuel could become another Lloyd Gaines and reminded Marshall that before her application, no one knew her name but now everyone was familiar with her, including those who wanted to stop her. Dunjee warned that continued filing delays could cost them their brave plaintiff.[77]

On April 6, 1946, two and half months after she first applied to the OU College of Law, Amos Hall filed a petition for a writ of mandamus on Sipuel's behalf in the District Court of Cleveland County. The petition listed Sipuel as the plaintiff and OU's board of regents, president, law and admissions deans, and registrar as defendants. In the petition, Sipuel reaffirmed under oath her desire to study law and her qualifications and maintained that OU officials had violated her constitutional guarantee of equal protection of the law because of her race.[78] Hall asked the court to compel OU to admit Sipuel.

As other states had done in earlier legal challenges to segregation in flagship public institutions, Oklahoma officials stalled for time to make Sipuel's case moot. The hearing on the mandamus was originally scheduled for April 26, but after state officials asked for more time and opposing counsel agreed, the hearing was pushed back until May 16. The state Board of Regents for Higher Education subsequently moved up its scheduled May 27 meeting two weeks early to discuss establishing a law school for Black Oklahomans before the court hearing. At that meeting, the regents discussed the costs of establishing a law school for Black Oklahomans but took no other action.[79]

Three months after Sipuel filed suit in district court, her trial began on July 9, 1946. An interracial crowd of spectators packed the courtroom to the point that audience members had to sit in the jury box. Ironically, the Black and white onlookers who gathered for a case about segregation sat integrated, probably for the first time in the history of Norman, Oklahoma.[80] Hall asked the court to admit Sipuel, basing his arguments on Donald Murray's case out of Maryland and the *Gaines* decision. Fred Hanson, Oklahoma's attorney general and counsel for the defendants, did not deny that Oklahoma had failed to provide equal educational facilities for Black and white residents, but he maintained that state law made it a crime for Black and white students to learn together. Sipuel's writ of mandamus was inappropriate, according to Hanson, since the court was being asked to order the defendants to violate rather than follow state law. Moreover, Hanson argued that Sipuel should have provided the Oklahoma Board of Regents for Higher Education with notice that she desired to study law and only if the board refused her request could she apply to OU.[81]

After a late afternoon recess, court resumed and Judge Ben T. Williams announced his verdict. He denied the writ of mandamus because Oklahoma's laws prohibited OU from admitting Sipuel. While making his ruling from the bench, Judge Williams failed to even mention the *Gaines* decision and Oklahoma's responsibility to provide equal opportunities. Hall immediately announced his plans to appeal and did so two days later.[82]

With her sights now squarely on the Oklahoma Supreme Court, Ada Sipuel could not have fathomed the great personal losses ahead of her. In a span of four months between May and September 1946, she suffered the death of W. A. J. Bullock, the man who had first approached the Sipuel family about a test case, and the death of her father, Bishop Travis Sipuel, from a heart attack.[83] Even as she fought a public battle to advance educational equality for all, she also fought a private battle of grief.

Racism and the slow pace of legal challenges continued to prevent Ada Sipuel from pursuing the legal education that she had dreamed of since childhood.

Rather than preparing for a semester at OU, she prepared for the state supreme court appeal. When the Oklahoma Supreme Court heard oral arguments in Ada's lawsuit on March 4, 1947, Thurgood Marshall assisted Amos Hall with the plaintiff's case before a bench where seven of the nine justices had graduated from OU Law. Marshall argued that segregation was inconsistent with the Fourteenth Amendment while the state's counsel maintained that Sipuel should have asked the state board of regents to establish a separate law school. By not doing so, state officials believed she had no real interest in law but merely wanted admission to OU.[84]

Affirming the lower court's ruling, the state Supreme Court decreed that the *Gaines* decision had not outlawed segregation and Sipuel had a responsibility to make her desire for law school education known so that state officials could create a law school for her. The court also maintained that Sipuel could have gone out of state for law school. The verdict meant a showdown in the court of last resort.[85] While Sipuel continued to be shut out of OU's law school, reaching the US Supreme Court was a celebration of sorts because of the national significance it gave her case.

NAACP attorneys Marshall and Hall prepared to take Sipuel's case to the US Supreme Court, where they would argue that the verdicts rendered in Oklahoma's courts were inconsistent with the *Gaines* decision. When they made those oral arguments on January 8, 1948, Sipuel joined them in Washington, DC. Fred Hanson and Maurice Merrill once again represented the University of Oklahoma, and the two lawyers found themselves grilled by the nine justices over the issue of Sipuel's failure to give notice of her desire to study law within Oklahoma's borders. Justice William O. Douglass asked Hanson and Merrill why the state had made no effort to set up a law school for Black residents when Sipuel first applied to OU's law school nearly two years earlier. Hanson could only explain that the state board of regents did not have the money to set up another law school. In doing so, the segregationist attorney admitted that separate but equal did not exist.[86]

Just four days after oral arguments, the Supreme Court issued a brief decision recognizing Sipuel's right to legal education at a state institution. The court ordered Oklahoma to provide it for her in compliance with the Fourteenth Amendment and to do so as soon as it does for applicants of other races. The call for a speedy remedy was key. Second semester classes at OU's College of Law were scheduled to begin on January 29, 1948, which was seventeen days away. Oklahoma had two choices: it could admit Sipuel to its historically white public law school or create a comparable law school at Langston.[87]

Don't Shout Too Soon

As University of Oklahoma dean of admissions J. E. Fellows, Thurgood Marshall, and Amos T. Hall look on, Ada Sipuel again applies for admission to the University of Oklahoma College of Law in 1948. Prints and Photographs Division, Library of Congress, Washington, DC.

The same segregationist recalcitrance that led southern states to set up segregation scholarship programs led Oklahoma officials to race against time to create a law school at Langston University before registration began at OU. By hook or by crook, state officials committed themselves to keeping Sipuel out of the OU College of Law, and on January 19, the Oklahoma Board of Regents for Higher Education passed a resolution establishing the Langston School of Law. The badly underfunded Langston was unaccredited and did not have the capacity to offer graduate and professional school courses. In fact, just a month earlier, the university was forced to close one week early for the winter break because the school lacked an adequate heating system.[88] Despite inside knowledge of these serious issues, five state regents, with a $15,000 appropriation from the governor's contingency fund, had rooms in the Oklahoma City state capitol building converted into a law school for Langston. The state law library doubled as the law school library. The regents hired three full-time private attorneys to serve as part-time faculty in the makeshift school. On the same day that regents established Langston University's law school, Ada Sipuel traveled to Norman and once again applied to OU's law school.[89]

The Langston School of Law opened its doors on January 26, 1948, with some white Oklahomans declaring that its facilities were "even better" than the ones at OU College of Law. On behalf of the thousands of Black southerners seeking advanced study who were forced to leave their home states because of segregation and for the sake of the many public Black college administrators who dared not publicly take on white state legislators, Ada Sipuel refused to accept the hurriedly created Langston School of Law. Acting as if the OU College of Law was still the only law school in the state, Sipuel arrived in Norman on January 26, 1948, to enroll for class. President Cross once again denied her admission. Despite the setback, Sipuel remained determined and refused to acknowledge or legitimate an act of subterfuge that was in no way equivalent to the historically white law school that she and other Black taxpayers had subsidized for generations. She and NAACP attorneys went back into court to prove that Langston's law school was not equal to OU's. Expert witnesses including the deans of the Harvard and University of Pennsylvania law schools testified that the legal education offered at Langston School of Law was substantially unequal to that offered at the OU College of Law.[90]

Though legal education continued to elude her, Ada Sipuel's fight created professional school opportunities for other African Americans. University officials in Delaware and Arkansas carefully followed her case and decided to desegregate in light of the *Sipuel* decision rather than face lengthy and costly legal battles. The University of Delaware Board of Trustees agreed to admit Black students to programs not offered at the all-Black and public Delaware State University, specifically mentioning the *Gaines* and *Sipuel* decisions in the resolution opening the flagship institution to African Americans.[91] Arkansas, which did not have a law forbidding Black and white students from learning together at the collegiate level, had provided Black residents with segregation scholarships since 1943 to pursue courses that were available at the University of Arkansas but were not available at the public and all-Black Arkansas Agricultural, Mechanical, and Normal College in Pine Bluff. The tuition aid came out of the Arkansas AM&N operating budget. In February 1948, the University of Arkansas admitted Silas Hunt, a twenty-five-year-old World War II veteran, to the law school. As an undergraduate, Hunt had attended the Pine Bluff campus, where he had served as president of the student body and editor of the campus newspaper, and where he and Sipuel had been classmates before she transferred to Langston. He had graduated from the college with honors in 1947.[92]

Hunt's admission to the previously all-white law school was certainly a "don't shout too soon" moment, as Arkansas continued to offer segregation scholarships. Moreover, the University of Arkansas maintained racial segregation by physically separating Silas Hunt from other students. University officials did not plan for Hunt to learn alongside his white classmates. Rather than sit alongside his peers, Hunt's professor offered him instruction privately after teaching the rest of the class. Hunt also did not have the same library privileges as white students. He had to use an intermediary to borrow books from the law library, where a special section was reserved for him. When he needed to use the restroom, he had to seek permission to use the dean's restroom rather than the facilities available to other students. Despite the isolation and challenges, Hunt persevered and did well academically, but an aggressive form of tuberculosis caused him to withdraw from school in July 1948. He died less than a year later. Hunt's withdrawal and death, however, did not stymy desegregation at the University of Arkansas. With each successive year, additional Black students entered the law school.[93]

During the fall of 1948, Edith Irby became the first Black student to enroll in a previously all-white southern medical school when she matriculated at the University of Arkansas College of Medicine. That semester, there were 6,500 medical school students throughout the United States. Only 185 of them were Black and 141 of that number attended either the Howard University College of Medicine or Meharry Medical College.[94]

Years later, Irby admitted that she had applied to several medical schools across the country because she was aware of Arkansas's segregation scholarship program. In addition to her home state's flagship medical school, she also applied to Northwestern, the University of Chicago, and Johns Hopkins. Tuition at the University of Arkansas's medical school was $300 per year, much cheaper than the cost at every other school where she had applied. Wagering that the state's segregation scholarship program would not pay full tuition at any of the northern schools, she stayed home and made history. Each medical school class at Arkansas consisted of ninety students, but in 1948, the first-year class had ninety-one students so that Irby's admission would not prevent a "white male student who could be a doctor from having a place in the class."[95] Most of the white students treated Irby cordially. Segregation laws banned her from using the campus dining hall or the public bathrooms used by other students, so university officials created a private dining room for her in one of the library study rooms. They also provided her with her own bathroom. In a reminder of the pride and support that Black communities had for academic trailblazers like Irby, the university's Black custodians daily placed bouquets of flowers in her private rooms.[96]

The legal challenge brought by a young Black woman in Oklahoma had cracked open the door of opportunity for a Black woman in Arkansas and for Black people in other parts of the South. Ada Sipuel's lawsuit also created graduate and professional school opportunities for Black Oklahomans. Within weeks of Sipuel's victory at the Supreme Court, six African Americans applied for graduate or professional school study at OU. OU denied admission to all six, including George McLaurin, an Oklahoma City native seeking a doctorate in educational administration. The sixty-one-year-old McLaurin had completed his undergraduate studies at Langston in 1928 and had earned a master's degree at the University of Kansas in 1943. At the time of his application to OU, he was a professor of English at Langston.[97] Thurgood Marshall mounted a legal challenge on McLaurin's behalf and was successful because of the earlier *Sipuel* ruling. Marshall probably chose McLaurin rather than any of the other five Black applicants who applied to OU at the same time because McLaurin already had a master's degree demonstrating his ability to do graduate-level work. Marshall sought legal redress for McLaurin in the Federal District Court for the Western District of Oklahoma. While waiting for court action, he had his client apply to OU once again in September 1948 to make obvious to the court that McLaurin had given the state adequate notice that he desired graduate study in a discipline not offered at Langston. That same month, a federal three-judge panel ruled that the *Sipuel* decision required the state to provide McLaurin with the education he sought as soon as the state provided it to applicants of other groups. The judges ordered OU to admit McLaurin without delay. He walked through a door that Ada Sipuel had pried open.

University officials did not challenge the ruling to admit George McLaurin but schemed to maintain a form of internal segregation after he matriculated.[98] When McLaurin enrolled at the University of Oklahoma on October 14, 1948, as that institution's first Black student, he quickly learned that school officials had no intention of allowing him the same opportunities as white students. Administrators assigned all four of his classes to a classroom that had a main section and a vestibule. McLaurin had to sit in the vestibule, where he could see the blackboard at a forty-five-degree angle. In addition to being separated from his peers during lectures, OU required him to use a separate bathroom, eat alone in a designated section of the student union, and study at a separate table, labeled with his name, in the library.[99]

Graduate student George McLaurin segregated in the vestibule of the classroom at the University of Oklahoma in 1948. In 1950, he challenged internal segregation, or the separate treatment of students based on their race at the university, with the US Supreme Court and won. Prints and Photographs Division, Library of Congress, Washington, DC.

Oklahoma could not afford to create separate graduate programs at Langston every time that a Black applicant requested it, so lawmakers amended the segregation statute to admit Black students at state-supported white institutions if the course of study desired was not offered at Langston. The legislation that Oklahoma governor Roy Turner signed into law on June 10, 1949, stipulated that Black students admitted to higher educational institutions other than Langston receive instruction on a segregated basis like McLaurin.[100] During the summer of 1949, twenty-three Black graduate students enrolled in classes at OU. The students sat roped off from their white peers in the classroom, except when white students occasionally removed the barricades to signal their displeasure with the arrangement. The separation of the races even extended to the OU football stadium, where a plywood barrier cordoned off a section of seats for Black spectators. Internal segregation also existed at Oklahoma's land-grant institution. Nancy Randolph Davis, an alumna of Langston and public school teacher, began graduate study in home economics at Oklahoma A&M College (Oklahoma State University) during the 1949 summer. Five additional Black graduate students enrolled at the Stillwater institution that fall. They sat just outside the classroom.[101]

While the half-hearted desegregation order allowed Black Oklahomans to remain in state for graduate study and take part in sporting events, it still did not open the OU College of Law to Ada Sipuel, since Langston continued to have a law school on the books. The Oklahoma Board of Regents for Higher Education announced its plans to close the Langston law school on June 30, 1949. During the school's eighteen month existence, only one student attended at a cost to the state of $28,000. The closure announcement led Sipuel to visit OU's law school on June 17 and once again apply for admission. Officials rejected her application on a technicality—the Langston School of Law was still open. Understanding that if Sipuel had to wait until the Black law school officially closed before being admitting to OU's law school, she might miss the summer term, President Cross directed university officials to admit her.[102] In taking this action, Cross did not remain neutral in the struggle over racial equality in higher education. He could have simply waited until Langston's law school closed so that he did not have to take a side with respect to desegregation and risk alienating trustees, alumni, and donors, but personal conviction and a commitment to the law compelled him to assist Sipuel.

Sipuel began law school at OU on June 20, 1949, more than three years after she first applied. Through drawn-out legal procedures and policy minutia, segregationists manipulated time and delayed her educational aspirations, but she refused to be denied. Sipuel secured the opportunity to learn Oklahoma law alongside people she would later practice with and against. In her initial term, she was the only woman and the only Black student. As if she did not already stick out, she was set apart from the rest of the class in a chair bearing a large sign that read "colored."[103]

While the NAACP had gotten Black students into OU, the organization went back into court seeking enforcement of not just the letter but also the spirit of the Fourteenth Amendment. Thurgood Marshall argued that OU's requiring Black students to sit apart from their white classmates was an equal protection violation and on June 5, 1950, a unanimous US Supreme Court agreed in *McLaurin v. Oklahoma State Regents*. The justices decreed that the differential treatment afforded McLaurin solely based on race "impair[ed] and inhibit[ed] his ability to study, to engage in discussions and exchange views with other students, and, in general, to learn his profession." The ruling ended the degrading internal segregation arrangement at all Oklahoma institutions of higher education.

Ada Sipuel Fisher later in life recalled that the day after the *McLaurin* decision, she began sitting in the front row of her law school classroom. Justice had been delayed but not denied, and after earning her law degree in August 1951, she practiced law for several years in Oklahoma before joining the faculty at Langston, where she taught for nearly thirty years. In 1992, Oklahoma's governor appointed Sipuel to the Board of Regents of the University of Oklahoma, the governing body that had once refused to admit her.[104]

On the same day that the US Supreme Court heard oral arguments in the *McLaurin* case, justices also heard arguments in the case of Heman Sweatt, the Black plaintiff who had applied to the University of Texas School of Law, the only public law school in the state, in February 1946. Sweatt met all admission requirements except for his race. He desired to be a lawyer at a time when there were only twenty-three Black attorneys in the entire state of Texas.[105] The only state-supported Black college in Texas, Prairie View Agricultural and Mechanical College, established in 1876, had never been adequately funded or designated as the state's university for African Americans as provided for in the state constitution. A "university" designation would have afforded Prairie View A&M access to money from the Permanent University Fund, which handsomely subsidized the all-white UT and Texas Agricultural and Mechanical University.[106]

Rather than invest in Prairie View A&M, in 1939 the Texas Legislature created a segregation scholarship program to provide African Americans with out-of-state graduate and professional school training, but Heman Sweatt had no desire to leave home to receive the same training that white Texans received locally. A 126th District Court judge in Travis County agreed that Sweatt should not have to and ordered Texas lawmakers to create a state-supported law school for African Americans within six months or admit Sweatt to UT Law.[107] The victory was a hollow one. On the one hand, the judge had acknowledged Texas's failure to provide equal educational opportunities for African Americans. On the other hand, the judge told Sweatt to wait six months for the state to create a Black law school. Once again, Black waiting operated as a tool to pacify segregationists and afford them time to create new ways to exclude African Americans from full citizenship.

When Sweatt, his counsel, and counsel for UT reappeared in district court six months later, Texas attorney general Grover Sellers announced that the state had complied with the judge's original order by setting up a law school in Houston that was affiliated with Prairie View. Black applicants had to obtain a certificate from the UT law school dean attesting to their scholastic qualifications before registering for courses at the makeshift law school.[108] Once again, segregation imposed a greater burden on Black students than on white students since white applicants to UT did not have to secure any kind of certification. The Prairie View law school, "born of conflict and not of long-range planning," operated in a two-room office suite with the bare basics. Not a single student applied to the new law school during its registration period.[109]

Unwilling to admit defeat and desegregate UT Law, Texas lawmakers went a step further and created an entire new university, at a cost of nearly $3.5 million, in response to Heman Sweatt's desire to become a lawyer. The legislature passed a bill in March 1947 purchasing the private Houston College for Negroes and establishing Texas State University for Negroes (present-day Texas Southern University) in Houston. Texas State would not be a branch of UT and therefore would not have access to the lucrative Permanent University Fund available to UT and Texas A&M. The new university included a temporary law school in Austin while a permanent facility was built in Houston. State officials created the temporary law school in order to have a school in operation before Sweatt's next court hearing to improve the state's position.[110] In September 1947, to the chagrin of Thurgood Marshall and other NAACP officials, three Black students enrolled in the hastily created law school in Austin.[111] While many considered these students to be race traitors, they, like Sweatt, had aspirations of being attorneys and did not want to go out of state or continue delaying their dreams.

The Texas State University for Negroes School of Law (present-day Thurgood Marshall School of Law at Texas Southern University) relocated to Houston in the summer of 1948. Only one of the three Black students who enrolled at the temporary law school in Austin was able to move with the school. Heman Sweatt and his attorneys continued to oppose the Texas State University School of Law because it was unaccredited, the library facilities were deficient, and because the case method of legal education required a large and diverse student population to foster robust discussion, which the school lacked.[112]

Unmoved by Texas officials' sudden interest in increasing educational opportunities for African Americans, Sweatt and his attorneys exhausted state appeals and took their case to the US Supreme Court, which heard oral arguments on April 4, 1950. Supporters of UT and of the NAACP filed amicus briefs in the case. At Marshall's request, more than 200 law school deans and professors filed a brief decrying the public Black law schools that southern states created out of thin air. Not to be outdone, eleven southern attorneys general filed briefs in support of Texas's and states' right to practice segregation.[113] Both sides presented the same arguments that had been made in lower courts, with UT attorneys maintaining that the state had made provision for African Americans' legal education and NAACP attorneys countering that the provision made fell short of separate but equal.

Ruling in favor of Sweatt, a unanimous Supreme Court found that racial segregation in law school admissions violated the Fourteenth Amendment because separate law school facilities were inherently unequal. Focusing on the intangibles of law schools, Chief Justice Fred Vinson wrote for a unanimous court: "The University of Texas Law School possesses to a far greater degree those qualities which are incapable of objective measurement but which make for greatness in a law school. Such qualities, to name but a few, include reputation of faculty, experience of the administration, position and influence of the alumni, standing in the community, traditions, and prestige. It is difficult to believe that one who had a free choice between these law schools would consider the question close."[114]

The justices ordered the University of Texas School of Law to admit Heman Sweatt. One person who did not get to see this landmark victory was Charles Hamilton Houston, who had died weeks earlier of heart failure. His star pupil secured the victory that he first pursued more than a decade earlier.[115]

The Supreme Court's ruling led Texas to desegregate UT graduate and professional schools that were not offered at Prairie View A&M or Texas State. Within days of the ruling, African Americans began applying for admission to postbaccalaureate programs during summer school. Eight Black graduate students—five women and three men—desegregated UT during the summer of 1950. In September 1950, Sweatt and five other African American students enrolled in the UT School of Law. He had first sought admission to that institution four years earlier.[116]

Reactions to the *McLaurin* and *Sweatt* decisions were mixed. OU president George Cross said the ruling affecting his school "knocks out all segregation in graduate schools at Oklahoma University." UT president Theophilus Painter pledged to comply with the court, while Georgia governor Herman Talmadge pledged resistance and South Carolina governor Strom Thurmond insisted that the rulings attacked states' rights.[117] Perhaps the clearest sign that southern states continued to have very little interest in Black education was the Texas Legislature's decision to slash funding at Texas State University for Negroes from $1.57 million to $958,672 in the legislative session immediately following *Sweatt*. The decrease in funds made clear that lawmakers never planned to fund the school at adequate levels and gave up the charade of doing so after legal defeat.[118]

Days after the US Supreme Court ruled in Ada Sipuel's favor in January 1948, Black and white newspapers alike throughout the United States carried headlines detailing an unfathomable proposed education deal. Citing financial woes, the Meharry Medical College Board of Trustees offered to sell the Nashville institution to fifteen southern states who would then operate the college as a regional medical school for African Americans. The arrangement served to keep the financially strapped Meharry open and, supporters alleged, would put southern states in compliance with US Supreme Court decisions that required them to provide equal educational opportunities for Black and white citizens. The scheme was yet another example of the great lengths to which southern states went to preserve segregation. And this time, a Black college, albeit one largely run by white businessmen, was complicit.[119]

Meharry Medical College opened its doors in Nashville, Tennessee, in 1876 as the first Black medical school in the South. The college was named for Samuel Meharry, an Irish American immigrant who first worked as a salt trader on the Kentucky-Tennessee frontier. In the 1820s, Samuel Meharry was hauling salt through Kentucky when he got stuck in the mud. He stumbled upon a cabin owned by a Black family who had recently gained their freedom. Despite the possibility that Meharry was a slave hunter looking to kidnap free Black people and sell them back into slavery, the Black family gave Meharry food and shelter. In return for their kindness, the story goes, Meharry vowed to do something for their race when he was able. More than forty years later, Meharry made good on his promise when he learned that Methodist clergy and laymen were organizing a school called Central Tennessee College. Meharry and his four brothers supported the college's medical department with a donation of $30,000 in cash and property.[120]

The Nashville medical school held its first classes in 1876 in the basement of a Methodist Episcopal Church while a building was constructed. In succeeding years, Meharry added dentistry and pharmacy. A nursing school opened in 1900 and a teaching hospital in the following year. In 1915, Meharry became an independent college, separating itself from the now defunct Walden University, which had formerly been Central Tennessee College.[121]

Financial instability plagued Meharry for decades. One of the main reasons why expenses exceeded revenues was because throughout its existence, Meharry had the "burden of carrying a hospital to furnish medical care to the indigent of the city and region."[122] By World War II, things had become dire, with a growing deficit from year to year. To shore up funding, Fisk University president Thomas Elsa Jones suggested that the medical college merge with his institution. Meharry's faculty, however, opposed the idea vigorously.[123]

One consistent and guaranteed stream of income that the professional school had enjoyed since the early 1940s was something akin to a few southern states underwriting segregation. In 1943, Tennessee began utilizing Meharry as its in-state medical school for African Americans by appropriating state funds annually to the private institution, so that Black state residents could study medicine and dentistry there free of charge. Black Tennesseans utilizing the funds would be enrolled at the public Tennessee Agricultural and Industrial College for Negroes while taking their classes at Meharry.[124] Prior to the new arrangement, Black residents had received segregation scholarships covering the difference in tuition and fees between Meharry and the University of Tennessee.[125] State commissioner of education B. O. Duggan hailed the full-ride arrangement as the first time that the state had provided its Black residents with education equivalent to that provided to white residents. He failed to mention that the funding was also an attempt by state officials to keep Black students out of the University of Tennessee and remain in compliance with the *Gaines* decision.[126]

One year after Tennessee implemented its medical education scheme, Virginia began subsidizing the cost of training Black physicians and dentists at Meharry by setting aside $16,000 annually to educate twenty-five Black Virginia medical school students and ten Black Virginia dental students at the Tennessee college. Virginia contributed $500 a year for each medical school student and $400 a year for each dental student.[127] These funds, paid directly to Meharry for overhead costs, were in addition to the segregation scholarships that Black Virginians received from the state. Meharry, in return, reserved a certain number of seats in each incoming class for residents from Virginia, so the state's lawmakers reasoned that they provided medical education to Black and white citizens alike. Black citizens, however, had to travel several hundred miles out of state to receive the same opportunity that white citizens enjoyed in state.

The concept of interstate regional education began in 1943 with a medical school arrangement between West Virginia and Virginia. West Virginia University had a two-year medical school, which required its students to complete the last two years of medical school out of state. Hoping to encourage more students to pursue medicine, the West Virginia Legislature contracted with the state of Virginia to transfer between fifteen and twenty WVU medical school students to the Medical College of Virginia for their final two years of medical school. West Virginia agreed to pay any costs exceeding what Virginia residents paid to attend the state-supported medical school. The arrangement kept West Virginia from expending large sums of money to secure the faculty and equipment needed for the final two years of medical school and provided a financial boon and a more diverse pool of students for the Medical College of Virginia.[128] This plan, though, was only available to white West Virginians, as the Virginia institutions did not admit African Americans.

Interstate regional education became very popular across the South after World War II for two reasons. First, the educational benefits provided by the federal government to returning veterans increased demand for higher education at all levels, including in graduate and professional schools. Second, as the NAACP continued its legal strategy to secure tax-supported postbaccalaureate opportunities in the South for African Americans, southern states began to look beyond their borders to secure graduate and professional school opportunities that did not exist at public Black colleges because the states did not have the will or the financial resources to build the necessary laboratories, libraries, and faculty necessary for advanced training.

Alabama governor Chauncey Sparks was one of the earliest proponents of regional education. At the opening of the 1945 Alabama legislative session, he urged the state legislature not only to set up a segregation scholarship program but also to authorize Alabama institutions to offer their facilities on a reciprocal basis to other states, so that Alabama could acquire educational facilities subject to small demand without having to build them in state at a hefty cost.[129] Both measures became law and Sparks began selling the regional idea to his fellow southern governors. In December 1945, he presented a report on regional education at the Southern Governors' Conference, where he explained the virtues of each state's maintaining a school with one specialty that would serve the entire South.

By early 1948, fourteen southern states had signed on in favor of regional education, proposing an organization called the Southern Regional Education Compact. To legitimize the takeover of Meharry, southern governors sought congressional approval of the compact. Their efforts inspired widespread Black opposition, with representatives from twelve national organizations testifying in Congress against the scheme. Witnesses included Thurgood Marshall of the NAACP, James Nabrit of the Conference of Presidents of Land Grant Colleges, Alma Vessels of the National Association of Colored Graduate Nurses, and representatives from the National Medical Association, the National Dental Association, the National Negro Insurance Association, the National Negro Publishers Association, and the Congress of Industrial Organizations' Committee against Discrimination.[130]

Outside of Washington, Black opposition came from many different arenas. Luther Jackson, president of the all-Black Virginia State College, argued that "a state cannot build culturally if the educational facilities are to be located in other states." Decrying the Meharry arrangement in particular, he pointed out that Howard's medical school enrolled four times as many Virginia residents as Meharry's, so in no way, shape, or form should Virginia officials consider Meharry to be their state-supported medical school for African Americans.[131] In a prominently placed editorial titled "Evading the Cost of Segregation," the editor of the *Pittsburgh Courier* wrote that southern governors were interested in regional education for African Americans because they wanted to evade Supreme Court rulings and because it was too costly to maintain graduate and professional school programs for African Americans in each state. "If southern states want segregation and discrimination, let them pay for it," the editor concluded.[132] Meharry alumni also opposed the plan in large numbers.

The US House of Representatives eventually approved the education compact 235–45, setting up a showdown in the Senate. Northern and southern Democrats supported the measure in a show of party solidarity, but liberal Republican senators, led by Wayne Morse of Oregon, remained steadfast in their opposition to the unconstitutional plan.[133] The US Supreme Court had already said that if a state provides education to its white students within its borders, it must do the same for its Black students. In the end, by a one-vote margin, the Southern Regional Education Compact failed in the US Senate.[134] Regional education, however, was not banned because congressional approval was not needed for interstate compacts related to areas reserved to state powers and education was one such area.[135]

The proposed compact, which eventually became the Southern Regional Education Board, exposed the challenges facing Black higher education in the post–World War II period. First, the unabashed enthusiasm with which southern states attempted to circumvent Supreme Court decisions demonstrated that white commitment to segregation could not easily be dismantled. Almost half of the US Senate approved of a scheme antithetical to the Constitution. Second, Black institutions such as Meharry needed a significant influx of funds so that financial insecurity did not make them susceptible to segregationists' offers of assistance, and the strings attached. Finally, the complicity of Meharry's white president, M. Don Clawson, in the proposal to sell the college to a southern pact called into question the appropriateness of continued white leadership at Black educational institutions. Clawson did not consult with Black faculty and administrators before endorsing the pact. White paternalism had no place in an institution whose purpose was to cultivate and deploy Black leadership.

Undeterred by the Capitol Hill defeat, southern state governors next sought state legislative approval for regional education and held the inaugural meeting of the Southern Regional Education Board (SREB) in June 1949. Veterinary medicine was the first field in which southern states contracted for service under the new overarching board. Tuskegee Institute, Alabama Polytechnic Institute

(Auburn), Oklahoma A&M, and the University of Georgia agreed to serve as regional schools for veterinary medicine, admitting a quota of qualified students from designated states other than the state in which it was located. Black students studied at Tuskegee and white students studied at one of the other three regional schools for veterinary medicine. Member states paid the regional board $1,000 a year per student, with each participating state having an annual admissions quota to a designated program. The participating schools retained complete control over admissions, and accepted students paid in-state tuition at public institutions and reduced tuition at private institutions. If a state's agreed-upon quota was not met each year, the state would still pay three-fourths of the agreed amount for every student allotted but not enrolled unless another cooperating state desired additional spaces and paid for the unused spaces of another state. The board served as the liaison between the states and the schools, collecting and disbursing funds and ensuring that both parties carried out the contract terms.

Southern students entered veterinary schools on regional contracts beginning in the fall of 1949. During that school year, Tuskegee reserved twenty-seven spaces for students from ten states affiliated with the SREB. North Carolina A&T president Ferdinand Bluford oversaw the contract with Tuskegee. North Carolina's quota during the 1949–50 academic year was four freshmen students, but only one student benefited because the program was late getting underway. Even though Tuskegee received a certain amount of money per North Carolina resident, Black North Carolinians still received segregation scholarships because the cost to attend Tuskegee was higher than the cost to attend the regional institution for white veterinary medicine students.[136]

Like the contracted services for veterinary medicine, southern states also provided regional medical and dental training in the fall of 1949. Schools designated as regional institutions agreed to admit a quota of qualified students from states participating in regional education and received $1,500 per student per year within the quota. Once again, several white schools with the desired professional school program became regional institutions for white students, while only one Black school, Meharry, served as a regional destination for Black students.[137]

During the inaugural year of regional education contracts, 149 Black students attended two Black institutions and 211 white students attended nine white institutions. Thus, regional education did not desegregate institutions or increase the facilities needed to train Black doctors, dentists, and veterinarians. Although southern states used it to evade Supreme Court decisions, the arrangement did help Black institutions with their bottom line. In one academic year, Meharry enrolled 47 dental students and 108 medical students under the regional education arrangement, and Tuskegee enrolled 27 veterinary students.[138] That same year,

Atlanta University became the third Black institution to participate in regional education. The AU School of Social Work admitted 53 students, and each participating state agreed to pay AU $750 for each student enrolled.[139] Tuskegee and AU received both regional education funds from the participating states and tuition dollars from the segregation scholarship recipients hailing from those states.

SREB leadership maintained that regional education was not a scheme to preserve segregation, a position they put on record during a lawsuit involving the University of Maryland School of Nursing. While Donald Murray had desegregated the University of Maryland's law school in 1936, the institution only admitted a handful of Black students after him and Maryland continued its segregation scholarship program. In 1949, eighteen-year-old Esther McCready applied to the University of Maryland School of Nursing. School officials rejected her application because of race. When McCready sued the university with the assistance of NAACP attorney Thurgood Marshall, university officials asserted that the state had made provision for African American nursing education through its SREB contract with Meharry Medical College. The contract allowed students to study medicine, dentistry, or nursing at Meharry and pay the same amount that non-Black students paid to pursue those courses at the University of Maryland. SREB officials met with Maryland authorities and asked them to withdraw the regional education defense because "that use of regional arrangements would endanger the future activities of the Board and throw it into racial politics."[140] When Maryland officials refused to change their defense, the SREB intervened in the suit as a friend of the court on behalf of McCready. The Maryland Court of Appeals ruled in McCready's favor and she desegregated the nursing program. Overcoming hostility from both students and faculty, she graduated in 1953. McCready's successful lawsuit led university officials to desegregate other professional school programs and the undergraduate college at the University of Maryland.[141]

Despite important Supreme Court victories involving Lloyd Gaines, Ada Sipuel, and George McLaurin, African Americans continued to fight uphill battles to enter state-supported graduate and professional school programs at historically white institutions in the South. With very little enforcement of court orders, the NAACP was compelled to go into court state-by-state to address educational inequality. It would not be until the late 1960s that all border and southern states admitted African Americans for postbaccalaureate degrees and disbanded their segregation scholarship programs. These states would continue to drag their feet on establishing graduate and professional school programs at their public Black institutions.

Conclusion

Just as segregation scholarship recipients often faced hostile environments while attending universities in the North, the Black pioneers who desegregated state-supported graduate and professional school programs in the South also endured racism, discrimination, and isolation. In June 1951, five African Americans—Harvey Beech, James Lassiter, J. Kenneth Lee, Floyd McKissick, and James Robert Walker—enrolled at the University of North Carolina law school for the first summer session after a lawsuit compelled the institution to admit them. In both housing and extracurricular activities, the students faced isolation and racial hostility. Despite a housing shortage on campus, the university reserved an entire floor of a dormitory for the three Black students who needed campus housing. At UNC's Kenan Stadium where football games were held, there were three separate seating sections: one for students, one for non-Black spectators, and one for Black spectators. Rather than give the five Black law school students tickets in the student section during the fall semester, the university sequestered them in the Black seating section. After appealing to the governor for redress, the five men received tickets to sit in the student section. These social slights were only the tip of the iceberg. The pioneering five endured constant harassment in the dining hall and daily threatening letters from the Ku Klux Klan.[1]

While UNC had not rolled out the welcome wagon for the five Black law school students, at least school officials allowed them to begin classes. A sixth African American student also journeyed to Chapel Hill that summer, but she was not as fortunate as her male counterparts. Gwendolyn Harrison, a twenty-five-year-old Kinston native, Spelman College graduate, and instructor at Johnson C. Smith University, gained admission to UNC's doctoral program in Spanish. Harrison, who also held a master's degree from the University of California, picked up her dorm key just as other enrolling students did and then proceeded to register for classes. When the registrar discovered that Harrison was Black, a fact that she had noted on her application for student housing weeks before

Gwendolyn Harrison's application for campus housing at the University of North Carolina in 1951. Records of the Chancellor, Robert Burton House Series, 1919–57, box 2: Integration, University Archives, Wilson Library, University of North Carolina at Chapel Hill.

arriving on campus, he prevented her from registering and eventually had UNC chancellor Robert House speak with her. House explained that there had been a mistake and that the university's board of trustees was still studying the question of admitting Black students to its graduate school. In April 1951, the trustees had voted to admit qualified Black students to UNC's graduate programs and professional schools when the programs were not available at North Carolina College or North Carolina A&T. Weeks later, they rescinded that policy and pledged to provide graduate work for African Americans at NCC.[2]

Humiliated but determined, Harrison gathered her luggage from the dorm room she had been assigned to and returned to Kinston, where she prepared for a legal challenge. Represented by a group of attorneys that included Conrad Pearson, who had represented Thomas Hocutt nearly twenty years earlier, Harrison sued UNC in federal district court, maintaining that she was denied admission because of her race. Before her case came to trial, UNC's trustees held an emergency meeting and voted to admit Gwendolyn Harrison to the university's second summer session.[3] She began classes at UNC during the second summer session of 1951, becoming the first Black woman to attend the flagship institution. She also attended UNC during the 1952 summer session but withdrew without completing the doctorate degree.[4]

Conclusion 169

The first African American to receive a doctorate from a historically white institution in the South was Walter Nathaniel Ridley, who earned a doctor of education degree from the University of Virginia in 1953. Born in 1910 in Newport News, Virginia, Ridley received his bachelor's and master's degrees from Howard University in 1931 and 1933, respectively. He sought to earn a doctorate at UVA and applied several times, but the university did not admit African Americans, so he accepted a segregation scholarship and began doctoral study at the University of Minnesota in 1939. His dissertation research explored whether the audiovisual materials used in schools contained content detrimental to Black students. His methodology required him to view countless hours of movies, a task that caused his eye to hemorrhage. Doctors advised him to stop his research, so he returned home without the degree he sought.[5]

The NAACP's US Supreme Court victories in higher education cases from Oklahoma and Texas led Lindley Stiles, the dean of UVA's Curry School of Education, to recruit prospective Black graduate students at Virginia State College. He met Ridley, who was then on faculty at the college, and encouraged him to apply. Ridley applied soon thereafter and was accepted. He took evening courses and received his degree in 1953. Ridley later served as the president of the historically Black Elizabeth City State Teachers College (present-day Elizabeth City State University) in North Carolina.[6]

While Ridley was UVA's first Black graduate, he was not the first Black student to enroll there. That distinction belongs to Gregory Swanson, a Black lawyer who sued for admission to take graduate courses in law. Swanson had earned bachelor's degrees in political science and law from Howard University before applying to UVA in 1949. In defiance of both the *Sweatt* and *McLaurin* decisions, the university denied Swanson admission based on his race. He sued in federal district court and won.[7] Swanson left UVA without earning a degree because of death threats and racial shunning, but his lawsuit undoubtedly opened the door for Walter Ridley.[8]

In the same year that Gregory Swanson matriculated at UVA, Gus Ridgel made history as one of nine Black students and the sole Black graduate student to desegregate the University of Missouri. More than a decade after Lloyd Gaines attempted to study at Mizzou, civil rights groups won a court ruling to break the color barrier. Ridgel had graduated first in his high school class in Poplar Bluff, Missouri, and finished Lincoln University magna cum laude. He excelled academically in Mizzou's graduate program in economics but found the institution to be challenging socially. Even though the campus had a housing shortage, he lived alone in a two-bed dormitory room because no white student would room with him. There was only one off-campus eatery where he could buy a meal. While the master's program in economics normally took two years to complete, Ridgel doubled up on courses and wrote his thesis in one year because of financial constraints. After earning his master's degree with honors in 1951, he earned a doctorate in economics from the University of Wisconsin and became an administrator at Kentucky State University.[9]

A segregation scholarship recipient desegregated graduate education at the University of Georgia. Mary Frances Early, a native of Atlanta, graduated valedictorian from Clark College (present-day Clark Atlanta University) in 1957 with a bachelor's degree in music education. She was a public school teacher who sought a postbaccalaureate education. She applied for and received a segregation scholarship from Georgia to take summer classes at the University of Michigan during the summer of 1958. She also attended during the summers of 1959 and 1960 before events at UGA led her to press for admission.[10]

In January 1961, Hamilton Holmes and Charlayne Hunter, two Black undergraduates at Morehouse College and Wayne University (present-day Wayne State University), desegregated the University of Georgia. Days after they arrived on campus, students rioted and university officials suspended Holmes and Hunter "for their own safety." As Early watched news of the campus unrest from the comfort of her home, she made the decision to help the two Black pioneers by transferring from Michigan to UGA. Against the wishes of her mother, Early applied and endured a demeaning interview process during which the university investigated her personal life to see if she had used drugs, shoplifted, been arrested, or had a child out of wedlock. The UGA registrar went so far as to ask her if she had ever visited a house of prostitution. After several months' delay, she was admitted. Though she was not the first Black student to apply for graduate admission to UGA, she was the first accepted, and she matriculated during the summer of 1961 as a master's student in music education. During her time at UGA, she experienced harassment and isolation but still managed to do well academically. She had not come to UGA to make friends, so she focused on studies and used her own version of intellectual warfare to break down the walls of racism. After a professor announced to the class that Early had scored the highest grade on an exam, a few white classmates began interacting with her during class, but never outside of it. In August 1962, she became the first known African American to receive a degree from UGA.[11]

As the UGA riots that sprung Early into action demonstrated, breaking the color barrier at southern flagships could be a dangerous enterprise. At the University of Mississippi, it was an undergraduate student, James Meredith, who desegregated the school in October 1962 under the protection of US deputy marshals, who stayed on detail until he graduated in August 1963. In June of 1963, two months before Meredith graduated, Cleve McDowell became the first Black law student at the University of Mississippi. McDowell did not feel safe there after Meredith graduated, since the marshals had also left campus. For one thing, he was isolated socially. He had an entire dormitory floor to himself because no white students would live near him. He also felt unsafe because he had purchased Meredith's car, a vehicle segregationists knew well. He asked university officials for permission to carry a gun and they denied his request. He secretly carried a gun anyway. One day while rushing up the steps of the law school building to attend class, he dropped his sunglasses. When he bent down to pick them up, his pistol fell out of his pocket and he was summarily expelled. Mississippi's flagship institution was once again all-white.[12]

In 1967, Reuben Anderson became the first Black graduate of the University of Mississippi's law school. He would go on to become the first African American justice on the Mississippi Supreme Court and the first Black president of the Mississippi Bar. In 1968, Robert Walker became the first Black graduate student to receive a degree at Mississippi's flagship institution. He earned a master's degree in history and later became the first African American mayor of Vicksburg.[13]

Black students' matriculation at historically white institutions was not inevitable. Both segregation scholarship recipients and the Black pioneers who desegregated historically white institutions were persistent in demanding and securing the educational opportunities due them as citizens. In leaving the only homes and communities they had ever known, enduring loneliness and harassment, and sometimes even delaying their academic pursuits in order to secure court decisions that expanded opportunity for others, they made citizenship claims against recalcitrant southern state governments and compelled state officials to act. Educational opportunity was their right as taxpayers and state residents, and they never conceded that fact, even if their methods of achieving a semblance of belonging differed.

The opening of historically white state-supported graduate and professional school programs in the South led some Black institutions and programs to close, foreshadowing what would happen to many Black elementary and secondary schools after *Brown*. When the University of Louisville began admitting Black students in the fall of 1950, university trustees announced that Louisville Municipal College, UL's Black branch, would close at the end of the academic year.[14] The closure exposed the vulnerability of Black educators in a Black institution.

The municipal college had seven Black professors, four of whom had doctorate degrees. The white university offered Ford Foundation fellowships to four professors, a position as a student advisor and instructor to another professor, and one semester of severance pay to two others. The sole retained professor was Charles H. Parrish, who had earned a PhD in sociology from the University of Chicago in 1944. He and three other Municipal College faculty members agreed to accept the offers made to them, but three others threatened legal action because they found the severance packages inadequate. William Bright, a Kentucky segregation scholarship recipient himself, was one of the faculty members offered a Ford Foundation fellowship. Bright, a full professor who had been at the college since it opened, requested a semester's salary of severance pay in addition to the fellowship. His two colleagues, George D. Wilson and Henry S. Wilson, who had been offered severance found the semester of pay inadequate and countered by asking for a faculty position at UL or severance pay at the rate recommended by the American Association of University Professors, which was one-and-a-half-month pay for each year of service. The professors had worked at Louisville Municipal College for twenty and seventeen years, respectively, and had doctorates from Ohio State and Indiana University, respectively. The three laid off professors planned to seek redress in the courts if UL did not accept the counterproposals.[15] UL trustees declined their requests.[16] The dismissed professors never waged a legal challenge and all of them eventually found new jobs at other Black colleges.

The University of Louisville's refusal to retain all the Municipal College faculty with terminal degrees was part of a larger, national trend of white universities—in the North and South—denying Black scholars faculty positions. While most southern states had laws requiring segregation of the races, in the North, historically white institutions excluded African Americans by custom. Many of these schools used bogus rationales to explain why they had not hired Black professors. One of the most common excuses was that Black scholars did not have much published work. Even a cursory examination of the important and groundbreaking scholarship that Black scholars published in the *Journal of Negro Education* and the *Journal of Negro History* exposed the lie embedded in such an excuse. While the leading journals of many predominately white professional organizations refused to publish or review the work of Black scholars, they continued to produce important scholarship. The truth was that historically white institutions simply did not want Black faculty, exposing the racism embedded in the academy, including at institutions that admitted segregation scholarship recipients.[17]

Like the Black faculty at Louisville Municipal College, Black public school teachers throughout the South lost their jobs with desegregation. As public school systems moved from dual to unitary school systems and closed Black schools, Black educators experienced firings, nonrenewal of contracts, and pressure to resign or retire early. Because of segregation scholarships, these principals and teachers usually had academic credentials and professional credentials that were superior to those of the white educators who replaced them.[18]

Another institutional casualty of postbaccalaureate desegregation was the law school at present-day South Carolina State University in Orangeburg. The historically white University of South Carolina School of Law began admitting Black students in 1964, and two years later the law school at the state's only public Black college closed. Despite a short existence from 1947 until 1966, South Carolina State College's law school trained a coterie of African Americans who went on to dismantle segregation in many arenas and bring about a more just society. One notable graduate was Matthew Perry Jr., the first Black lawyer from the Deep South to serve as a federal judge.[19]

The entrance of Black students into state-supported graduate and professional schools in the South did not automatically end segregation scholarships. Most historically white border and southern state universities admitted only handfuls of Black students during the early years of desegregation. Moreover, segregation scholarship recipients who had already started programs in the North before their home states desegregated continued their studies "abroad" with state assistance even after their native state flagship institutions began admitting Black students. It would not be until the late 1960s that all states did away with the tuition assistance programs created to maintain segregation. Today, Arkansas, Delaware, Georgia, Kentucky, Louisiana, Mississippi, and South Carolina participate in a regional contract program that allows qualified students pursuing health degrees to pay in-state tuition at participating out-of-state public universities and reduced tuition at private universities.[20]

Decades of diverting southern tax dollars to colleges and universities in the North to preserve segregation led to curricular underdevelopment at public Black colleges. Many southern states continued to avoid establishing graduate and professional school programs at public Black institutions even after the states began desegregating their university systems. Take for instance the case of veterinary education in North Carolina. After the Civil Rights Office of the Department of Health, Education, and Welfare (HEW) found that the University of North Carolina System, composed of eleven historically white institutions and five historically Black institutions and managed by a board of governors, still had vestiges of racial segregation, North Carolina's university system pledged in 1974 not to establish any new programs that would "impede elimination of the dual system of higher education" in the state.[21] That same year, UNC System officials announced the creation of a state school of veterinary medicine. Both North Carolina State University in Raleigh and the historically Black North Carolina A&T State University in Greensboro submitted proposals to house the school.

To speed along higher education desegregation in the state, HEW required North Carolina officials to study the racial impact of a veterinary school on student enrollment at both institutions before deciding on a location. The study suggested that placing the vet school on the historically Black campus would bring about greater student desegregation than placing the vet school on the historically white campus. Unsatisfied with that study, the UNC Board of Governors contracted with consultants from Ohio State who studied both institutions and asserted that North Carolina State was better equipped than North Carolina A&T to support a new program. Neither the consultants nor the board of governors considered the fact that racially based funding disparities had existed between the two institutions since their founding. In the end, the UNC System established its school of veterinary medicine at North Carolina State, passing up the opportunity to appropriate significant resources and establish an advanced degree program at a Black university. UNC System president William Friday admitted that "the state probably does not have or would not be willing to commit the amount of money required to establish a veterinary medicine program at NC A&T."[22] When presented with an opportunity to redress racial discrimination and curricular neglect in higher education, North Carolina chose to perpetuate the status quo. This was not the first or the last time that state officials lacked the will to invest in graduate and professional school programs at their Black institutions.[23]

Several public historically Black colleges and universities in the South have demanded financial redress from state governments for the decades of racist neglect and underfunding. In 1975, Jake Ayers, a civil rights activist in Glen Allan, Mississippi, sued the state on behalf of his son, a student at Jackson State University. Ayers alleged that the state had not provided adequate and equitable resources to its three publicly funded historically Black colleges and universities, Jackson State University, Alcorn State University, and Mississippi Valley State University. Mississippi's underfunding resulted in major disparities between Black and white institutions, including severely limited academic offerings at the Black institutions. The case went all the way to the US Supreme Court, which instructed Mississippi to eliminate all effects of previous state-mandated racial segregation in its state university system. The court instructed historically white institutions to increase their Black student populations, and it instructed historically Black institutions to accept more non-Black students.

In 2002, state officials and plaintiffs in the *Ayers* case reached a $503 million settlement that provided funding for new academic programs, infrastructure, and endowments at the state's three historically Black institutions over seventeen years. The Black universities used a significant portion of the funding to increase their curricular offerings and expand existing programs to attract more non-Black students. For example, Mississippi Valley used settlement funds to create a graduate program in special education, while Alcorn State created a master's degree program in biotechnology. While the programs were a welcome addition, many supporters of the school maintained that the settlement amount was an inadequate remedy for such gross underfunding.[24]

The *Ayers* case was just the tip of the iceberg in terms of exposing systematic underfunding of Black colleges and universities. In 2006, students and alumni from Maryland's four public Black universities—Morgan State University, Coppin State University, Bowie State University, and the University of Maryland Eastern Shore—brought a lawsuit against Maryland for underfunding the institutions and allowing historically white universities to duplicate academic programs at the Black institutions, hindering the schools' ability to attract students. After a fifteen-year legal battle, Maryland officials agreed to a $577 million settlement to the four Black institutions of higher education over a ten-year period. Even that amount, while significant and a powerful acknowledgement of wrongdoing, still did not make up for the long-term denial of equitable state funding and duplication of academic programs.[25]

It would not be surprising in the coming years to see other southern states attempt to make amends for deliberately funding Black institutions of higher education at lower rates than their historically white counterparts. Recently, the Tennessee Office of Legislative Budget Analysis found that the state owed Tennessee State University, a historically Black land-grant institution, between $150 and $544 million in land-grant funds unpaid between 1957 and 2007. Land-grant institutions receive an annual state dollar-to-dollar match to their federal land grants for food and agriculture research. Not only did the historically white University of Tennessee receive its full state funding every year, but in some years it received more than the required funding from the state.[26] The deliberate withholding of state land-grant funds prevented Tennessee State from establishing new programs and recruiting faculty and students just as Tennessee's segregation scholarship program prevented the university from creating graduate and professional school programs.

While the figure that Tennessee officials admitted to owing Tennessee State was staggering, according to the Biden administration the actual number is substantially higher. In September 2023, US education secretary Miguel Cardona and agriculture secretary Thomas Vilsack sent letters to the governors of the sixteen states that had had segregation scholarship programs informing them that their state governments had underfunded their Black land-grant institutions by more than $13 billion in the last three decades. Federal officials found that Tennessee State had a $2.1 billion disparity compared to the historically white University of Tennessee, Knoxville, and that astounding figure only considered the years 1987 until 2020. Federal data showed that Missouri underfunded Lincoln University by $361 million as compared to the funding per student provided to its historically white counterpart, the University of Missouri, between 1987 and 2020. If traced back to the early twentieth century, the fund disparity would be substantially more, as Walthall Moore had warned when sounding the alarm about racial inequity in 1921.[27]

The underfunding of Black land-grant institutions is also in the billions in states such as North Carolina, Florida, and Texas. North Carolina A&T State University has a $2 billion funding disparity compared with North Carolina State University. Florida A&M University, an 1890 land-grant HBCU, has a $1.9 billion funding gap, according to federal officials, while Prairie View A&M's gap is $1.1 billion.[28] The withholding of these funds prevented Black educational institutions from making critical investments in campus infrastructure, research, and student support services. For certain, southern state governments owe an enormous debt to state-sponsored Black institutions of higher education. Even before the recent discovery of systemic underfunding of Black land-grants, many public Black institutions of higher education were denied key investments of public dollars for several generations by hook-or-crook schemes such as segregation scholarships that were financed out of the already meager operating budgets of Black colleges.

At the very time that more states began phasing out their segregation scholarship programs and admitting Black students to historically white institutions, white public officials in southern communities developed ways to use tuition grants from the state to evade school desegregation. In 1959, after the Fourth US Circuit Court of Appeals ordered Prince Edward County, Virginia, to desegregate its public schools, the Virginia General Assembly created a voucher system that provided vouchers of $125 for white elementary school students and $150 for high school students to attend nonsectarian private schools or nearby public schools. Soon thereafter, Prince Edward County closed all its public schools in defiance of the court's order to desegregate and abdicated to private enterprise its responsibility to provide education to its residents. White students in the county, armed with vouchers, received instruction at the newly established Prince Edward Academy. The Black students could not attend the segregation academy and were not granted vouchers to attend other private schools. From

1959 until 1964, Black children had to attend school in other localities or forgo education altogether. Prince Edward County's public schools only reopened by order of the US Supreme Court. In 1965, the US District Court for the Eastern District of Virginia ruled that state vouchers could not be used to fund schools that practiced racial discrimination.[29]

What happened in Virginia was not an anomaly. By 1969, more than 200 private schools created with the sole purpose of excluding African Americans operated in the South. Seven states passed legislation that made public money available to pay tuition at these segregation academies.[30] Many scholars rightly point to this diversion of public funds for private education as the beginning of school choice movements and voucher systems in the United States. These scholars, however, fail to acknowledge segregation scholarships as the ideological progenitors of vouchers.

Segregation scholarships introduced the pattern of diverting badly needed resources from public (and Black) institutions and using them elsewhere to preserve segregation. This history necessitates that southern state lawmakers contend with what is just compensation for public Black colleges today. Appropriate remedies might include southern states making endowment contributions to public Black universities equal to the cumulative amount, adjusted for inflation, that respective states spent on segregation scholarships. Additionally, these states could provide public Black colleges with equity funding for the decades of underinvestment. States should also pursue policies that prohibit duplicative academic programs at historically white institutions that are already available at public Black colleges and polices that require one-to-one state matching of federal research extension formula funds to Black land-grant institutions.

The history of segregation scholarships requires all of us to consider who is pushed aside and harmed by education funding policies that replace direct government-provided educational services. Most important, this history should compel all those who believe in equity and inclusion in education to go to the same lengths, if not surpass the lengths that segregationists took, to ensure that public Black colleges are funded fairly and adequately and that Black students at all levels are afforded the same educational opportunities as their peers. At a time when there is a federal assault on affirmative action, nothing less is acceptable.

NOTES

Abbreviations

Ernest Lindley Papers
  Ernest Lindley Papers, Records of the University of Kansas Chancellor's Office, University Archives, Kenneth Spencer Research Library, University of Kansas, Lawrence.
Papers of the NAACP-A
  Papers of the NAACP, part 3: The Campaign for Educational Equality, series A: Legal Department and Central Office Records, 1913–1940, Center for Research Libraries, Chicago.
Papers of the NAACP-B
  Papers of the NAACP, part 3: The Campaign for Educational Equality, series B: Legal Department and Central Office Records, 1940–1950, Center for Research Libraries, Chicago.

Introduction

1. "Remarks by President Biden at Presentation of the Presidential Medal of Freedom," The White House, July 7, 2022, www.whitehouse.gov/briefing-room/speeches-remarks/2022/07/07/remarks-by-president-biden-at-presentation-of-the-presidential-medal-of-freedom/#:~:text=That%27s%20the%20soul%20of%20our,our%20nation%27s%20highest%20civilian%20award.
2. Gray, *Bus Ride to Justice*, 14–15.
3. Gray, *Bus Ride to Justice*, 13.
4. Gray, *Bus Ride to Justice*, 16–17.
5. Jackson, "Financial Aid Given," 33–37.
6. Gray, *Bus Ride to Justice*, 28.
7. Lavergne, *Before "Brown,"* 199.
8. Clement, "Impact of the War," 365–66; McCuistion, *Graduate Instruction for Negroes*, 8. Howard and Fisk had conferred master's degrees in the liberal arts in the late nineteenth century on an "in-course basis," which meant students who presented evidence that they had made satisfactory progress in liberal studies after graduation from the institution were eligible for the degree. Most students completed this advanced work as nonresidents. These institutions did not formalize resident graduate study until the late 1920s. Logan, *Howard University*, 55–56; and Richardson, *History of Fisk University*, 116–18. North Carolina College was the first Black institution to confer a PhD, doing so in 1955. The doctoral program began in 1952 in the areas of administration and

supervision, elementary education, and guidance. For more information, see Gershenhorn, "Stalling Integration."
9. For more on Charles Hamilton Houston, see McNeil, *Groundwork*; Ogletree, *All Deliberate Speed*, 111–18, quote on 117.
10. Charles Hamilton Houston, "Cracking Closed University Doors," *The Crisis* (New York), December 1935, 370; Anderson, "Race, Meritocracy, and the American Academy," 157.
11. For more on the Great Migration, see Wilkerson, *Warmth of Other Suns*.
12. For more on alternate sources of educational funding for African Americans during Jim Crow, see Embree and Waxman, *Investment in People*; Fosdick, *Story of the Rockefeller Foundation*; Fisher, *Fundamental Development of the Social Sciences*; Masghati, "Patronage Dilemma."
13. For more on the double tax, see Anderson, *Education of Blacks in the South*.
14. For more on *Gaines*, see Endersby and Horner, *Lloyd Gaines*.
15. The Carolina Story: A Virtual Museum of University History, accessed May 20, 2022, https://museum.unc.edu. My use of the term "historically white institutions" is a riff on Jarvis Givens's use of the term in "Invisible Tax."
16. Brown, "Graduate and Professional Education"; "Drops Journalism Course to Keep Colored Out," *Philadelphia Tribune*, April 4, 1942.
17. Lucas, "Mississippi Legislature," 79.
18. Ward, *Black Physicians in the Jim Crow South*, 47.
19. Watson, *Against the Odds*, 23.
20. W. Montague Cobb, "Medical Care and the Plight of the Negro," *The Crisis* (New York), July 1947, 202.
21. Public medical schools in Delaware and Arkansas began admitting Black students in 1948. Thomas, *Deluxe Jim Crow*, 210–11.
22. "Dearth of Negro Lawyers Is Challenge to Youth: Howard Figures Show Only One to Every 9,667 Persons," *Norfolk (VA) Journal and Guide*, August 4, 1934.
23. For more on traveling while Black, see Bay, *Traveling Black*.
24. Du Bois, *Autobiography of W. E. B. Du Bois*, 135.
25. *Sixteenth Biennial Report of State Superintendent of Public Instruction, Oklahoma State Board of Education*.
26. Franklin, *Mirror to America*, 62. For more on the experiences of Black students at Ivy League institutions, see Bradley, *Upending the Ivory Tower*.
27. Franklin, *Mirror to America*, 62.
28. Purnell and Theoharis, with Woodard, *Strange Careers of the Jim Crow North*, 4. Other works that consider racism and freedom movements in the North include Biondi, *To Stand and Fight*; and Countryman, *Up South*.
29. Titus, *Brown's Battleground*, 35–36.
30. Favors, *Shelter in the Time of Storm*. Other research on HBCUs includes Frazier, "Graduate Education in Negro Colleges and Universities"; Johnson, *Negro College Graduate*; Brown, "Graduate and Professional Education in Negro Institutions"; Wolters, *New Negro on Campus*; Preer, *Lawyers v. Educators*; Anderson, *Education of Blacks in the South*; Williamson, *Radicalizing the Ebony Tower*.
31. Devlin, *Girl Stands at the Door*; Bradley, *Upending the Ivory Tower*. The historiography

on Black firsts also includes Barbara Lewinson, "Black Students in Eastern Colleges, 1895–1940," *The Crisis* (New York), March 1974, 84–87; Perkins, "African American Female Elite"; Stephenson, "Unsung Heroes"; and Wallenstein, "Black Southerners and Non-Black Universities."

32. Langston Hughes referred to the North as a supposedly "kinder mistress" in the 1926 poem "The South."
33. Williamson-Lott, *Radicalizing the Ebony Tower*; Cole, *Campus Color Line*.
34. Fenwick, *Jim Crow's Pink Slip*, xvi–xvii, 37–41; Walker, *Their Highest Potential*; Givens, *Fugitive Pedagogy*.
35. "UI Alumna Makes History," *Daily Iowan* (Iowa City), September 27, 1996; Martin, "Jewel Limar Prestage," 95–97. Some consider Merze Tate to be the first Black woman to earn a PhD in political science, but her 1941 doctorate degree from Harvard's Radcliffe College was in government and international relations.
36. Perkins, "Merze Tate," 520; Evans, *Black Women in the Ivory Tower*, 110; Pirkle, "Study of the State Scholarship Aid." Despite gender constraints in the early twentieth century, Black women pursued advanced study. In 1921, three Black women became the first to earn PhD degrees from American universities (Eva Beatrice Dykes from Radcliffe College, Sadie T. Mossell Alexander from the University of Pennsylvania, and Georgiana Rose Simpson from the University of Chicago).

Chapter One

1. Asa Hutson, "First Negro Given Prominent Seat in Missouri Legislature," *St. Louis Globe-Democrat*, January 6, 1921.
2. For more on equalization strategies, see Tushnet, *NAACP's Legal Strategy against Segregated Education*.
3. For more on white hostility to Black education, see, for example, Williams, *Self-Taught*; Eagles, *Price of Defiance*; and Titus, *Brown's Battleground*.
4. The phrase "passive recipients of whites' actions" was coined by Glenda Gilmore in a discussion of southern historiography. See Gilmore, *Gender and Jim Crow*, xvi.
5. Painter, *Exodusters*.
6. For more on the Great Migration, see Wilkerson, *Warmth of Other Suns*.
7. Jack, *St. Louis African American Community*, 129.
8. Jack, *St. Louis African American Community*, 128–29. Notable alumni of Sumner High School include tennis star Arthur Ashe, Alpha Kappa Alpha Sorority Incorporated founder Ethel Hedgemon Lyle, comedian Dick Gregory, and singer Tina Turner.
9. Walthall Moore's exact date of birth is not known, but he was probably born in the mid-1870s. He lists May 1, 1878, as his birthdate on a World War I draft registration card. His death certificate lists his birth year as 1886, but this is unlikely since he is listed as six years old in the 1880 US Census.
10. Missouri Secretary of State's Office, *Official Manual of the State of Missouri 2001–2002*.
11. Richardson, "Missouri and the Negro."
12. Savage, *History of Lincoln University*, 1–9.
13. Savage, *History of Lincoln University*, 70, 145.

14. Savage, *History of Lincoln University*, 61–62. For more on land-grant colleges, see Nash, "Entangled Pasts"; and Wheatle, "Ward of the State."
15. Savage, *History of Lincoln University*, 71, 127–28.
16. *Laws of Missouri*, 51st Sess. (1921), 86–87. In later years, Missouri lawmakers maintained that any state in the Midwest constituted an "adjacent" state. See Savage, *History of Lincoln University*, 169.
17. "Missouri Fools Voters, Giving Them Gold Brick," *Chicago Defender*, May 13, 1922.
18. "Lincoln Univ. Sues for Half Million Fund," *Baltimore Afro-American*, May 19, 1922; "Lincoln University Bill Found Defective," *St. Louis Post-Dispatch*, June 20, 1922.
19. "Moore Seeks $500,000 for Pa. University," *Pittsburgh Courier*, February 7, 1925; "Race Men Jim Crowed by Senate," *Pittsburgh Courier*, April 18, 1925.
20. Boone County Circuit Court Trial Transcript, Papers of the NAACP-A.
21. West Virginia Board of Education, *Record of Proceedings*, July 21–22, 1954.
22. Posey, *Negro Citizen of West Virginia*.
23. Harlan, *History of West Virginia State College*, 5–6; Haught, "Institute"; Posey, *Negro Citizen of West Virginia*, 101–2.
24. Reynolds, "Rise and Fall," 4.
25. "W. VA. to Pay Tuition of Law and Medical Students," *Baltimore Afro-American*, May 7, 1927; "Progressive West Virginia," *Pittsburgh Courier*, May 14, 1927; "From Farmhand to Legislator," *Pittsburgh Courier*, March 23, 1929.
26. Wright, *American Hunger*, 2.
27. "N.Y. School of Social Work Drops West Virginia Co-ed," *Pittsburgh Courier*, March 21, 1931.
28. Murray, *Song in a Weary Throat*, 83; Ella Baker and Marvel Cooke, "The Bronx Slave Market," *The Crisis* (New York), November 1935.
29. "N.Y. School of Social Work Drops West Virginia Co-ed."
30. "N.Y. School of Social Work Drops West Virginia Co-ed."
31. Posey, *Negro Citizen of West Virginia*, 44.
32. "West Virginia to Aid Students," *New York Amsterdam News*, May 11, 1927.
33. "W. Va. Graduate Students Flock to Foreign Colleges," *Pittsburgh Courier*, November 6, 1937; "Information Desired from Certain States Relative to Graduate Instruction for Negroes—West Virginia," September 2, 1938, special subject file, box 1, folder: Graduate Study for Negroes, Division of Negro Education, Department of Public Instruction, State Archives of North Carolina, Raleigh; Letter from Charles Hamilton Houston to K. Norman Diamond, April 14, 1936, Papers of the NAACP-A.
34. "H.U. Quits Penn Law Meet," *Baltimore Afro-American*, March 16, 1935; "West Virginia Sets New Pace for Education of Race," *Atlanta Daily World*, July 3, 1935.
35. "West Virginia Sets New Pace"; Cohen, *When the Old Left Was Young*, 208.
36. Caroline Wasson Thomason, "Will Prejudice Capture Oberlin?," *The Crisis* (New York), December 1934, 360–61.
37. "Dr. Theodore Phillips Is Master of Music," *Pittsburgh Courier*, June 29, 1935.
38. Bacote, *Story of Atlanta University*, 264–76. See earlier note about master's degrees that Fisk conferred in the late nineteenth century. Richardson, *History of Fisk University*, 116–18.

39. Bacote, *Story of Atlanta University*, 276–79.
40. Bacote, *Story of Atlanta University*, 280, 372; Bond, "Some Aspects of Graduate and Professional Education for Negroes," 395; "Dr. Hope Resigns as Morehouse President," *Norfolk (VA) Journal and Guide*, June 13, 1931; "Atlanta U Rated Class A in South," *Chicago Defender*, December 17, 1932. For more information on the role of Black librarians in diversifying reading material, see Dennis, "'Weapons for Building a Better World.'" After SACSS began rating Black colleges in 1930, the organization stipulated that a Black college's favorable rating would not entail admission to the Southern Association even though the standard policy was that approval of a school automatically came with membership in the association. See Winston, "Through the Back Door."
41. Howard had first embarked upon graduate education in the liberal arts in the late nineteenth century when the Howard Board of Trustees adopted a provision permitting a thesis or examination by the faculty for the master's degree. In 1902, the board required that the degree not be granted less than three years after the conferring of the bachelor's degree. Nevertheless, Howard did not yet have a graduate school or a graduate faculty. See Logan, *Howard University*, 119, 275–76; and "Howard to Enlarge Graduate School," *Norfolk (VA) Journal and Guide*, December 24, 1938. For information on the graduate council membership of Howard's graduate school, see Winston, "Through the Back Door."
42. Logan, *Howard University*, 420.
43. *Laws of Missouri*, 55th Sess. (1929), 61; *Laws of Missouri*, 56th Sess. (1931), 27–28.
44. See "Direct Examination of E. R. Adams," *State ex rel. Gaines v. Canada*, Circuit Court of Boone County, no. 34337, 1936, 89–91.
45. Louis Lautier, "Graduate Study Denied Youth of Southern States—Houston," *Norfolk (VA) Journal and Guide*, May 8, 1937.
46. Savage, *History of Lincoln*, 253. Lincoln's president requested $947,880.
47. Information taken from E. R. Adams's testimony in *State ex rel. Gaines v. Canada*, Circuit Court of Boone County, no. 34337, 1936, 90–92.
48. The 1921 law creating Lincoln University stipulated that the Lincoln Board of Curators would administer the scholarships, but the state superintendent of education's office actually did so. See "Finding of Facts in the Circuit Court of Boone County, Missouri," June 1936, 4, box 2, folder SC35286, record group 600, Missouri State Archives, Jefferson City; Letter from L. Amasa Knox to Charles H. Houston, December 13, 1935, Papers of the NAACP-A.
49. Loupe, "Storming and Defending the Color Barrier," 22.
50. Lucile Bluford, interview by Fern Ingersoll, May 13, 1989, interview no. 1, transcript, Washington Press Club Foundation Women in Journalism Oral History Project Collection, Columbia Center for Oral History, Columbia University Libraries, New York; Devlin, *Girl Stands at the Door*, 4.
51. Bluford, interview; Devlin, *Girl Stands at the Door*, 4.
52. Bluford, interview; Devlin, *Girl Stands at the Door*, 6.
53. "Negroes Receiving Tuition from the State during 1935," Papers of the NAACP-A.
54. Haldeman-Julius, "What Negro Students Endure in Kansas"; "Henderson Swings—No Negroes Allowed," *The Dove* (Lawrence, KS), November 21, 1938; Devlin, *Girl Stands at the Door*, 7.

55. Letter from E. H. Lindley to H. C. Herman, May 11, 1928, series 2/9/3, box 6, folder 1927, Ernest Lindley Papers.
56. Letter from Doxey Wilkerson to KU Chancellor, January 1926, Ernest Lindley Papers; Letter from Doxey Wilkerson to KU Chancellor, May 2, 1926, Ernest Lindley Papers.
57. Breaux, "New Negro Arts," 155; "Our Jim Crow Laws," *The Dove* (Lawrence, KS), March 27, 1930; Devlin, *Girl Stands at the Door*, 8.
58. Information taken from Ann Arbor, MI, city directories, the 1930 US Census, and University of Michigan Official Publication: General Register, issue 40, no. 66 (February 15, 1939).
59. University of Kansas *Jayhawker* Yearbooks, 1932 and 1936, Kenneth Spencer Research Library, University of Kansas; *Appendix to the House and Senate Journals of the Sixtieth General Assembly, State of Missouri*, 1939, 9; Board of Visitors Minutes, May 5, 1937, University of Virginia Library.
60. *Michiganensian*, University of Michigan yearbook, 1937.
61. "G. S. Bluford, Engineering Teacher, Mourned by Many," *Philadelphia Tribune*, October 14, 1967.
62. Letter from W. E. B. Du Bois to Ernest Lindley, November 17, 1930, series 2/9/1, box 1, folder C, Ernest Lindley Papers.
63. Letter from Ernest Lindley to W. E. B. Du Bois, December 11, 1930, series 2/9/1, box 1, folder C, Ernest Lindley Papers.
64. Letter from W. E. B. Du Bois to Ernest Lindley, December 15, 1930 and Letter from Ernest Lindley to W. E. B. Du Bois, December 23, 1930, series 2/9/1, box 1, folder C, Ernest Lindley Papers; Annual Catalogue of the University of Kansas, 1930–1931, Kenneth Spencer Research Library, University of Kansas.
65. University of Kansas School of Medicine Administrative Committee Minutes, December 1930, Lindley Correspondence, Departmental 1930/31, series 2/9/5, box 2, folder: Medicine, Ernest Lindley Papers; "Comments on the Petition of the Citizens' League of Kansas Relative to Negro Medical Schools," [1931], Lindley Correspondence, Departmental 1930/31, series 2/9/5, box 2, folder: Medicine, Ernest Lindley Papers.
66. Obituary for Dr. Geraldine Mowbray in author's possession.
67. Taylor, *Overground Railroad*, 11–14; Bay, *Traveling Black*, 141–48.
68. "Actress to Sue L & N Railroad," *Atlanta Daily World*, January 18, 1939; "Mother and Child Assaulted on Train," *Atlanta Daily World*, December 5, 1945.
69. Karen Lathen Sabur, telephone interview by author, December 21, 2020.
70. Sabur, interview.
71. Sabur, interview.
72. Sabur, interview.
73. 1936 *Collegian* (Lincoln University yearbook); Briscoe, "Study of Living Conditions among Negroes."
74. Dungy, "African American Graduate School Experiences at the University of Iowa," 135.
75. Briscoe, "Study of Living Conditions among Negroes in Wagoner County," 86.
76. Hallstoos, "'Excellent Work and Superior Traits of Personality,'" 18.
77. *Appendix to the House and Senate Journals of the Sixtieth General Assembly, State of Missouri*, 9; Dungy, "African American Graduate School Experiences," 94.

78. From 1946 until 1949, only Black women with residency status in Iowa were allowed to live in campus dormitories. Black women from the South continued having to live off campus. See Breaux, "Maintaining a Home for Girls," 250; and Edwards, "Fine Art," 60.
79. Breaux, "Maintaining a Home for Girls."
80. Breaux, "Maintaining a Home for Girls," 236–55.
81. Information taken from Iowa City directories and the 1930 US Census.
82. Dungy, "African American Graduate School Experiences at the University of Iowa," 122.
83. "UI Alumna Makes History," *Daily Iowan* (Iowa City), September 27, 1996.
84. "UI Alumna Makes History"; Jewel Prestage, interview by Shelby Faye Lewis, October 31, 1992, Louis B. Nunn Center for Oral History, University of Kentucky Libraries, Lexington.
85. "UI Alumna Makes History"; Obituary for James Jordan Prestage, accessed November 22, 2023, https://obits.theadvocate.com/us/obituaries/theadvocate/name/james-prestage-obituary?id=31122335.
86. "Mrs. Hardiman, Mrs. Evans Are Sorority Guests," *Baltimore Afro-American*, July 8, 1944.
87. *Appendix to the House and Senate Journals of the Sixtieth General Assembly, State of Missouri*, 1939, 9; Alisa D. Perdue, "Dr. Laurence Boyd, 91, Professor Emeritus at Morris Brown College," *Atlanta Constitution*, September 8, 1989.
88. "MBC Professor Gets Honorary Degree," *Atlanta Daily World*, June 9, 1972; Perdue, "Dr. Laurence Boyd."
89. *Appendix to the House and Senate Journals of the Sixtieth General Assembly, State of Missouri*, 1939, 9; Wesley, Price, and Morris, *Lift Every Voice and Sing*, 63.
90. Information about John Royston's Tuskegee years taken from author's email correspondence with Tuskegee's archivist, August 2018.
91. Letter from Sherman Scruggs to Adell M. Deboe, July 23, 1942, Papers of the NAACP-B; Letter from Ruth Greene to Roy Wilkins, August 23, 1942, Papers of the NAACP-B.
92. Letter from Sherman Scruggs to Adell M. Deboe, July 23, 1942, Papers of the NAACP-B.
93. "St. Louisan Got School Raised to College Rank," *St. Louis Globe-Democrat*, September 14, 1958.

Chapter Two

1. C. C. Spaulding to Walter White, February 6, 1933, Papers of the NAACP-A.
2. Conrad Pearson and Cecil McCoy to Walter White, February 6, 1933, Papers of the NAACP-A.
3. Conrad Pearson and Cecil McCoy to Walter White, February 6, 1933, Papers of the NAACP-A.
4. Tushnet, *NAACP's Legal Strategy against Segregated Education*, 13–14. For more on African Americans' support of fully funded segregated education, see Brown-Nagin,

Courage to Dissent; Walker, *Lost Education of Horace Tate*; and Burkholder, *African American Dilemma*.

5. By 1933, UNC had begun admitting non-Black minorities. For example, Henry Owl, a member of the Eastern Band of Cherokee Indians, received a master's degree in history from UNC in 1929.
6. Walter White to Conrad Pearson and Cecil McCoy, February 8, 1933, Papers of the NAACP-A.
7. Conrad Pearson, interview by Walter Weare, April 18, 1979, Southern Oral History Program Collection, Southern Historical Collection, Wilson Library, University of North Carolina at Chapel Hill.
8. Kapur, *To Drink from the Well*.
9. Cecil McCoy to Walter White, February 11, 1933, Papers of the NAACP-A.
10. Pearson, interview; Kluger, *Simple Justice*, 193; Gershenhorn, "*Hocutt v. Wilson*," 291–92.
11. Pearson, interview.
12. "Negroes Will Ask Admittance to Law Courses at U.N.C.," *Greensboro (NC) Daily News*, February 13, 1933.
13. Letter from James E. Shepard to John C. B. Ehringhaus, March 17, 1933; Letter from James E. Shepard to John C. B. Ehringhaus, May 31, 1934, James Shepard Papers, University Archives, James E. Shepard Memorial Library, North Carolina Central University, Durham.
14. Ellis, *Between Washington and Du Bois*.
15. For more on Shepard's opposition and roadblocks erected by Durham's Black community, see Gershenhorn, "*Hocutt v. Wilson*."
16. *Thomas R. Hocutt v. Thomas J. Wilson and the University of North Carolina*, Durham County Superior Court, no. 6439, 1933.
17. Ware, *William Hastie*, 49; McNeil, *Groundwork*, 131–32.
18. Ware, *William Hastie*, 49–50.
19. Gershenhorn, "*Hocutt v. Wilson*."
20. Gershenhorn, "*Hocutt v. Wilson*"; Ware, "*Hocutt*," 233.
21. "Bill in North Carolina House Would Pay Tuition for Negroes," *Philadelphia Tribune*, April 20, 1933.
22. "Schools and Colleges: Bill to Break U. of Md. Jim Crow Is Prepared," *Baltimore Afro-American*, April 27, 1935; James, *Root and Branch*, 66–68; Weems, "Alpha Phi Alpha."
23. McNeil, *Groundwork*.
24. James, *Root and Branch*, 16.
25. James, *Root and Branch*, 55–78.
26. "Drum Major for Justice," *Baltimore Sun*, February 18, 1999.
27. Bogen, "First Integration."
28. Letter to Donald Murray from Raymond Pearson, December 14, 1934, https://msa.maryland.gov/megafile/msa/speccol/sc2200/sc2221/000011/000004/pdf/d007006a.pdf.
29. Wheatle, "Ward of the State"; italics added.

Notes to Chapter Two

30. Putney, "Black Colleges," 335–36.
31. Wheatle, "Ward of the State."
32. Wheatle, "Ward of the State," 115.
33. Wheatle, "Ward of the State."
34. Wheatle, "Ward of the State," 132–33, 140–41.
35. Wheatle, "Ward of the State," 128.
36. Wheatle, "Ward of the State," 146–57.
37. Wheatle, "Ward of the State," 146–57; Preer, *Lawyers v. Educators*, 41.
38. "Walks 250 Mi. to College to Save Carfare," *Baltimore Afro-American*, February 11, 1933.
39. "U. of Md. Fund Committee Not on the Job Yet," *Baltimore Afro-American*, September 9, 1933.
40. Letter to Donald Murray from Raymond Pearson, December 14, 1934, https://msa.maryland.gov/megafile/msa/speccol/sc2200/sc2221/000011/000004/pdf/d007006a.pdf.
41. "Defends Jim Crow Schools in Maryland," *Norfolk (VA) Journal and Guide*, May 18, 1935; Kluger, *Simple Justice*, 234–35; Letter to Donald Murray from Raymond Pearson, March 8, 1935, https://msa.maryland.gov/megafile/msa/speccol/sc2200/sc2221/000011/000004/pdf/d007006a.pdf.
42. "Bill to Break U. of Md. Jim Crow Is Prepared," *Baltimore Afro-American*, April 27, 1935.
43. "To Sue University of Maryland," *Baltimore Afro-American*, April 19, 1935; "Sues to Enter University," *Baltimore News and the Baltimore Post*, April 20, 1935; "Md. University Seeks to Defend Jim Crow Policy," *Baltimore Afro-American*, May 7, 1935.
44. Wheatle, "Ward of the State," 158–59.
45. Wheatle, "Ward of the State," 163–64.
46. "Maryland Legislature Votes Scholarships for High School Graduates," *Baltimore Afro-American*, April 13, 1935; "Interviews with Students Begun by Commission," *Baltimore Afro-American*, August 3, 1935. In the first year, 284 Black residents submitted applications for tuition assistance. By 1940, Carl Murphy believed that Maryland should discontinue its segregation scholarship program. See Cole, *Campus Color Line*, 27.
47. Frances Murphy, interview by Fern Ingersoll, December 3, 1992, Washington Press Club Foundation Women in Journalism Oral History Project Collection, Columbia Center for Oral History, Columbia University Libraries, New York.
48. Ware, "Setting the Stage for *Brown*," 649. Various sources refer to the legal challenge Donald Murray brought against the University of Maryland—and the subsequent Maryland Court of Appeals ruling—with different names such as *Murray v. Pearson*, *Murray v. University of Maryland*, *Pearson v. Murray*, etc. For clarity, I refer to the case as *Murray v. Pearson* and use the year of the opinion to differentiate between the original trial and the appeals trial.
49. Transcript of *Murray v. Pearson*, Baltimore City Court, June 18, 1935.
50. Transcript of *Murray v. Pearson*, Baltimore City Court, June 18, 1935.
51. Transcript of *Murray v. Pearson*, Baltimore City Court, June 18, 1935.

52. Transcript of *Murray v. Pearson*, Baltimore City Court, June 18, 1935, 6.
53. Transcript of *Murray v. Pearson*, Baltimore City Court, June 18, 1935.
54. Transcript of *Murray v. Pearson*, Baltimore City Court, June 18, 1935.
55. James, *Root and Branch*, 73–74.
56. "University of Maryland Applicant Gets Threatening Letter," *Baltimore Afro-American*, June 29, 1935.
57. Kuebler, "Desegregation of the University of Maryland," 46.
58. Weems, "Alpha Phi Alpha"; Kuebler, "Desegregation of the University of Maryland," 47.
59. Transcript of *Raymond A. Pearson, et al. v. Donald G. Murray*, Maryland Court of Appeals, January 1936.
60. Transcript of *Raymond A. Pearson, et al. v. Donald G. Murray*, Maryland Court of Appeals, January 1936.
61. Transcript of *Raymond A. Pearson, et al. v. Donald G. Murray*, Maryland Court of Appeals, January 1936.
62. Transcript of *Raymond A. Pearson, et al. v. Donald G. Murray*, Maryland Court of Appeals, January 1936.
63. Ware, "Setting the Stage for *Brown*," 650.
64. "Maryland U. Cannot Fire Two Law Students," *Baltimore Afro-American*, July 31, 1937.
65. "Approve Morgan College Sale to State," *Chicago Defender*, September 30, 1939; "138 Scholarships Awarded in Md.," *Baltimore Afro-American*, July 12, 1947; "189 Md. Students Given Scholarships Totaling $19,000," *Baltimore Afro-American*, September 6, 1947.
66. Kuebler, "Desegregation of the University of Maryland," 49; "Open U. of Md.: Court of Appeals Reverses City Judge," *Baltimore Afro-American*, April 22, 1950.
67. "State Board of Education for the Fiscal Year Ending June 30, 1936"; "A Service of Memory for Dr. Wadaran L. Kennedy," New Farmers of America Collection, Archives and Special Collections, F. D. Bluford Library, North Carolina A&T State University.
68. "Tuition Bill in Kentucky Gets Partial Okay," *Norfolk (VA) Journal and Guide*, February 15, 1936; Patterson, *Langston University*, 147.
69. "Early Court Action Seen in University Case," *Baltimore Afro-American*, September 28, 1935.
70. "NAACP Will Force Virginia Univ. to Drop Color Line," *Baltimore Afro-American*, September 28, 1935; "State Besieged by Educational Aid Requests: More Than Thirty Are Seeking Tuition and General Expenses," *Norfolk (VA) Journal and Guide*, August 1, 1936. "Information Desired from Certain States Relative to Graduate Instruction for Negroes—Virginia," September 1, 1938, special subject file, box 1, folder: Graduate Study for Negroes, Division of Negro Education, Department of Public Instruction, State Archives of North Carolina. Graduate courses began at Virginia State University during the summer of 1937. See "Preparation for Useful Lives Chief Aim of Colleges," *Norfolk (VA) Journal and Guide*, May 22, 1937.
71. "Dentists Urge Youths to Qualify under Tuition Bill," *Norfolk (VA) Journal and Guide*, April 25, 1936.

72. Letter from Alice Jackson to Walter White, August 25, 1936, Papers of the NAACP-A.
73. Letter from George Ferguson to Alice Jackson, September 15, 1936, Papers of the NAACP-A.
74. "30 Negroes Get Educational Aid under New Law," *Richmond (VA) Times-Dispatch*, July 30, 1936; "Tribute to Old North State," *Rocky Mount (NC) Evening Telegram*, August 25, 1956; "Address by Helen Edmonds," March 18, 1983, University Archives, Ohio State University.
75. "Information Desired from Certain States Relative to Graduate Instruction for Negroes—Virginia," September 1, 1938, special subject file, box 1, folder: Graduate Study for Negroes, Division of Negro Education, Department of Public Instruction, State Archives of North Carolina; Board of Visitors Minutes, June 11, 1938, University of Virginia Library; Williams, *Thurgood Marshall*, 195–96.
76. Pirkle, "Study of the State Scholarship Aid," 91; "Va. Ends Aid to H.U., Meharry Medic Students," *Baltimore Afro-American*, October 22, 1938. The actual amount during the 1936 fiscal year was $9,356.63. The following year, the amount was $18,017.87.
77. *K.N.E.A. Journal* 6, no. 1 (October–November 1935): 12, 28, Special Collections Research Center, University of Kentucky Libraries, Lexington.
78. *K.N.E.A. Journal* 7, no. 1 (October–November 1936): 24–25, Special Collections Research Center, University of Kentucky Libraries, Lexington.
79. Letter from Charles Hamilton Houston to K. Norman Diamon, April 14, 1936, folder 001509-002-0470, Papers of the NAACP-A.
80. Notable Kentucky African Americans Database, accessed March 20, 2021, https://nkaa.uky.edu/nkaa/items/show/1057.
81. K'Meyer, *Civil Rights in the Gateway to the South*, 10.
82. "KY 'Lynch' Jailer Is Ousted: Thrown Out by Governor after Quiz," *Chicago Defender*, March 10, 1934.
83. "Louisville Attorney Proposes New State Educational Law," *Louisville Leader*, April 8, 1933.
84. "Kentucky Negro Legislator Has Three Degrees," *Sun Democrat* (Paducah, KY), November 7, 1935.
85. "Contest Seat of Kentucky's First Race Assemblyman," *Chicago Defender*, January 11, 1936.
86. Wright, *History of Blacks in Kentucky*.
87. Wright, *History of Blacks in Kentucky*, 2:127.
88. For more on the Day Law, see Hardin, *Fifty Years of Segregation*, 1–16.
89. "Voters Put Anderson Back in Legislature: Returned to Assembly," *New York Amsterdam News*, November 18, 1939.
90. *Biennial Report of the Superintendent of Public Instruction of Kentucky*.
91. "Ky. Legislators Maps Program to Help Race," *Philadelphia Tribune*, February 27, 1936.
92. "Kentucky Legislature Passes Scholarship Bill," Papers of the NAACP-A.
93. Letter from Charles Hamilton Houston to Charles Anderson, February 18, 1936, Papers of the NAACP-A.

94. Letter from Charles Anderson to Charles Hamilton Houston, February 21, 1936, Papers of the NAACP-A.
95. Smith, *Black Educator in the Segregated South*, 49.
96. Untitled article, *Louisville (KY) Courier-Journal*, September 27, 1936; *Biennial Report of the Superintendent of Public Instruction of Kentucky*.
97. *Biennial Report of the Superintendent of Public Instruction of Kentucky*.
98. *Biennial Report of the Superintendent of Public Instruction of Kentucky*; Greene, *Holders of Doctorates among American Negroes*, 186; "Municipal College Aide Preparing Scrapbook," *Louisville (KY) Courier-Journal*, May 11, 1951.
99. Franke, "Injustice Sheltered," 49–50.
100. Jones, *Library Service to African Americans in Kentucky*; J. Howard Henderson, "Kentucky Test of Negro Student's Status Would Have High Barriers to Cross," *Louisville (KY) Courier-Journal*, December 18, 1938.
101. Undated newspaper clipping, Rufus B. Atwood Collection, Records and Special Collections Department, Paul G. Blazer Library, Kentucky State University, Frankfort.
102. Undated newspaper clipping, Rufus B. Atwood Collection; 1930 University of Minnesota Commencement Program (degree was conferred on July 27, 1929); Author correspondence with Columbia University Archives.
103. "Charles W. Anderson Seeks Re-election," *Louisville Leader*, July 8, 1939.
104. "Governor Chandley Aids Education Fund with $1600," *Atlanta Daily World*, February 7, 1939; "Gaines Ruling Encourages Newspaper Woman: Kentucky Has Similar Race Case," *Atlanta Daily World*, February 4, 1939.

Chapter Three

1. "A Race Financing Plan," *St. Louis Globe-Democrat*, January 1, 1928.
2. Sidney Redmond, interview by Richard Resh and Franklin Rother, July 6, 1970, Black Community Leaders Project, State Historical Society of Missouri, Columbia; Endersby and Horner, *Lloyd Gaines*, 18; Memorandum Regarding Educational Discrimination in the State of Missouri, Papers of the NAACP-A. The monetary amount spent on segregation scholarships was listed in the transcript of Lloyd Gaines's Missouri Supreme Court trial, Papers of the NAACP-A.
3. Mack, "Rethinking Civil Rights Lawyering," 81.
4. Letter to Charles Hamilton Houston from Sidney Redmond, August 17, 1935, Papers of the NAACP-A; Letter to Charles Hamilton Houston from Sidney Redmond, August 27, 1935, Papers of the NAACP-A.
5. Lloyd Gaines, biographical sketch, Papers of the NAACP-A.
6. Lloyd Gaines, biographical sketch, Papers of the NAACP-A; "Direct Examination of Lloyd L. Gaines," *State ex rel. Gaines v. Canada*, Circuit Court of Boone County, no. 34337, 1936, 12.
7. "Direct Examination of Lloyd L. Gaines." Sidney Redmond, a Black St. Louis attorney and the grandson of Hiram Revels, the first Black US senator.
8. "Direct Examination of Lloyd L. Gaines"; mileage and fare costs taken from transcript of Missouri Supreme Court case.

9. Endersby and Horner, *Lloyd Gaines*, 18, 68–69.
10. "Depositions from Respondents," *State ex rel. Gaines v. Canada*, Circuit Court of Boone County, no. 34337, 1936.
11. "Missouri University Raises New Defense: Attack Standing of Negro Applicant's Alma Mater," *Norfolk (VA) Journal and Guide*, June 6, 1936.
12. James, *Root and Branch*, 107–8.
13. Kluger, *Simple Justice*, 253.
14. Kluger, *Simple Justice*, 254.
15. Kluger, *Simple Justice*, 255.
16. Boone County Circuit Court Trial Transcript, Papers of the NAACP-A.
17. Boone County Circuit Court Trial Transcript, Papers of the NAACP-A.
18. Endersby and Horner, *Lloyd Gaines*, 85–86.
19. The Missouri Supreme Court had seven members and two divisions. One division of judges only heard criminal cases and the other division heard both criminal and civil cases. In complex or important cases, court sessions are heard en banc with all judges present. Letter from Charles Hamilton Houston to Osmond Fraenkel, July 14, 1938, Papers of the NAACP-A.
20. Letter from William B. Hogsett to Frederick A. Middlebush, January 5, 1938, Lloyd L. Gaines case, 1936–1939. University of Missouri, President's Office, Papers, 1892–1966 (C2582), folder 2597, State Historical Society of Missouri.
21. Western Union telegram to Black newspapers, October 10, 1938, Papers of the NAACP-A.
22. Letter from Frederick A. Middlebush to William B. Hogsett, October 12, 1938, Lloyd L. Gaines case, 1936–1939. University of Missouri, President's Office, Papers, 1892–1966 (C2582), folder 2597, State Historical Society of Missouri.
23. Letter from William B. Hogsett to Frederick A. Middlebush, October 13, 1938, Lloyd L. Gaines cases, 1936–1939. University of Missouri, President's Office, Papers, 1892–1966 (C2582), folder 2597, State Historical Society of Missouri.
24. Endersby and Horner, *Lloyd Gaines*, 90–92.
25. "U.S. Supreme Court Hears Arguments in University of Missouri Law School Case," *Black Dispatch*, November 19, 1938.
26. "U.S. Supreme Court Hears Arguments in University of Missouri Law School Case," *Black Dispatch*, November 19, 1938.
27. Endersby and Horner, *Lloyd Gaines*, 113.
28. There were only eight justices on the US Supreme Court during the Gaines case because Justice Benjamin Cardoza died during the 1938 summer. NAACP Press Release, November 11, 1938, Papers of the NAACP-A; James, *Root and Branch*, 116.
29. *Missouri ex rel. Gaines v. Canada*, 305 US 337 (1938).
30. *Missouri ex rel. Gaines v. Canada*, 305 US 337 (1938).
31. *Missouri ex rel. Gaines v. Canada*, 305 US 337 (1938).
32. The Taylor Act established the $200,000 fund to establish new departments at Lincoln as demand necessitated. R. C. Fisher, "St. Louis Gets Lincoln Uni. Law School," *Chicago Defender*, August 26, 1939; "Missouri vs. the Supreme Court," *Atlanta Daily World*, August 28, 1939.

33. "Missourians Picket Lincoln Law School," *Norfolk (VA) Journal and Guide*, September 30, 1939.
34. "Missourians Picket Lincoln Law School"; "Stalling in Missouri," *Pittsburgh Courier*, August 12, 1939; Endersby and Horner, *Lloyd Gaines*, 201.
35. "New Lincoln Law School Passed Its First 'Exam,'" *Baltimore Afro-American*, October 14, 1939.
36. Folder 001509-024-0921, Papers of the NAACP-A.
37. Letter from Lloyd Gaines to Callie Gaines, March 3, 1939, Gaines Family Correspondence, Lloyd L. Gaines Digital Collection, University of Missouri School of Law Library, Columbia.
38. Endersby and Horner, *Lloyd Gaines*, 212–14.
39. "LU Law School to Close Doors," *Pittsburgh Courier*, August 14, 1954.
40. "Seeks Admission to Tenn. U. Grad School," *Chicago Defender*, May 9, 1936; "Tenn. School Says It Isn't Affected by 14th Amendment," *Norfolk (VA) Journal and Guide*, May 23, 1936.
41. For more on William Redmond, see Tina Cahalan Jones's blog, "From Slaves to Soldiers and Beyond: Williamson County, Tennessee's African American History," usctwillcotn.blogspot.com.
42. Internal memorandum by the NAACP, "What Is the Aim of the Educational Campaign?," March 5, 1937, Papers of the NAACP-A.
43. "Seeks Admission to Tenn. U. Grad School."
44. Sarvis, "Leaders in the Court and Community."
45. "Supreme Court to Get Case of Tenn. Student," *Norfolk (VA) Journal and Guide*, April 24, 1937.
46. "Public Acts of the State of Tennessee"; "Bill Providing Negro School Aid Approved," *Philadelphia Tribune*, May 13, 1937.
47. "Tennesseans Seek Out of State Study Scholarships," *Norfolk (VA) Journal and Guide*, September 25, 1937.
48. "University of Tennessee Refuses to Enroll Six," *Atlanta Daily World*, October 1, 1939; "Rush Tennessee U. Campus; Demand Admittance," *Chicago Defender*, October 7, 1939; "Tenn. State to Get Graduate Schools," *Pittsburgh Courier*, June 13, 1942; "New Program Is Outlined for Tenn. State College," *Atlanta Daily World*, September 23, 1943; Lovett, *"Touch of Greatness,"* 97.
49. "Services Set for William Redmond, Jr., Who Fought UT's Segregation but Lost," *Tennessean* (Nashville), March 12, 1993.
50. Paul Oldham, "Obstacles in World Can't Hold Him Down," *Tennessean* (Nashville), April 3, 1991.
51. "Kansas Citians Hear Youth Who Won M.U. Case," *Call* (Kansas City, MO), March 3, 1939.
52. Loupe, "Storming and Defending the Color Barrier," 23; Devlin, *Girl Stands at the Door*, 10–11.
53. Letter from Silas Canada to Lucile Bluford, January 19, 1939, Papers of the NAACP-A; Letter from Lucile Bluford to Frederick Middlebush, February 2, 1939, Papers of the

NAACP-A; "NAACP Plans New Attempt to Pry Open Doors of Missouri U.," *Baltimore Afro-American*, October 14, 1939.
54. Lucile Bluford, interview by Fern Ingersoll, May 13, 1989, interview no. 1, transcript, Washington Press Club Foundation Women in Journalism Oral History Project Collection, Columbia Center for Oral History, Columbia University Libraries, New York; "Negroes Receiving Tuition from the State during 1935," Papers of the NAACP-A.
55. "Judge Reserves Decision in Bluford Case," Papers of the NAACP-A.
56. Letter from Charles Houston to Lucile Bluford, April 26, 1940, Papers of the NAACP-B.
57. Lucile Bluford, "Nothing Will Happen When Negro Student Is Admitted to M.U.," *Call* (Kansas City, MO), February 3, 1939.
58. Loupe, "Storming and Defending the Color Barrier," 25.
59. "Miss Bluford to Carry On Fight," *Baltimore Afro-American*, July 19, 1941; "University of Missouri," *Chicago Defender*, April 25, 1942; Loupe, "Storming and Defending the Color Barrier," 26.
60. "Drops Journalism Course to Keep Colored Out," *Philadelphia Tribune*, April 4, 1942; "Univ. Finds a Way to Oppose Lucile Bluford: Graduate Work in Journalism Is Discontinued," *Atlanta Daily World*, April 4, 1942; Lucile Bluford, interview by Fern Ingersoll, May 15, 1989, interview no. 2.
61. Letter from Harold Wilkie to Lucile Bluford, May 1, 1942, Papers of the NAACP-B.
62. Daniela Sirtori, "After Years of Struggle, African-American Journalist Lucile Bluford May Get Her Day in Missouri," *Columbia Missourian*, March 19, 2015. For more on Black waiting, see Fleming, *Black Patience*.
63. Donald Bradley, "Lucile Bluford Fought for Decades to Help African-American Community in Kansas City," *Kansas City Star*, October 17, 2016.
64. Kalme, "Racial Desegregation and Integration in American Education," 82–86.
65. Kalme, "Racial Desegregation and Integration in American Education," 148.
66. Frazier, *Negro in the United States*, 472–73.
67. Kalme, "Racial Desegregation and Integration."
68. Kalme, "Racial Desegregation and Integration," 130, 147, 149; Shetterly, *Hidden Figures*, 74–76; Rice, *Our Monongalia*, 130.
69. West Virginia Board of Education, *Record of Proceedings*, July 9, 1954. West Virginia desegregated all its colleges and universities in May 1954. The state agreed to continue giving segregation scholarships to Black residents enrolled in out-of-state institutions prior to May 17, 1954, when the Supreme Court outlawed racial segregation in public education. See West Virginia Board of Education, *Record of Proceedings*, July 21–22, 1954, and December 1–2, 1954; and Rice, *Our Monongalia*, 130–31.
70. Owens, "Financial Assistance for Negro College Students," 166–67.
71. West Virginia State Board of Education minutes, July 21–22, 1954.
72. "Governor Chandley Aids Education Fund with $1600," *Atlanta Daily World*, February 7, 1939.
73. Hardin, "Kentucky Is More or Less Civilized," 329, 333.
74. Smith, *Black Educator in the Segregated South*.

75. Letter from Charles Anderson to Charles Hamilton Houston, February 8, 1939; Letter from Thurgood Marshall to Charles Anderson, February 27, 1939; Letter from Thurgood Marshall to Charles Anderson, April 5, 1939, Papers of the NAACP-A.
76. "Negro Leaders as Enemies of the Race," *Louisville Leader*, February 11, 1939.
77. Wright, *History of Blacks in Kentucky*, 2:172–73.
78. McMillan, "Negro Higher Education," 14.
79. Letter to Walter White from Rufus B. Atwood, March 13, 1939, Papers of the NAACP-A.
80. Hardin, *Onward and Upward*, 39.
81. *Biennial Report of the Superintendent of Public Instruction of Kentucky*.
82. *Biennial Report of the Superintendent of Public Instruction of Kentucky*.
83. *Biennial Report of the Superintendent of Public Instruction of Kentucky*.
84. State Aid, box 1, folder 2, Rufus Atwood Collection.
85. State Aid, box 1, folder 4, Rufus Atwood Collection.
86. Walker, *Their Highest Potential*, 81.
87. Benjamin F. Shobe, interview by Constance Ard, October 18, 2013, Louie B. Nunn Center for Oral History, University of Kentucky Libraries.
88. Shobe, interview.
89. Shobe, interview.
90. "The Anderson-Mayer Law," *Louisville Leader*, January 15, 1944; "10 Reasons Why the Republican Party Has Built America," *Louisville Leader*, November 1, 1947.
91. Letter from Prentice Thomas to Thurgood Marshall, July 30, 1941, folder 001512-011-0687, Papers of the NAACP-B.
92. All correspondence taken from folder 001512-011-0687, Papers of the NAACP-B.
93. All correspondence taken from folder 001512-011-0687, Papers of the NAACP-B.
94. All correspondence taken from folder 001512-011-0687, Papers of the NAACP-B.
95. Folder 001512-011-0687, Papers of the NAACP-B.
96. Folder 001512-011-0871, Papers of the NAACP-B.
97. "U.K. Contends Negro's Suit Moot Case," January 29, 1943, folder 001512-011-0943, Papers of the NAACP-B.
98. Folder 001512-011-0943, Papers of the NAACP-B.
99. Folder 001512-011-0943, Papers of the NAACP-B.
100. Hardin, "Kentucky Is More or Less Civilized."
101. "Kentucky OKs Mixed School Plan," *Chicago Defender*, March 4, 1944.
102. "Kentucky OKs Mixed School Plan"; "Equalization of Educational Opportunities and Integration vs. Expansion of Present Negro Facilities," folder: Anderson-Atwood Educational Debate 1945–1946, Charles Anderson Papers, Archives and Special Collections, University of Louisville Libraries, University of Louisville, Louisville, KY.
103. Hardin, *Fifty Years of Segregation*, 74–75.
104. "The Anderson Bill Is More Practical," *Louisville (KY) Courier-Journal*, February 22, 1944.
105. Hardin, "Kentucky Is More or Less Civilized"; Letter from Charles Anderson to R. H. Jordan, March 19, 1944, Charles Anderson Papers, Archives and Special Collections, University of Louisville Libraries, University of Louisville, Louisville, KY.

Notes to Chapter Four

106. "Negro Applicant to Kentucky University Face [sic] Rejection," *Norfolk (VA) Journal and Guide*, April 10, 1948; Hardin, *Fifty Years of Segregation*, 94–95, 97.
107. Wesley, "Graduate Education for Negroes," 88–89.

Chapter Four

1. Kapur, *To Drink from the Well*, 120. We do not know how Pauli Murray would identify today and which pronouns Murray would use. As of 2024, "the Pauli Murray Center chooses to use he/him and they/them pronouns when discussing Pauli Murray's early life and she/her/hers when discussing Dr. Murray's later years. When discussing Pauli Murray in general, we interchangeably use she/her/hers, he/him/his, and they/them/theirs pronouns, or we refer to Pauli Murray by their name and title(s)." For more information, see www.paulimurraycenter.com/pronouns-pauli-murray.
2. Kapur, *To Drink from the Well*, 119, 135.
3. Gershenhorn, "Hocutt v. Wilson," 296.
4. Bay, *Traveling Black*, 82.
5. Letter from W. W. Pierson to Edwina Thomas, April 27, 1938, folder 521: Race and Ethnic Relations: Negroes: Admission to Graduate and Professional Schools, 1933–1941, Office of President of the University of North Carolina (System): Frank Porter Graham Records, 1932–1949, Records no. 40007, University Archives, Wilson Library, University of North Carolina at Chapel Hill.
6. Letter from Edwina Thomas to Frank Porter Graham, May 17, 1938, folder 521: Race and Ethnic Relations: Negroes: Admission to Graduate and Professional Schools, 1933–1941, Office of President of the University of North Carolina (System): Frank Porter Graham Records, 1932–1949, Records no. 40007, University Archives, Wilson Library, University of North Carolina at Chapel Hill.
7. Letter from Frank Porter Graham to Edwina Thomas, May 25, 1938, folder 521: Race and Ethnic Relations: Negroes: Admission to Graduate and Professional Schools, 1933–1941, Office of President of the University of North Carolina (System): Frank Porter Graham Records, 1932–1949, Records no. 40007, University Archives, Wilson Library, University of North Carolina at Chapel Hill.
8. Letter from Edwina Thomas to Frank Porter Graham, August 11, 1938, and letter from Frank Porter Graham to Edwina Thomas, August 15, 1938, folder 521: Race and Ethnic Relations: Negroes: Admission to Graduate and Professional Schools, 1933–1941, Office of President of the University of North Carolina (System): Frank Porter Graham Records, 1932–1949, Records no. 40007, University Archives, Wilson Library, University of North Carolina at Chapel Hill.
9. "Columbus Urban League Adds to Staff," *Cleveland Call and Post*, September 18, 1943.
10. Murray, *Song in a Weary Throat*, 108–10.
11. Murray, *Song in a Weary Throat*, 117–21.
12. Murray, *Song in a Weary Throat*, 124–25.
13. "Mrs. For [FDR] Favors Lynch Bill," *Norfolk (VA) Journal and Guide*, January 21, 1939.
14. "N.C. College Offers Graduate Study," May 6, 1939, *Norfolk (VA) Journal and Guide*; "Graduate and Professional Training of Negroes: North Carolina," special subject file,

Notes to Chapter Four

box 1, born in 1905, Instruction, State Archives of North Carolina; Clement, "Impact of the War."

15. "Graduate and Professional Training of Negroes: North Carolina," folder: Graduate Study for Negroes, box 1, special subject file, Division of Negro Education, Department of Public Instruction.
16. Letter from Nathan Newbold to Frank Porter Graham, January 4, 1939, and "Nine Recommendations of the Commission to Study Public Schools and Colleges for Negroes in North Carolina," folder 545, box 13, Office of President of the University of North Carolina System: Frank Porter Graham Records, 1932–1949.
17. Corbett, *Addresses, Letters, and Papers of Clyde Roark Hoey*, 38.
18. Louis Austin, "Graduate Courses for Negroes," *Carolina Times* (Durham, NC), January 14, 1939.
19. "Wilson Pharmacist Honored," *Wilson (NC) Times*, August 24, 1917; Twenty-Eighth Annual Catalog of the Leonard Medical School, Digital NC, accessed May 17, 2020, https://lib.digitalnc.org/record/32295?ln=en#?xywh=-1838%2C-158%2C5433%2C3152; "913 East Green Street," Black Wide-awake website, accessed May 17, 2020, https://afamwilsonnc.com/2017/03/20/913-east-green-street/.
20. "Has Doctor's Degree from Michigan Univ.," *Norfolk (VA) Journal and Guide*, July 26, 1952.
21. Woodland Ellroy Hall Fellowship Program, accessed June 1, 2020, www.ncat.edu/tgc/prospective-students/grad-funding/woodland-ellroy-hall-fellowship-progam.php.
22. "N.C. College to Have Graduate Courses," *Carolina Times* (Durham, NC), March 4, 1939; Kapur, *To Drink from the Well*, 149.
23. Houston, "Need for Negro Lawyers," 49–50.
24. "North Carolina Moves to Evade High Court Rule," *New York Amsterdam News*, September 16, 1939; "North Carolina Closes Jim Crow Law School," *Chicago Defender*, October 14, 1939.
25. White, "Some Tactics Which Should Supplement Resort to the Courts," 342.
26. "North Carolina Closes Jim Crow Law School," *Chicago Defender*, October 14, 1939.
27. Murray, *Song in a Weary Throat*, 126.
28. Murray, *Song in a Weary Throat*, 96, 99.
29. Murray, *Song in a Weary Throat*, 127.
30. Burns, "Graduate Education," 197.
31. Letter from James E. Shepard to N. C. Newbold, September 26, 1940, special subject file, box 1, folder: Graduate Study for Negroes, Division of Negro Education, Department of Public Instruction, State Archives of North Carolina.
32. Letter from Alphonso Elder to Harry McMullan, April 24, 1950, General Correspondence of the Director, box 18, folder: Out-of-State Aid, Division of Negro Education, Department of Public Instruction, State Archives of North Carolina.
33. Letter from James E. Shepard to Clyde A. Erwin, September 6, 1939, special subject file, box 1, folder: Graduate Study for Negroes, Division of Negro Education, Department of Public Instruction, State Archives of North Carolina; Letter from James E. Shepard to N. C. Newbold, September 26, 1940, special subject file, box 1, folder: Graduate

Study for Negroes, Division of Negro Education, Department of Public Instruction, State Archives of North Carolina.
34. "Prof. J. B. McRae Named L.U. Dean," *Philadelphia Tribune*, August 30, 1949; Letter from James E. Shepard to Clyde A. Erwin, September 22, 1939, special subject file, box 1, folder: Graduate Study for Negroes, Division of Negro Education, Department of Public Instruction, State Archives of North Carolina.
35. Letter from James E. Shepard to Clyde A. Erwin, September 22, 1939, special subject file, box 1, folder: Graduate Study for Negroes, Division of Negro Education, Department of Public Instruction, State Archives of North Carolina.
36. "Study Together for PhD Degree," *Norfolk (VA) Journal and Guide*, April 27, 1940.
37. Steward, "Time Not Ripe."
38. "Dr. Sarah Martin Pereira," *Charlotte (NC) Observer*, April 6, 1995.
39. "Charles R. Eason, Retired Physicist," *Coast Star* (Manasquan, NJ), September 20, 1984.
40. "Mrs. Gleason Is Awarded Doctorate," *Baltimore Afro-American*, April 6, 1940.
41. Letter from James E. Shepard to Clyde Erwin, August 19, 1940, special subject file, box 1, folder: Graduate Study for Negroes, Division of Negro Education, Department of Public Instruction, State Archives of North Carolina; Wedgeworth, *ALA World Encyclopedia*, 313.
42. Withers, *Balm in Gilead*, 58, 67.
43. Withers, *Balm in Gilead*, 58, 68–71.
44. Withers, *Balm in Gilead*, 373.
45. Withers, *Balm in Gilead*, 71.
46. Patricia Sullivan, "John Withers; Lieutenant Took In Refugees," *Boston Globe*, October 18, 2007; Letter from James E. Shepard to Clyde Erwin, September 6, 1939, special subject file, box 1, folder: Graduate Study for Negroes, Division of Negro Education, Department of Public Instruction, State Archives of North Carolina; "Bulletin of the University of Wisconsin," 1939–40. After one year of paying nonresident tuition, the University of Wisconsin allowed out-of-state graduate students who hailed from states that charged Wisconsin students less than $200 to pay $100 in tuition. Withers benefited from this policy in his second year.
47. Wilkerson, *Warmth of Other Suns*, 192.
48. Withers, *Balm in Gilead*, 73–74.
49. Withers, *Balm in Gilead*, 72–73, 75.
50. Withers, *Balm in Gilead*, 77.
51. Withers, *Balm in Gilead*, 76–77.
52. Withers *Balm in Gilead*, 78–82.
53. Withers, *Balm in Gilead*, 82–83.
54. Withers, *Balm in Gilead*, 83.
55. Withers, *Balm in Gilead*, 83.
56. Withers, *Balm in Gilead*, 285, 337.
57. "1941 Fall Semester," special subject files, box 1, folder: Graduate Study for Negroes, Division of Negro Education, Department of Public Instruction, State Archives of North Carolina.

58. Information gathered from correspondence with BUSM archivist A'Llyn Ettien, October 25, 2017.
59. Letter from Charles F. Carroll to Alphonso Elder, October 25, 1954, General Correspondence of the Director, box 22, folder: Charles F. Carroll Out-of-State Aid, Division of Negro Education, Department of Public Instruction, State Archives of North Carolina; "Three North Carolina Colleges to Seek Major Degrees," *Atlanta Daily World*, June 20, 1953.
60. Eaton, *Every Man Should Try*, 18, 201–2.
61. Eaton, *Every Man Should Try*; Board of Visitors Minutes, June 11, 1938, University of Virginia Library.
62. Eaton, *Every Man Should Try*.
63. "Record of Graduate Aid Awarded 1939–1940," special subject file, box 1, folder: Graduate Study of Negroes, Division of Negro Education, Department of Public Instruction, State Archives of North Carolina.
64. Letter from James E. Shepard to Elizabeth A. Young, February 5, 1940, folder 544, James Shepard Papers, University Archives, James E. Shepard Memorial Library, North Carolina Central University, Durham.
65. Letter from Charles A. Ray to Alfonso Elder, March 20, 1952; Letter from Charles Ray to Alfonso Elder, October 3, 1952; Letter from Charles F. Carrol to Alfonso Elder, October 27, 1952, General Correspondence of Director, box 20, folder: Charles Carroll, Out-of-State Aid, Division of Negro Education, Department of Public Instruction, State Archives of North Carolina.
66. "Dr. Charles A. Ray Dead at 72," *Baltimore Afro-American*, February 22, 1986.
67. Letter from Edgar W. Knight to Chairman and Board of Trustees at North Carolina College, September 15, 1950, General Correspondence of the Director, box 19, folder: Alfonso Elder, Division of Negro Education, Department of Public Instruction, State Archives of North Carolina.
68. Frances L. Murphy II, interview by Larry Crowe, June 3, 2003, interview A2003.117, HistoryMakers Digital Archive.
69. Letter from Charles Carroll to Alfonso Elder, April 21, 1953, General Correspondence of the Director, box 20, folder: Charles Carroll, Out-of-State Aid, Division of Negro Education, Department of Public Instruction, State Archives of North Carolina.
70. "North Carolina College Enjoys University Status," *Norfolk (VA) Journal and Guide*, June 21, 1969; Gershenhorn, "Stalling Integration, 175."
71. Correspondence between Roger D. Russell and North Carolina College officials, May–September 1953, General Correspondence of the Director, box 20, folder: Out-of-State Aid, Division of Negro Education, Department of Public Instruction, State Archives of North Carolina; "Gets Degree," *Carolina Times* (Durham, NC), February 22, 1958.
72. Evers with Peters, *For Us, the Living*, 47–49. Quote comes from Fairclough, "Black College Presidents," 72.
73. Waite and Crocco, "Fighting Injustice through Education."
74. Letter from Alphonso Elder to Members of the Advisory Budget Commission, August 14, 1950, special subject file, box 18, folder: Out-of-State Aid, Division of Negro Education, Department of Public Instruction, State Archives of North Carolina.

Notes to Chapter Four

75. "Columbia Univ. Is Mecca for 18,000 Teachers," *Chicago Defender*, August 2, 1947.
76. Weiler, "Mabel Carney at Teachers College."
77. Anderson, "Toward a History and Bibliography of the Afro-American Doctorate"; "254 Tan Graduates Get M.A. Degrees in New York University Class of 9,158," *Baltimore Afro-American*, June 24, 1950.
78. Walker, *Their Highest Potential*, 146–47.
79. Annemarie Mountz, "Her Heart Never Left Penn State," *Penn State News* (State College, PA), June 2, 2020, https://news.psu.edu/story/621702/2020/06/02/her-heart-never-left-penn-state?utm_source=newswire&utm_medium=email&utm_term=622476_HTML&utm_content=06-08-2020-07-58&utm_campaign=Diversity%20Headlines; Walker, *Their Highest Potential*.
80. Author personal correspondence with Vanessa Siddle Walker, June 2020 and December 2023.
81. "West Charlotte Teaching 'Legend' Mertye Rice," *Charlotte (NC) Observer*, April 24, 1986; Letter from Charles F. Carroll to Alfonso Elder, February 15, 1955, General Correspondence of the Director, box 22, folder: Charles F. Carroll Out-of-State Aid, Division of Negro Education, Department of Public Instruction, State Archives of North Carolina.
82. Frazier, *Negro in the United States*, 472.
83. "White University Professors Will Teach Law Students in North Carolina College," *Pittsburgh Courier*, April 20, 1940; Jeffries, "History of Struggle."
84. "22 Law Students at N.C. College," *Norfolk (VA) Journal and Guide*, October 19, 1946.
85. "N.C. Negro Law School Graded Sub-standard," *Asheville (NC) Citizen-Times*, April 17, 1948.
86. "N.C.C. Gets $35,000 Library," *Norfolk (VA) Journal and Guide*, October 7, 1944; Burns, "Graduate Education," 209–10; A. M. Rivera, "N.C. Whites Fighting to Keep Jim Crow Law School," *Pittsburgh Courier*, September 3, 1949; "Separate School Is Unequal Judge Morris A. Sopher Says," *Baltimore Afro-American*, April 7, 1949.
87. Sanders, "First March on Raleigh."
88. "Procedure for Administering Out-of-State Aid through North Carolina College at Durham," April 13, 1950, General Correspondence of the Director, box 18, folder: Out-of-State Aid, Division of Negro Education, Department of Public Instruction.
89. Letter from Robert C. Leathers to Alphonso Elder, February 11, 1954, General Correspondence of the Director, box 20, folder: Charles Carroll, Out-of-State Aid, Division of Negro Education, Department of Public Instruction, State Archives of North Carolina.
90. "Procedure for Administering Out-of-State Aid through North Carolina College at Durham," April 13, 1950, General Correspondence of the Director, box 18, folder: Out-of-State Aid, Division of Negro Education, Department of Public Instruction.
91. A Bill to Be Entitled an Act to Amend G.S. 116–100 Relating to Graduate and Professional Studies for Negro Students, ratified March 4, 1953, General Correspondence of the Director, box 18, folder: Out-of-State Aid, Division of Negro Education, Department of Public Instruction.
92. Letter from Alfonso Elder to E. W. Knight, May 31, 1950, General Correspondence

of the Director, box 20, folder: Charles Carroll, Out-of-State Aid, Division of Negro Education, Department of Public Instruction, State Archives of North Carolina.
93. Letter from Alfonso Elder to E. W. Knight, May 31, 1950, General Correspondence of the Director, box 20, folder: Charles Carroll, Out-of-State Aid, Division of Negro Education, Department of Public Instruction, State Archives of North Carolina.
94. McMillan, *Negro Higher Education*, 290.
95. "Table 1: Areas of Major Concentration of Eighty-Nine Students Granted Out-of-State Aid," September 10, 1954, special subject file, box 18, folder: Out-of-State Aid, Division of Negro Education, Department of Public Instruction.

Chapter Five

1. Charles H. Houston, "Don't Shout Too Soon," *The Crisis* (New York), March 1936, 79.
2. Dailey, Gilmore, and Simon, *Jumpin' Jim Crow*, 5.
3. Anderson, "Race, Meritocracy, and the American Academy," 154; Greene, *Holders of Doctorates among American Negroes*, 55. Charles Reason was the first Black college professor in the United States. He taught at New York Central College. Julien H. Lewis is often recognized as the first African American to hold a faculty position at a historically white university. He rose from instructor to associate professor in the University of Chicago's Sprague Memorial Institute but only had a nominal appointment in the university's pathology department. Neither Reason nor Lewis was hired in a permanent faculty position.
4. Dalton, "Music Department, 58–61; Pirkle, "Study of the State Scholarship Aid"; "Ala. Grants Out-of-State College Funds for Negroes," *Chicago Defender*, October 20, 1945; "Watson Favors Negro Attending White Colleges," *Tallahassee (FL) Democrat*, October 16, 1945; "Retirement Plan Voted," *Shreveport (LA) Journal*, July 2, 1946; McMillan, *Negro Higher Education*, 286–87; "Leadership Still Opposed to Regional School Plan," *Atlanta Daily World*, October 24, 1947.
5. Ladson-Billings, "Landing on the Wrong Note," 3.
6. "Seeks Post-graduate Funds for Georgians," *Pittsburgh Courier*, December 2, 1944.
7. "Speaking Out: From the New South 'Differential Scholarships,'" *Chicago Defender*, February 1, 1947; "Out of State Scholarships," *Atlanta Daily World*, October 25, 1946.
8. "Leadership Still Opposed to Regional School Plan."
9. Annie Brown Kennedy, interview by Joseph Mosnier, December 6, 1995, interview A-0400, Southern Oral History Program Collection no. 4007, Southern Historical Collection, Wilson Library, University of North Carolina at Chapel Hill.
10. Kennedy, interview.
11. Farris, *Through It All*, 43.
12. Farris, *Through It All*, 44–47.
13. Farris, *Through It All*, 47–48.
14. Farris, *Through It All*, 48–49; Christine King Farris, interview by Julieanna L. Richardson, July 11, 2010, interview A2010.074, session 1, tape 3, story 6, HistoryMakers Digital Archive.

15. Serena Williams (daughter of Willarena Lamar), telephone interview by author, February 11, 2021.
16. Williams, interview; letter from Willarena Lamar to her children (copy in author's possession), February 26, 1992.
17. Williams, interview; letter from Lamar to her children.
18. Williams, interview; letter from Lamar to her children.
19. Louis Sullivan, telephone interview by author, December 28, 2021.
20. Sullivan, interview.
21. Sullivan, interview.
22. Sullivan, interview.
23. Sullivan, interview.
24. Gasman with Sullivan, *Morehouse Mystique*.
25. Sullivan, interview.
26. Carrie P. Meek, interview by Julieanna L. Richardson, June 19, 2001, interview A2001.049, session 1, tape 2, story 4, HistoryMakers Digital Archive.
27. "Negro Students Get Aid Despite Protest," *Atlanta Daily World*, October 27, 1945.
28. Meek, interview, session 1, tape 3, story 1.
29. Meek, interview, session 1, tape 3, story 1.
30. "Negroes to Fight Exclusion from State University," *Fort Lauderdale (FL) News*, May 14, 1949.
31. "Equal Facilities Cost Described," *Tampa (FT) Daily Times*, May 13, 1949.
32. "Equal Facilities Cost Described."
33. "State Board of Control Rules on Negro Tuition," *Miami (FL) News*, July 20, 1951.
34. Matthew J. Perry, interview by Joseph Mosnier, June 7, 2011, Civil Rights History Project, Library of Congress Archive of Folk Culture, Washington, DC. The Colored Normal, Industrial, Agricultural and Mechanical College of South Carolina School of Law opened after a Black student, John Howard Wrighten, applied to the University of South Carolina School of Law and was denied admission based on race. He sued and a district judge ordered South Carolina to admit Wrighten to USC's law school or build a law school that he could attend.
35. Clark, *Schoolhouse Door*, 11–12; "All But Two Administration Bills Offered," *Dothan (AL) Eagle*, May 6, 1945; "Ala. Grants Out-of-State College Funds for Negroes"; "Out of State Aid Offered by Alabama," *Atlanta Daily World*, December 13, 1945; "Negroes Ask College Aid," *Decatur (AL) Daily*, December 9, 1945; Trenholm, "Some Background and Status of Higher Education" Tuskegee Institute/University is an independent and state-related educational institution. Auburn University's name was Alabama Polytechnic Institute until 1960, although it was popularly called Auburn for many years before the official name change.
36. Trenholm, "Some Background and Status of Higher Education"; "Negroes to Get Only 12 Percent Ala. School Fund," *Alabama Citizen* (Tuscaloosa), February 5, 1949; "State University for Ala. Negroes Recommended," *Alabama Citizen* (Tuscaloosa), April 30, 1949.
37. Andersen and Thomas, *Living Art*.
38. Andersen and Thomas, *Living Art*.

Notes to Chapter Five

39. Letter from William F. Adams to Paul R. Jones, February 4, 1949, in author's possession; "Paul Jones," accessed March 20, 2021, https://paulrjones.museums.ua.edu/paul-jones.
40. Evers with Peters, *For Us, the Living*, 98–102, 115. Medgar Evers was the second African American to apply to the University of Mississippi Law School. The first, Charles Dubra, did so in 1953 and was not admitted on the grounds that his undergraduate institution, Claflin, was not accredited although Dubra had a master's degree from Boston University.
41. Gwendolyn DuBose Rogers, interview by Larry Crowe, December 15, 2003, interview A2003.299, session 1, tape 2, story 7, HistoryMakers Digital Archive.
42. Rogers, interview, session 1, tape 2, story 7.
43. Rogers, interview, session 1, tape 2, story 8.
44. Thomas N. Todd, interview by Larry Crowe, June 6, 2002, interview A2002.094, session 1, tape 1, note 44, HistoryMakers Digital Archive.
45. Todd, interview, session 1, tape 1, story 12.
46. Todd, interview, session 1, tape 1, story 13.
47. Todd, interview, session 1, tape 2, story 6.
48. "Law School to Southern U.," *Chicago Defender*, September 6, 1947.
49. Todd, interview, session 1, tape 2, stories 6 and 7.
50. Todd, interview, session 1, tape 2, story 7.
51. "The Trials, Tribulations, and Tenacity of U.W. Clemon '68," *Columbia Law School News*, August 17, 2022, www.law.columbia.edu/news/archive/trials-tribulations-and-tenacity-judge-uw-clemon-68.
52. "Trials, Tribulations, and Tenacity."
53. "Alabama Law School Grads Seek Licenses," *New York Amsterdam News*, October 15, 1949. Other recipients of segregation scholarships from Alabama to study law included Philander Butler, Manley E. Banks, Henry C. Moss, Clarence E. Moses, and Henry L. Person.
54. "State Bar Assn. Refuses to Licence Negro Lawyers," *Alabama Citizen* (Tuscaloosa), December 17, 1949.
55. "They Did Not Apply," *Alabama Citizen* (Tuscaloosa), July 15, 1950.
56. Bruce Carver Boynton, interview by Jared Morris, May 18, 2018, transcript, Oral History Project of the United States District Court Middle District of Alabama.
57. Boynton, interview; "Bruce Boynton, Who Inspired 1961 Freedom Rides, Dies at 83," *Brownsville (TX) Herald*, November 26, 2020.
58. "Bruce Boynton, Who Inspired 1961 Freedom Rides"; Bay, *Traveling Black*, 269. For more on the Freedom Rides, see Arsenault, *Freedom Riders*.
59. Memorandum from Thurgood Marshall to State Conferences of Branches, June 29, 1945, folder 001512-001-0595, Papers of the NAACP-B.
60. "Discrimination and Segregation at the University of Texas," folder 001512-015-0001, Papers of the NAACP-B.
61. The Oklahoma territory passed a school segregation law in 1897 before statehood in 1907. Wattley, *Step toward "Brown,"* 8–14.
62. For more on the history of Langston University, see Patterson, *Langston University*.

63. Edith Johnson, "Let Us Give Negroes Hope," *Daily Oklahoman* (Oklahoma City), March 25, 1947.
64. Wattley, *Step toward "Brown,"* 176.
65. Johnson, "Let Us Give Negroes Hope."
66. "Equality Sought in Negro Attempt at OU Enrollment," *Oklahoma Daily* (Norman), November 6, 1945.
67. University of Oklahoma Board of Regents Minutes, November 7, 1945, https://digital.libraries.ou.edu/regents/minutes/1945_11_07.pdf.
68. Fisher, *Matter of Black and White*, 3–13, 75–76.
69. Fisher, *Matter of Black and White*.
70. Fisher, *Matter of Black and White*, 77–78.
71. Fisher, *Matter of Black and White*; Wattley, *Step toward "Brown."*
72. Fisher, *Matter of Black and White*.
73. Fisher, *Matter of Black and White*, 82–83.
74. Fisher, *Matter of Black and White*, 83–85.
75. Cross, *Blacks in White Colleges*, 37–39.
76. Fisher, *Matter of Black and White*, 85.
77. Letter from Thurgood Marshall to Amos T. Hall, January 24, 1946, "Discrimination and Segregation at the University of Oklahoma," folder 001512-013-0340, Papers of the NAACP-B.
78. Wattley, *Step toward "Brown,"* 91–92; Cross, *Blacks in White Colleges*, 40.
79. "Regents Speed Study for Negro School of Law," *Daily Oklahoman* (Oklahoma City), May 9, 1946, 16.
80. "Oklahoma Court Crowd Colorful and Intent," *Norfolk (VA) Journal and Guide*, July 20, 1946.
81. Fisher, *Matter of Black and White*, 101–2.
82. Fisher, *Matter of Black and White*.
83. Fisher, *Matter of Black and White*, 103–4.
84. Wattley, *Step toward "Brown,"* 107–8; Cross, *Blacks in White Colleges*, 44–45.
85. Wattley, *Step toward "Brown,"* 107–8; Cross, *Blacks in White Colleges*, 44–45.
86. Fisher, *Matter of Black and White*, 119–21.
87. Wattley, *Step toward "Brown,"* 122–23; Cross, *Black in White Colleges*, 46–47.
88. "Poor Langston! Buildings So Cold, School Let Out Early," *Black Dispatch*, December 20, 1947.
89. Wattley, *Step toward "Brown,"* 130–38.
90. Fisher, *Matter of Black and White*, 128–29, 138.
91. Wattley, *Step toward "Brown,"* 193–94.
92. Arkansas Legislative Act 345 of 1943; Nichols, "Breaking the Color Barrier"; Kilpatrick, "Desegregating the University of Arkansas School of Law."
93. Nichols, "Breaking the Color Barrier"; Kilpatrick, "Desegregating the University of Arkansas School of Law."
94. Gamble, "No Struggle, No Fight."
95. Edith Irby Jones, interview by Denise Gines, March 10, 2008, interview A2008.041, session 1, tape 4, story 1, HistoryMakers Digital Archive.

96. Jones, interview.
97. Cross, *Blacks in White Colleges*, 91.
98. "Six Negroes Apply at OU; Segregation Law Faces Showdown," *Daily Oklahoman* (Oklahoma City), January 29, 1948; Cross, *Blacks in White Colleges*, 91.
99. Cross, *Blacks in White Colleges*, 93–95.
100. "Governor Signs Negro School Law," *Okmulgee (OK) Daily Times*, June 11, 1949.
101. Cross, *Backs in White Colleges*, 116–17, 125–26; Wallenstein, "Black Southerners and Non-Black Universities," 129.
102. "Langston Law School Closes," *Shawnee (OK) News-Star*, July 1, 1949 Cross, *Blacks in White Colleges*, 113–14.
103. Fisher, *Matter of Black and White*, 145–48.
104. Fisher, *Matter of Black and White*, 152; Paul English, "New OU Regent Appointment Ends 45-year Cycle," *Daily Oklahoman* (Oklahoma City), April 28, 1992.
105. Lavergne, *Before "Brown,"* 127.
106. Lavergne, *Before "Brown,"* 65–69, 83–85.
107. "Texas To Provide Professional Training for Negro Graduates," *Corpus Christi (TX) Caller Times*, June 17, 1939; Lorraine Barnes, "Houston Considered as Site for New Negro Law School," *Austin American-Statesman*, June 18, 1946.
108. Lorraine Barnes, "Judge Extends Deadline for Negro Law School," *Austin American-Statesman*, December 17, 1946.
109. The quote was in reference to the makeshift law school created at South Carolina A&M College (present-day South Carolina State University), but I found it applicable to Prairie View Law School. Taken from McMillan, *Negro Higher Education*, 213. Lavergne, *Before "Brown,"* 142.
110. "Negro Law School Is Ready but No Students in Sight," *Waco (TX) News Tribune*, March 5, 1947; Pitre, *Born to Serve*; "Sweatt Appeal Delayed," *Austin American-Statesman*, March 5, 1947; "Law School for Negroes to Open in Week," *Fort Worth (TX) Star-Telegram*, March 2, 1947.
111. "Negro Woman 3rd to Enroll at Law School in Houston," *Fort Worth (TX) Star-Telegram*, September 27, 1947.
112. Lavergne, *Before "Brown,"* 220.
113. Lavergne, *Before "Brown,"* 241–42.
114. *Sweatt v. Painter*, 339 US 629 (1950).
115. *Sweatt v. Painter*, 339 US 629 (1950).
116. "8 Negroes Now Enrolled at University of Texas," *Fort-Worth Star Telegram*, July 21, 1950; Holland, *Texas Book*.
117. Mercer Bailey, "Reaction to Supreme Court Ruling," *Petaluma (CA) Argus-Courier*, June 6, 1950.
118. Pitre, *In Struggle against Jim Crow*, 103.
119. John N. Popham, "Medical College Offered to South," *New York Times*, January 19, 1948; "Meharry Trustees Offer School to Dixie Governors," *Philadelphia Tribune*, January 20, 1948; "$8,000,000 Meharry Plant Offered to South," *Norfolk (VA) Journal and Guide*, January 24, 1948.
120. Summerville, *Educating Black Doctors*.

121. Summerville, *Educating Black Doctors*.
122. Givens, "Our Medical Colleges," 170.
123. Summerville, *Educating Black Doctors*, 97.
124. "Tenn. A&I Now a 'Real' University," *Chicago Defender*, March 20, 1943; "Negroes of State Get College Plan," *Chattanooga (TN) Daily Times*, March 4, 1943.
125. "Graduate Courses Offered at A&I," *Tennessean* (Nashville), May 1, 1942.
126. "Negroes of State Get College Plan."
127. "Virginia Sets a Precedent," *Richmond (VA) Times-Dispatch*, April 24, 1944; "Governor Would Help Negro Students," *Richmond (VA) Times-Dispatch*, January 21, 1945.
128. "Virginia Sets a Precedent"; Sugg and Jones, *Southern Regional Education Board*, 9.
129. "Conference of 3 Governors on Negro Education Halted," *Montgomery (AL) Advertiser*, April 13, 1945; "Sparks Proposes End to Poll Tax Accumulation," *Dothan (AL) Eagle*, May 1, 1945.
130. "House Group OK's Regional Plan," *Norfolk (VA) Journal and Guide*, March 13, 1948; "Negroes Testify against Proposed Regional Plan," *Atlanta Daily World*, March 16, 1948.
131. "Dr. Foster, State College Head, Condemns Regional School Idea," *Norfolk (VA) Journal and Guide*, December 22, 1945.
132. "Evading the Costs of Segregation," *Pittsburgh Courier*, January 31, 1948.
133. "Sen. Morse to Talk S.R. 191 to Death: Bulletin," *Pittsburgh Courier*, May 15, 1948.
134. The Senate vote was 38 to 37. "Urge New President for Meharry College; Dixie Regional School Pack Loses, 38–37," *Pittsburgh Courier*, May 22, 1948.
135. Sugg and Jones, *Southern Regional Education Board*, 19.
136. Letter to G. H. Ferguson from F. D. Bluford, April 15, 1950, box 18, folder: Out-of-State Aid, General Correspondence of Director, Division of Negro Education, Department of Public Instruction, State Archives of North Carolina.
137. Sugg and Jones, *Southern Regional Education Board*, 25–26.
138. "Atlanta U. to Participate in Regional Education Program," folder 001588-001-0300, Claude A. Barnett Papers: The Associated Negro Press, 1918–1967, part 3: Subject Files on Black Americans, 1918–1967, series B: Colleges and Universities, 1918–1966.
139. "Atlanta U. to Participate in Regional Education Program." The breakdown of states represented at the AU School of Social Work in 1951 were Alabama (5), Arkansas (5), Florida (5), Louisiana (3), Mississippi (5), North Carolina (10), South Carolina (5), Tennessee (5), and Virginia (10).
140. Suggs and Jones, *Southern Regional Education Board*, 45.
141. Laura Hager, "Remembering Esther McCready, a Nursing Pioneer," *UMB News* (Baltimore), September 4, 2020, www.umaryland.edu/news/archived-news/september-2020/remembering-esther-mccready-a-nursing-pioneer.php.

Conclusion

1. Harvey Beech, interview by Anita Foye, September 25, 1996, interview J-0075, Southern Oral History Program Collection no. 4007, Southern Historical Collection, Wilson Library, University of North Carolina at Chapel Hill; Nixon, "Integration of

UNC–Chapel Hill." For more on the desegregation of historically white colleges and universities in the South, see Pratt, *We Shall Not Be Moved*; Wallenstein, *Higher Education and the Civil Rights Movement*; Kean, *Desegregating Private Higher Education in the South*; and Kapur, *To Drink from the Well*.

2. "Ask Court to Order Admission of Negro," *Cleveland Call and Post*, July 21, 1951; "Negro Denied Study at UNC," *News and Observer* (Raleigh, NC), June 13, 1951; Kapur, *To Drink from the Well*, 243–45.

3. "Rejected Coed Files U.S. Suit," *Chicago Defender*, July 21, 1951; Kapur, *To Drink from the Well*, 245.

4. Nicholas Graham, "Remembering Gwendolyn Harrison, the First African American Woman to Attend UNC," *For the Record* (Spring City, PA), April 17, 2017, https://blogs.lib.unc.edu/uarms/2017/04/17/remembering-gwendolyn-harrison-the-first-african-american-woman-to-attend-unc/.

5. "The Life of Walter Ridley," Ridley Scholarship Program, accessed February 25, 2023, https://aig.alumni.virginia.edu/ridley/about/history/life-walter-n-ridley/.

6. "The Life of Walter Ridley"; Apprey and Poe, *Key to the Door*, 19.

7. Carter Jewell, "Request to Va. Univ. Ignored," *Atlanta Daily World*, July 12, 1950; "File Suit to End Virginia Univ. Jimcrow," *Cleveland Call and Post*, August 19, 1950; P. Bernard Young Jr., "Univ. of VA Ordered to Admit Swanson," *Norfolk (VA) Journal and Guide*, September 9, 1950.

8. Apprey and Poe, *Key to the Door*, 18.

9. Michael Wines, "A Real Missouri 'Concerned Student 1950' Speaks, at Age 89," *New York Times*, November 10, 2015.

10. Early, *Quiet Trailblazer*.

11. Early, *Quiet Trailblazer*.

12. Lambert, "Black Students," 58–59.

13. Tom Brennan, "Reuben Anderson Sworn In as State's First Black Justice," *Clarion-Ledger* (Jackson, MS), January 17, 1985; "The Mission Continues: Building upon the Legacy," University of Mississippi, 2022, https://60years.olemiss.edu.

14. "Louisville Univ. to Admit Negroes, Close Municipal," *Atlanta Daily World*, April 26, 1950.

15. "3 Threaten Court Action over Loss of College Jobs," *Louisville (KY) Courier-Journal*, June 15, 1951.

16. "U.L. Rejects 3 Professors' Pay Requests," *Louisville (KY) Courier-Journal*, June 21, 1951.

17. Anderson, "Race, Meritocracy, and the American Academy." For more on how professional organizations and their journals excluded Black scholars, see Morris, *Scholar Denied*.

18. Fenwick, *Jim Crow's Pink Slip*, xvi–xvii, 16.

19. Lee Henden, "Seeking Restoration," *Times and Democrat* (Orangeburg, SC), April 3, 2006. The University of South Carolina School of Law admitted Black students during Reconstruction.

20. "Regional Contract Program," Southern Regional Education Board, accessed November 25, 2023, www.sreb.org/regional-contract-program.

21. Angela Davis, "UNC, HEW Officials Discuss Bias Plan," *News and Observer* (Raleigh, NC), April 12, 1974; Cathy Steele Roche, "HEW Objections May Block Vet School Plans," *Durham (NC) Sun*, April 15, 1975.
22. "UNC President Defends Vet School Construction," *Robesonian* (Lumberton, NC), August 20, 1975.
23. Eric Ferreri, "Plan Would Help Train More Pharmacists," *Chapel Hill (NC) Herald*, March 17, 2002; Crystal Sanders, "A School Shortchanged," *News and Observer* (Raleigh, NC), June 1, 2014.
24. Patrice Sawyer, "Ayers: It's Over," *Clarion-Ledger* (Jackson, MS), January 19, 2002; "Ayers Accountability Manual," September 2021, www.mississippi.edu/ayers/downloads/2021_ayers_manual.pdf.
25. Danielle Douglass-Gabriel and Ovetta Wiggins, "Hogan Signs Off on $577 Million for Maryland's Historically Black Colleges and Universities," *Washington Post*, March 24, 2021.
26. Sara Weissman, "A Debt Long Overdue," *Inside HigherEd* (Washington, DC), April 26, 2021.
27. Ariana Figueroa, "Missouri Has Reportedly Underfunded Lincoln University in Jefferson City by $361 Million," *Georgia Recorder* (Atlanta), September 18, 2023.
28. Figueroa, "Missouri Has Reportedly Underfunded Lincoln."
29. Titus, *Brown's Battleground*; Green, *Something Must Be Done*; Ford, Johnson, and Partelow, "Racist Origins of Private School Vouchers."
30. "Private Schools: The Last Refuge," *Time* (New York), November 14, 1969; Hershkoff and Cohen, "School Choice and the Lessons of Choctaw County," 2.

BIBLIOGRAPHY

Primary Sources

MANUSCRIPT AND ARCHIVAL COLLECTIONS
Ann Arbor, Michigan
    Bentley Historical Library
        African American Student Project
        Michiganensian
Chapel Hill, North Carolina
    University of North Carolina at Chapel Hill, Wilson Library, University Archives
        Office of President of the University of North Carolina (System)
        Office of the Vice President for Finance
        Frank Porter Graham Papers
Charlottesville, Virginia
    University of Virginia, Albert and Shirley Small Special Collections Library, University of Virginia Archives
        Board of Visitors Minutes
Columbia, Missouri
    State Historical Society of Missouri
        Black Community Leaders Project
            Sidney Redmond
    University of Missouri
        President's Office
    University of Missouri School of Law Library
        Lloyd L. Gaines Digital Collection
Columbus, Ohio
    Ohio State University, University Libraries, University Archives
        Office of the President
            Commencement Addresses
Durham, North Carolina
    North Carolina Central University, James E. Shepard Memorial Library, University Archives
        James E. Shepard Papers
Frankfort, Kentucky
    Kentucky State University, Paul G. Blazer Library
        Records and Special Collections Department
            Rufus Atwood Collection

Greensboro, North Carolina
    North Carolina Agricultural and Technical State University, F. D. Bluford Library
        Archives and Special Collections
            New Farmers of America Collection
Jefferson City, Missouri
    Lincoln University, Inman E. Page Library
        Archives and Special Collections
            Alumni Vertical Files
            LU Yearbooks
    Missouri State Archives
        Official Manual of the State of Missouri—The Blue Book Collection
        Supreme Court of the State of Missouri
Lawrence, Kansas
    University of Kansas, Kenneth Spencer Research Library, University Archives
        Annual Catalogues
        Jayhawker Yearbooks
        Records of the University of Kansas Chancellor's Office
Lexington, Kentucky
    University of Kentucky, University of Kentucky Libraries
        Louis B. Nunn Center for Oral History
            Benjamin F. Shobe Papers
            Jewel Prestage Papers
        Special Collections Research Center
            Kentucky Negro Educational Association Journal
Louisville, Kentucky
    University of Louisville, University of Louisville Libraries
        Archives and Special Collections
            Charles Anderson Papers
Montgomery, Alabama
    Alabama Department of Archives and History
        Annual Reports of the State Superintendent of Education
        House and Senate Journals of Alabama
Raleigh, North Carolina
    State Archives of North Carolina
        Division of Negro Education, Department of Public Instruction
Washington, DC
    Library of Congress
        National Association for the Advancement of Colored People Papers

PUBLISHED MEMOIRS

Cross, George Lynn. *Blacks in White Colleges: Oklahoma's Landmark Cases*. Norman: University of Oklahoma Press, 1975.

Eaton, Hubert A. *Every Man Should Try*. Wilmington, NC: Bonaparte, 1984.

Evers, Myrlie B. with William Peters. *For Us, the Living*. Garden City, NY: Doubleday, 1967.
Farris, Christine King. *Through It All: Reflections on My Life, My Family, and My Faith*. New York: Atria, 2009.
Fisher, Ada Lois Sipuel. *A Matter of Black and White: The Autobiography of Ada Lois Sipuel Fisher*. Norman: University of Oklahoma Press, 1996.
Gray, Fred D. *Bus Ride to Justice: The Life and Works of Fred D. Gray*. Montgomery, AL: New South, 2021.

ORAL INTERVIEWS

Beech, Harvey. Interview by Anita Foye. September 25, 1996. Interview J-0075, Southern Oral History Program Collection no. 4007, Southern Historical Collection, Wilson Library, University of North Carolina at Chapel Hill.
Bluford, Lucile. Interview by Fern Ingersoll. May 13 and 15, 1989. Interview no. 1 and no. 2. Transcript. Washington Press Club Foundation Women in Journalism Oral History Project Collection, Columbia Center for Oral History, Columbia University Libraries, New York.
Boynton, Bruce Carver. Interview by Jared Morris. May 18, 2018. Transcript. Oral History Project of the United States District Court, Middle District of Alabama.
Farris, Christine King. Interview by Julieanna L. Richardson. July 11, 2010. Interview A2010.074, HistoryMakers Digital Archive.
Jones, Edith Irby. Interview by Denise Gines. March 10, 2008. Interview A2008.041, HistoryMakers Digital Archive.
Kennedy, Annie Brown. Interview by Joseph Mosnier. December 6, 1995. Interview A-0400, Southern Oral History Program Collection no. 4007, Southern Historical Collection, Wilson Library, University of North Carolina at Chapel Hill.
Meek, Carrie. Interview by Julieanna L. Richardson. June 19, 2001. Interview A2001.049, HistoryMakers Digital Archive.
Murphy, Frances. Interview by Fern Ingersoll. December 3, 1992. Washington Press Club Foundation Women in Journalism Oral History Project Collection, Columbia Center for Oral History, Columbia University Libraries, New York.
Murphy, Frances L., II. Interview by Larry Crowe. June 3, 2003. Interview A2003.117, HistoryMakers Digital Archive.
Pearson, Conrad. Interview by Walter Weare. April 18, 1979. Southern Oral History Program, University of North Carolina at Chapel Hill.
Perry, Matthew J. Interview by Joseph Mosnier. June 7, 2011. Civil Rights History Project, Library of Congress Archive of Folk Culture, Washington, DC.
Prestage, Jewel. Interview by Shelby Faye Lewis. October 31, 1992. Louis B. Nunn Center for Oral History, University of Kentucky Libraries, Lexington.
Redmond, Sidney. Interview by Richard Resh and Franklin Rother. July 6, 1970. Black Community Leaders Project, State Historical Society of Missouri, Columbia.
Rogers, Gwendolyn DuBose. Interview by Larry Crowe. December 15, 2003. Interview A2003.299, HistoryMakers Digital Archive.
Sabur, Karen Lathen. Telephone interview by author. December 21, 2020.

Shobe, Benjamin F. Interview by Constance Ard. October 18, 2013. Louie B. Nunn Center for Oral History, University of Kentucky Libraries, Lexington.
Sullivan, Louis. Telephone interview by author. December 28, 2021.
Todd, Thomas N. Interview by Larry Crowe. June 6, 2002. Interview A2002.094, HistoryMakers Digital Archive.
Williams, Serena. Telephone interview by author. February 11, 2021.

NEWSPAPERS AND PERIODICALS

Alabama Citizen (Tuscaloosa)
Asheville (NC) Citizen-Times
Atlanta Constitution
Atlanta Daily World
Austin American-Statesman
Baltimore Afro-American
Baltimore News and the Baltimore Post
Baltimore Sun
Black Dispatch
Boston Globe
Brownsville (TX) Herald
Call (Kansas City, MO)
Carolina Times (Durham, NC)
Chapel Hill (NC) Herald
Charlotte (NC) Observer
Chattanooga (TN) Daily Times
Chicago Defender
Clarion-Ledger (Jackson, MS)
Cleveland Call and Post
Coast Star (Manasquan, NJ)
Columbia Law School News
Columbia Missourian
Corpus Christi (TX) Caller-Times
The Crisis (New York)
Daily Iowan (Iowa City)
Daily Oklahoman (Oklahoma City)
Decatur (AL) Daily
Dothan (AL) Eagle
The Dove (Lawrence, KS)
Durham (NC) Sun
For the Record (Spring City, PA)
Fort Lauderdale (FL) News
Fort Worth (TX) Star-Telegram
Georgia Recorder (Atlanta)
Greensboro (NC) Daily News
Inside HigherEd (Washington, DC)
Kansas City Star
Louisville (KY) Courier-Journal
Louisville (KY) Leader
Miami (FL) News
Montgomery (AL) Advertiser
News and Observer (Raleigh, NC)
New York Amsterdam News
New York Times
Norfolk (VA) Journal and Guide
Oklahoma Daily (Norman)
Okmulgee (OK) Daily Times
Penn State News (State College, PA)
Petaluma (CA) Argus-Courier
Philadelphia Tribune
Pittsburgh Courier
Richmond (VA) Times-Dispatch
Robesonian (Lumberton, NC)
Rocky Mount (NC) Evening Telegram
Shawnee (OK) News-Star
Shreveport (LA) Journal
St. Louis Globe-Democrat
St. Louis Post-Dispatch
Sun Democrat (Paducah, KY)
Tallahassee (FL) Democrat
Tampa (FL) Daily Times
Tennessean (Nashville)
Time (New York)
Times and Democrat (Orangeburg, SC)
UMB News (Baltimore)
Waco (TX) News Tribune
Washington Post
Wilson (NC) Times

GOVERNMENT DOCUMENTS

Acts, Concurrent Resolutions, and Memorials of the Fifty-Fourth General Assembly of the State of Arkansas. Little Rock: Arkansas Printing and Lithography, 1948.

Appendix to the House and Senate Journals of the Sixtieth General Assembly, State of Missouri, 1939. Jefferson City: Missouri General Assembly, 1939.

Berea College v. Kentucky, 211 U.S. 45 (1908).

Biennial Report of the Superintendent of Public Instruction of Kentucky for the Biennium Ended June 30, 1937. Lexington: Kentucky Board of Education, 1937.

Boynton v. Virginia, 364 U.S. 454 (1960).

Brown v. Board of Education of Topeka, 347 U.S. 483 (1954).

Donald G. Murray v. Raymond A. Pearson, et al., Baltimore City Court, June 18, 1935. Transcript.

Laws of Missouri, 51st Sess. (1921).

Laws of Missouri, 55th Sess. (1929).

Laws of Missouri, 56th Sess. (1931).

McLaurin v. Oklahoma State Regents, 339 U.S. 637 (1950).

Missouri ex rel. Gaines v. Canada, 305 U.S. 337 (1938).

Missouri Secretary of State's Office. *Official Manual of the State of Missouri 1921–1922*. Jefferson City: Charles U. Becker, Secretary of State, 1922.

——. *Official Manual of the State of Missouri 2001–2002*. Edited by Rob Davis. Jefferson City: Matt Blunt, Secretary of State, 2002.

Morgan v. Virginia, 328 U.S. 373 (1946).

Murray v. Pearson, 169 Md. 478, 182 A. 590 (1936).

Plessy v. Ferguson, 163 U.S. 537 (1896).

Public Acts of the State of Tennessee Passed by the Seventieth General Assembly, Extra Session, 1936 and Regular Session, 1937. Nashville: Tennessee General Assembly, 1937.

Raymond A. Pearson, et al v. Donald G. Murray, Maryland Court of Appeals, January 1936. Transcript.

Simkins v. City of Greensboro, 246 F.2d 425 (4th Cir. 1957).

Sixteenth Biennial Report of State Superintendent of Public Instruction, Oklahoma State Board of Education for the Fiscal Year Ending June 30, 1936. Oklahoma City: Oklahoma State Department of Education, 1936.

State ex rel. Gaines v. Canada, Circuit Court of Boone County, no. 34337, 1936.

Sweatt v. Painter, 339 U.S. 629 (1950).

Thomas R. Hocutt v. Thomas J. Wilson and the University of North Carolina, Durham County Superior Court, no. 6439, 1933.

West Virginia Board of Education. *Record of Proceedings*. July 21–22 and December 1–2, 1954. Charleston: West Virginia Board of Education, 1954.

Secondary Sources

Andersen, Margaret, and Neil F. Thomas. *Living Art: The Life of Paul R. Jones, African American Art Collector*. Newark: University of Delaware Press, 2009.

Anderson, James D. *The Education of Blacks in the South*. Chapel Hill: University of North Carolina Press, 1988.

———. "Race, Meritocracy, and the American Academy during the Immediate Post–World War II Era." *History of Education Quarterly* 33, no. 2 (Summer 1993): 157.

———. "Toward a History and Bibliography of the Afro-American Doctorate and Professoriate in Education, 1896 to 1980." In *The Black Education Professoriate*, edited by Ayers Bagley, 149–72. Minneapolis: SPE Monograph Series, 1984.

Apprey, Maurice, and Shelli M. Poe. *The Key to the Door: Experiences of Early African American Students at the University of Virginia*. Charlottesville: University of Virginia Press, 2017.

Arsenault, Raymond. *Freedom Riders: 1961 and the Struggle for Racial Justice*. New York: Oxford University Press, 2007.

Bacote, Clarence. *The Story of Atlanta University: A Century of Service, 1865–1965*. Atlanta: Atlanta University, 1969.

Bay, Mia. *Traveling Black: A Story of Race and Resistance*. Cambridge, MA: Belknap, 2021.

Biondi, Martha. *To Stand and Fight: The Struggle for Civil Rights in Postwar New York City*. Cambridge, MA: Harvard University Press, 2003.

Bogen, David Skillen. "The First Integration of the University of Maryland School of Law." *Maryland Historical Magazine* 84 (Spring 1989): 39–46.

Bond, J. Max. "Some Aspects of Graduate and Professional Education for Negroes." *Phylon* 10 (1949): 392–96.

Bradley, Stefan M. *Upending the Ivory Tower: Civil Rights, Black Power, and the Ivy League*. New York: New York University Press, 2018.

Breaux, Richard M. "Maintaining a Home for Girls: The Iowa Federation of Colored Women's Clubs at the University of Iowa, 1919–1950." *Journal of African American History* 87 (2002): 236–55.

———. "The New Negro Arts and Letters Movement among Black Universities in the Midwest, 1914–1940." *Great Plains Quarterly* 24, no. 3 (2004): 147–62.

Briscoe, Mineola. "A Study of Living Conditions among Negroes in Wagoner County, Oklahoma, as a Basis for Home Economics Instruction." Master's thesis, State University of Iowa, 1938.

Brown, Aaron. "Graduate and Professional Education in Negro Institutions." *Journal of Negro Education* 27, no. 3 (Summer 1958): 233–42.

Brown-Nagin, Tomiko. *Courage to Dissent: Atlanta and the Long History of the Civil Rights Movement*. New York: Oxford University Press, 2011.

Burkholder, Zoe. *An African American Dilemma: A History of School Integration in the Civil Rights North*. New York: Oxford University Press, 2021.

Burns, Augustus M., III. "Graduate Education for Blacks in North Carolina, 1930–1951." *Journal of Southern History* 46, no. 2 (May 1989): 195–218.

Clark, E. Culpepper. *The Schoolhouse Door: Segregation's Last Stand at the University of Alabama*. New York: Oxford University Press, 1993.

Clement, Rufus E. "The Impact of the War upon Negro Graduate and Professional Schools." *Journal of Negro Education* 11, no. 3 (July 1942): 365–66.

Cohen, Robert. *When the Old Left Was Young: Student Radicals and America's First Mass Student Movement, 1929–1941*. New York: Oxford University Press, 1993.

Cole, Eddie R. *The Campus Color Line: College Presidents and the Struggle for Black Freedom*. Princeton, NJ: Princeton University Press, 2020.

Cole, Eddie R., and Cameron L. Burris-Greene. "Black Higher Education: A Historiography of Perseverance and Triumph." In *Higher Education: Handbook of Theory and Research* 39, edited by Laura W. Perna, 21–73. Cham, Switzerland: Springer Nature, 2024.

Corbett, David Leroy, ed. *Addresses, Letters, and Papers of Clyde Roark Hoey, Governor of North Carolina, 1937–1941*. Raleigh: Council of State, State of North Carolina, 1944.

Countryman, Matthew. *Up South: Civil Rights and Black Power in Philadelphia*. Philadelphia: University of Pennsylvania Press, 2006.

Dailey, Jane, Glenda Elizabeth Gilmore, and Bryant Simon, eds. *Jumpin' Jim Crow: Southern Politics from Civil War to Civil Rights*. Princeton, NJ: Princeton University Press, 2000.

Dalton, Ulysses Grant, III. "The Music Department of the University of Arkansas at Pine Bluff: Its Development and Role In Music Education in the State of Arkansas, 1873–1973." PhD diss., University of Michigan, 1981.

Dennis, Ashley. "'Weapons for Building a Better World': Black Children's Books and the Fight for Democracy." In *New Histories of Black Chicago*, edited by Erik Gellman, Marcia Chatelain, and Simon Balto. Urbana: University of Illinois Press, forthcoming.

Devlin, Rachel. *A Girl Stands at the Door: The Generation of Young Women Who Desegregated America's Schools*. New York: Basic Books, 2018.

Du Bois, W. E. B. *The Autobiography of W. E. B. Du Bois: A Soliloquy on Viewing My Last Decade of Its First Century*. New York: International, 1968.

Dungy, Madgetta Thornton. "African American Graduate School Experiences at the University of Iowa, 1937–1959." PhD diss., University of Iowa, 1997.

Eagles, Charles W. *The Price of Defiance: James Meredith and the Integration of Ole Miss*. Chapel Hill: University of North Carolina Press, 2009.

Early, Mary Frances. *The Quiet Trailblazer: My Journey as the First Black Graduate of the University of Georgia*. Athens: Mary Frances Early College of Education; University of Georgia Libraries, 2021.

Edwards, Kathleen A. "The Fine Art of Representing Black Heritage." In *Invisible Hawkeyes: African Americans at the University of Iowa during the Long Civil Rights Era*, edited by Lena M. Hill and Michael D. Hill, 51–66. Iowa City: University of Iowa Press, 2016.

Ellis, Reginald. *Between Washington and Du Bois: The Racial Politics of James Edward Shepard*. Gainesville: University Press of Florida, 2017.

Embree, Edwin, and Julia Waxman. *Investment in People: The Story of the Julius Rosenwald Fund*. New York: Harper and Brothers, 1949.

Endersby, James W., and William T. Horner. *Lloyd Gaines and the Fight to End Segregation*. Columbia: University of Missouri Press, 2016.

Evans, Stephanie Y. *Black Women in the Ivory Tower, 1850–1954: An Intellectual History*. Gainesville: University Press of Florida, 2007.

Fairclough, Adam. "The Black College Presidents Who Tried to Thwart the Racial

Integration of Higher Education." *Journal of Blacks in Higher Education* 55 (April 2007): 71–75.

Favors, Jelani. *Shelter in the Time of Storm: How Black Colleges Fostered Generations of Leadership and Activism*. Chapel Hill: University of North Carolina Press, 2019.

Fenwick, Leslie T. *Jim Crow's Pink Slip: The Untold Story of Black Principal and Teacher Leadership*. Cambridge, MA: Harvard Education Press, 2022.

Fisher, Donald. *Fundamental Development of the Social Sciences: Rockefeller Philanthropy and the United States Social Science Research Council*. Ann Arbor: University of Michigan Press, 1993.

Fleming, Julius. *Black Patience: Performance, Civil Rights, and the Unfinished Project of Emancipation*. New York: New York University Press, 2022.

Ford, Chris, Stephanie Johnson, and Lisette Partelow. "The Racist Origins of Private School Vouchers." Center for American Progress, July 12, 2017.

Fosdick, Raymond B. *The Story of the Rockefeller Foundation*. New York: Harper, 1952.

Franke, Carrie. "Injustice Sheltered: Race Relations at the University of Illinois and Champaign-Urbana, 1945–1962." PhD diss., University of Illinois, 1991.

Franklin, John Hope. *Mirror to America: The Autobiography of John Hope Franklin*. New York: Farrar, Straus and Giroux, 2005.

Frazier, E. Franklin. "Graduate Education in Negro Colleges and Universities." *Journal of Negro Education* 2, no. 3 (July 1933): 329–41.

———. *The Negro in the United States*. New York: Macmillan, 1949.

Gamble, Vanessa Northington. "'No Struggle, No Fight, No Court Battle': The 1948 Desegregation of the University of Arkansas School of Medicine." *Journal of the History of Medicine and Allied Sciences* 68, no. 3 (July 2013): 377–415.

Gasman, Marybeth, with Louis Sullivan. *The Morehouse Mystique: Becoming a Doctor at the Nation's Newest African American Medical School*. Baltimore: Johns Hopkins University Press, 2012.

Gershenhorn, Jerry. "*Hocutt v. Wilson* and Race Relations in Durham, North Carolina, during the 1930s." *North Carolina Historical Review* 78 (July 2001): 275–308.

———. "Stalling Integration: The Ruse, Rise, and Demise of North Carolina College's Doctoral Program in Education, 1951–1962." *North Carolina Historical Review* 82, no. 2 (April 2005): 156–92.

Gilmore, Glenda. *Gender and Jim Crow: Women and the Politics of White Supremacy in North Carolina, 1896–1920*. Chapel Hill: University of North Carolina Press, 1996.

Givens, Jarvis. *Fugitive Pedagogy: Carter G. Woodson and the Art of Black Teaching*. Cambridge, MA: Harvard University Press, 2021.

———. "The Invisible Tax: Exploring Black Student Engagement at Historically White Institutions." *Berkeley Review of Education* 6, no. 1 (2016): 55–78.

Givens, John T. "Our Medical Colleges and Medical Education." *Journal of the National Medical Association* 40, no. 4 (July 1948): 170.

Green, Kristen. *Something Must Be Done about Prince Edward County*. New York: HarperCollins, 2015.

Greene, Harry Washington. *Holders of Doctorates among American Negroes*. Boston: Meador, 1946.

Haldeman-Julius, Marcet. "What Negro Students Endure in Kansas." *Haldeman-Julius Monthly* 7 (January 1928): 5–16, 147–59.

Hallstoos, Brian. "'Excellent Work and Superior Traits of Personality': Composing an Integrated Music Department." In *Invisible Hawkeyes: African Americans at the University of Iowa during the Long Civil Rights Era*, edited by Lena M. Hill and Michael D. Hill, 17–44. Iowa City: University of Iowa Press, 2016.

Hardin, John. *Fifty Years of Segregation: Black Higher Education in Kentucky*. Lexington: University Press of Kentucky, 1997.

———. "Kentucky Is More or Less Civilized: Alfred Carroll, Charles Eubanks, Lyman Johnson, and the Desegregation of Kentucky Higher Education, 1939–1949." *Register of the Kentucky Historical Society* 109, no. 3–4 (Summer–Autumn 2011): 327–50.

———. *Onward and Upward: A Centennial History of Kentucky State University, 1886–1986*. Frankfort: Kentucky State University, 1987.

Harlan, John Clifford. *History of West Virginia State College, 1891–1965*. Dubuque, IA: William C. Brown, 1968.

Harris, Adam. *The State Must Provide: Why America's Colleges Have Always Been Unequal—and How to Set Them Right*. New York: Ecco, 2021.

Haught, James A. "Institute: Its Spring from Epic Love Story." *West Virginia History* 32, no. 2 (January 1971): 101–7.

Hershkoff, Helen, and Adam S. Cohen. "School Choice and the Lessons of Choctaw County." *Yale Law and Policy Review* 10 (Winter–Spring 1992): 1–29.

Holland, Richard A. *The Texas Book: Profiles, History, and Reminisces of the University*. Austin: University of Texas Press, 2006.

Houston, Charles H. "The Need for Negro Lawyers." *Journal of Negro Education* 4, no. 1 (January 1935): 49–52.

Jack, Bryan M. *The St. Louis African American Community and the Exodusters*. Columbia: University of Missouri Press, 2007.

Jackson, Reid E. "Financial Aid Given by Southern States to Negroes for Out-of-State Study." *Journal of Negro Education* 13, no. 1 (Winter 1944): 30–39.

James, Rawn, Jr. *Root and Branch: Charles Hamilton Houston, Thurgood Marshall, and the Struggle to End Segregation*. New York: Bloomsbury, 2010.

Jeffries, Deborah Mayo. "A History of Struggle: NCCU School of Law Library." *North Carolina Central Law Review* 36, no. 2 (2013): 168–277.

Johnson, Charles S. *The Negro College Graduate*. Chapel Hill: University of North Carolina, 1938.

Jones, Reinette F. *Library Service to African Americans in Kentucky, from the Reconstruction Era to the 1960s*. Jefferson, NC: McFarland, 2002.

Kalme, Albert P. "Racial Desegregation and Integration in American Education: The Case History of West Virginia State College, 1891–1973." PhD diss., University of Ottawa, 1977.

Kapur, Geeta. *To Drink from the Well: The Struggle for Racial Equality at the Nation's Oldest Public University*. Durham, NC: Blair, 2021.

Kean, Melissa. *Desegregating Private Higher Education in the South: Duke, Emory, Rice, Tulane, and Vanderbilt*. Baton Rouge: Louisiana State University Press, 2008.

Kilpatrick, Judith. "Desegregating the University of Arkansas School of Law: L. Clifford Davis and the Six Pioneers." *Arkansas Historical Quarterly* 68 (Summer 2009): 123–56.

Kluger, Richard. *Simple Justice: The History of "Brown v. Board of Education" and Black America's Struggle for Equality.* New York: Vintage, 2004.

K'Meyer, Tracy E. *Civil Rights in the Gateway to the South: Louisville, Kentucky, 1945–1980.* Lexington: University Press of Kentucky, 2010.

Kuebler, Edward J. "The Desegregation of the University of Maryland." *Maryland Historical Magazine* 71 (1976): 37–49.

Ladson-Billings, Gloria. "Landing on the Wrong Note: The Price We Paid for *Brown*." *Educational Researcher* 33, no. 7 (October 2004): 3–13.

Lambert, Frank. "The Black Students Who Followed in the Footsteps of James Meredith at Ole Miss." *Journal of Blacks in Higher Education*, no. 66 (Winter 2009/2010): 58–63.

Lavergne, Gary M. *Before "Brown": Heman Marion Sweatt, Thurgood Marshall, and the Long Road to Justice.* Austin: University of Texas Press, 2010.

Logan, Rayford W. *Howard University: The First Hundred Years, 1867–1967.* New York: New York University Press, 1969.

Loupe, Diane. "Storming and Defending the Color Barrier at the University of Missouri School of Journalism: The Lucile Bluford Case." *Journalism History* 16 (April 1989): 20–31.

Lovett, Bobby L. *"A Touch of Greatness": A History of Tennessee State University.* Macon, GA: Mercer University Press, 2012.

Lucas, Aubrey Keith. "The Mississippi Legislature and Mississippi Public Higher Education, 1890–1960." PhD diss., Florida State University, 1966.

Mack, Kenneth J. "Rethinking Civil Rights Lawyering and Politics in the Era before *Brown*." *Yale Law Journal* 115, no. 2 (November 2005): 256–354.

Martin, Sheila Harmon. "Jewel Limar Prestage: Political Science Trailblazer and the Mother of Black Political Science." *PS: Political Science and Politics* 38 (January 2005): 95–97.

Masghati, Emily. "The Patronage Dilemma: Allison Davis's Odyssey from Fellow to Faculty." *History of Education Quarterly* 60, no. 4 (2020): 581–610.

McCuistion, Fred. *Graduate Instruction for Negroes in the United States.* Nashville, TN: George Peabody College for Teachers, 1939.

McMillan, Lewis. "Negro Higher Education as I Have Known It." *Journal of Negro Education* 8, no. 1 (January 1939): 9–18.

———. *Negro Higher Education in the State of South Carolina.* Orangeburg, SC: Lewis K. McMillan, 1952.

McNeil, Genna Rae. *Groundwork: Charles Hamilton Houston and the Struggle for Civil Rights.* Philadelphia: University of Pennsylvania Press, 1983.

Morris, Aldon. *The Scholar Denied: W. E. B. Du Bois and the Birth of Modern Sociology.* Oakland: University of California Press, 2015.

Murray, Pauli. *Song in a Weary Throat: An American Pilgrimage.* New York: Harper and Row, 1987.

Nash, Margaret. "Entangled Pasts: Land Grant Colleges and American Indian Dispossession." *History of Education Quarterly* 59, no. 4 (November 2019): 437–67.

Nichols, Guerdon D. "Breaking the Color Barrier at the University of Arkansas." *Arkansas Historical Quarterly* 27 (Spring 1968): 3–21.

Nixon, Donna L. "The Integration of UNC–Chapel Hill: Law School First." *North Carolina Law Review* 97, no. 6 (September 2019): 1741–93.

Ogletree, Charles J. *All Deliberate Speed: Reflections on the First Half Century of Brown v. Board of Education*. New York: W. W. Norton, 2004.

Owens, Robert Lee, III. "Financial Assistance for Negro College Students in America: A Social Historical Interpretation of the Philosophy of Negro Higher Education." PhD diss., University of Iowa, 1953.

Painter, Nell. *Exodusters: Black Migration to Kansas after Reconstruction*. New York: Knopf, 1977.

Patterson, Zella J. Black. *Langston University: A History*. Norman: University of Oklahoma Press, 1979.

Perkins, Linda. "The African American Female Elite: The Early History of African American Women in the Seven Sister Colleges, 1880–1960." *Harvard Educational Review* 67, no. 4 (December 1997): 718–57.

———. "Merze Tate and the Quest for Gender Equity at Howard University, 1942–1977." *History of Education Quarterly* 54, no. 4 (November 2014): 516–51.

Pirkle, William Broughton. "A Study of the State Scholarship Aid Program for Negroes in Georgia, 1944–1955." PhD diss., Alabama Polytechnic Institute, 1956.

Pitre, Merline. *Born to Serve: A History of Texas Southern University*. Norman: University of Oklahoma Press, 2018.

———. *In Struggle against Jim Crow: Lulu B. White and the NAACP, 1900–1957*. College Station: Texas A&M University Press, 1999.

Posey, Thomas E. *The Negro Citizen of West Virginia*. Institute: Press of West Virginia State College, 1934.

Pratt, Robert. *We Shall Not Be Moved: The Desegregation of the University of Texas*. Athens: University of Georgia Press, 2002.

Preer, Jean L. *Lawyers v. Educators: Black Colleges and Desegregation in Public Higher Education*. Westport: Greenwood Press, 1982.

Purnell, Brian, and Jeanne Theoharis, with Komozi Woodard, eds. *The Strange Careers of the Jim Crow North: Segregation and Struggle outside of the South*. New York: New York Press, 2019.

Putney, Martha S. "The Black Colleges in the Maryland State College System: Quest for Equal Opportunity, 1908–1975." *Maryland Historical Magazine* 75, no. 4 (December 1980): 335–43.

Reynolds, Colin E. "The Rise and Fall of West Virginia's Bureau of Negro Welfare and Statistics, 1921–1957." *West Virginia History: A Journal of Regional Studies* 9, no. 1 (Spring 2015): 1–22.

Rice, Connie Park. *Our Monongalia: A History of African Americans in Monongalia County, West Virginia*. Terra Alta, WV: Headline, 1999.

Richardson, Clement. "Missouri and the Negro." *Southern Workman* 50, no. 8 (August 1921): 366–69.

Richardson, Joe M. *A History of Fisk University, 1865–1946*. Tuscaloosa: University of Alabama Press, 1980.

Sanders, Crystal R. "The First March on Raleigh: North Carolina College School of Law and the Fight for Educational Equality." *North Carolina Historical Review* 99 (October 2022): 375–401.

Sarvis, Will. "Leaders in the Court and Community: Z. Alexander Looby, Avon N. Williams, Jr., and the Legal Fight for Civil Rights in Tennessee, 1940–1970." *Journal of African American History* 88, no. 1 (Winter 2003): 42–58.

Savage, Sherman W. *The History of Lincoln University*. Jefferson City, MO: Lincoln University, 1939.

Shetterly, Margot Lee. *Hidden Figures: The American Dream and the Untold Story of the Black Women Mathematicians Who Helped Win the Space Race*. New York: HarperCollins, 2016.

Smith, Gerald L. *A Black Educator in the Segregated South: Kentucky's Rufus B. Atwood*. Lexington: University Press of Kentucky, 1994.

Stephenson, Gail S. "The Unsung Heroes of the Desegregation of American Law Schools." *Journal of Law and Education* 51, no. 1 (April 2022): 118–93.

Steward, Tyran Kai. "Time Not Ripe: Black Women's Quest for Citizenship and the Battle for Full Inclusion at Ohio State University." *Ohio History* 121 (2014): 4–34.

Sugg, Redding S., and George Hilton Jones. *The Southern Regional Education Board*. Baton Rouge: Louisiana State University Press, 1960.

Summerville, James. *Educating Black Doctors: A History of Meharry Medical College*. Tuscaloosa: University of Alabama Press, 1983.

Taylor, Candacy. *Overground Railroad: The* Green Book *and the Roots of Black Travel in America*. New York: Abrams, 2020.

Thomas, Karen Kruse. *Deluxe Jim Crow: Civil Rights and American Health Policy, 1935–1954*. Athens: University of Georgia Press, 2011.

Titus, Jill. *Brown's Battleground: Students, Segregationists, and the Struggle for Justice in Prince Edward County, Virginia*. Chapel Hill: University of North Carolina Press, 2011.

Trenholm, H. Councill. *Some Background and Status of Higher Education for Negroes in Alabama*. Montgomery: Alabama State Teachers Association, 1949.

Tushnet, Mark V. *The NAACP's Legal Strategy against Segregated Education, 1925–1950*. Chapel Hill: University of North Carolina Press, 1987.

Waite, Cally, and Margaret Smith Crocco. "Fighting Injustice through Education." *History of Education Quarterly* 33, no. 5 (September 2004): 573–83.

Walker, Vanessa Siddle. *The Lost Education of Horace Tate: Uncovering the Hidden Heroes Who Fought for Justice in Schools*. New York: New Press, 2020.

———. *Their Highest Potential: An African American School Community in the Segregated South*. Chapel Hill: University of North Carolina Press, 1996.

Wallenstein, Peter. "Black Southerners and Non-Black Universities: Desegregating Higher Education, 1935–1967." In *History of Higher Education Annual*, edited by Roger Geiger, 121–48. University Park: Pennsylvania University, 1999.

———, ed. *Higher Education and the Civil Rights Movement: White Supremacy, Black Southerners, and College Campuses*. Gainesville: University Press of Florida, 2008.

Ward, Thomas J., Jr. *Black Physicians in the Jim Crow South*. Fayetteville: University of Arkansas Press, 2003.

Ware, Gilbert. "*Hocutt*: Genesis of *Brown*." *Journal of Negro Education* 52, no. 3 (Summer 1983): 227–33.

———. *William Hastie: Grace under Pressure*. New York: Oxford University Press, 1985.

Ware, Leland. "Setting the Stage for *Brown*: The Development and Implementation of the NAACP's School Desegregation Campaign, 1930–1950." *Mercer Law Review* 52, no. 2 (Winter 2001): 631–73.

Watson, Wilbur H. *Against the Odds: Blacks in the Profession of Medicine in the United States*. New York: Transaction, 1998.

Wattley, Cheryl Elizabeth Brown. *A Step toward "Brown v. Board of Education": Ada Lois Sipuel Fisher and Her Fight to End Segregation*. Norman: University of Oklahoma Press, 2014.

Wedgeworth, Robert, ed. *ALA World Encyclopedia of Library and Information Services*. London: American Library Association, 1986.

Weems, Robert E., Jr. "Alpha Phi Alpha, the Fight for Civil Rights, and the Shaping of Public Policy." In *Alpha Phi Alpha: A Legacy of Greatness, the Demands of Transcendence*, edited by Gregory S. Parks and Stefan M. Bradley, 233–62. Lexington: University Press of Kentucky, 2012.

Weiler, Kathleen. "Mabel Carney at Teachers College: From Home Missionary to White Ally." *Teachers College Record* 107, no. 12 (1970): 2599–633.

Wesley, Charles H. "Graduate Education for Negroes in Southern Universities." *Harvard Educational Review* 10, no. 1 (January 1940): 82–94.

Wesley, Doris, Wiley Price, and Ann Morris, eds. *Lift Every Voice and Sing: St. Louis African-Americans in the Twentieth Century*. Columbia: University of Missouri Press, 1999.

Wheatle, Katherine Ica Elizabeth. "Ward of the State: The Politics of Funding Maryland's Black Land-Grant College, 1886–1939." PhD diss., Indiana University, 2018.

White, Walter. "Some Tactics Which Should Supplement Resort to the Courts in Achieving Racial Integration in Education." *Journal of Negro Education* 21, no. 3 (Summer 1952): 340–44.

Wilkerson, Isabel. *The Warmth of Other Suns: The Epic Story of America's Great Migration*. New York: Vintage, 2011.

Williams, Heather Andrea. *Self-Taught: African American Education in Slavery and Freedom*. Chapel Hill: University of North Carolina Press, 2005.

Williams, Juan. *Thurgood Marshall: American Revolutionary*. New York: Times Books, 1998.

Williamson, Joy Ann. *Radicalizing the Ebony Tower: Black Colleges and the Black Freedom Struggle in Mississippi*. New York: Teachers College Press, 1998.

Winston, Michael R. "Through the Back Door: Academic Racism and the Negro Scholar in Historical Perspective." *Daedalus* 100, no. 3 (Summer 1971): 678–719.

Withers, John, II. *Balm in Gilead: A Story from the War.* Morrisville, NC: Lulu, 2020.

Wolters, Raymond. *The New Negro on Campus: Black College Rebellions of the 1920s.* Princeton: Princeton University Press, 1975.

Wright, George C. *In Pursuit of Equality, 1890–1980.* Vol 2 of *A History of Blacks in Kentucky.* Frankfort: Kentucky Historical Society, 1992.

Wright, Richard. *American Hunger.* New York: Harper and Row, 1944.

INDEX

Page numbers in italics refer to illustrations.

affirmative action, 177
African Methodist Episcopal Church, 111
Agricultural, Mechanical, and Normal College in Pine Bluff. *See* University of Arkansas at Pine Bluff
Agricultural and Technical College of North Carolina. *See* North Carolina Agricultural and Technical State University
Alabama, 1, 2, 3, 13, 14, 17, 19, 78, 103, 131, 135, 139, 140–43; creation of segregation scholarships in, 128, 137–38; and regional education, 162
Alabama A&M University, 138
Alabama Legislature, 138, 142
Alabama Polytechnic Institute. *See* Auburn University
Alabama State College for Negroes. *See* Alabama State University
Alabama State Teachers College. *See* Alabama State University
Alabama State University, 1, 139; graduate courses at, 138
Albany State College. *See* Albany State University
Albany State University, 129
Alcorn State University, 33, 120, 174–75
Alexander, Sadie T. Mossell, 181n36
Allen, MD, 51
Alpha Kappa Alpha Sorority, 32, 34, 35, 36
Alpha Phi Alpha Fraternity, 32, 48, 49, 53, 56, 73, 81–82, 139
American Association of University Professors, 172

American Bar Association, 48, 80, 123
American Society of Mechanical Engineers, 33
American Tennis Association, 117
Amherst College, 48, 134
Anderson, Charles W., Jr., 62–66, 69, 92, 95, 97, 98
Anderson, Reuben, 171
Anderson-Mayer State Aid Act, 62, 65, 67, 68, 69, 94, 98
Ann Arbor, MI, 33, 34, 117, 121, 135
Arkansas, 3, 152, 154, 173; creation of segregation scholarships in, 128, 152
Arkansas Teachers Association, 128. *See also* Black public school teachers; Colored Teachers Associations
Armstrong, William Oscar, 90
Art Institute of Chicago, 93
Ashe, Arthur, 181n8
Atkins, Oleona Pegram, 111
Atkins, Simon Green, 111
Atlanta, GA, 28, 84, 129, 130, 131, 132, 170
Atlanta University, 5, 39, 59, 67, 93, 94, 99, 110, 129, 138; and move to graduate study only, 27–29; and regional education, 165; School of Library Science, 112; School of Social Work, 165
Atwood, Rufus B., 91–94, 95, 96, 98
Auburn University, 138, 201n35; and regional education, 163–64
Augusta, GA, 131, 132, 134
Austin, Louis, 46, 104–5
Austin, TX, 158

Index

Ayers, Jake, 174
Ayers case, 174–75

Bailey, Joseph, 2
Baltimore, MD, 48, 49, 50, 53, 58, 104
Baltimore Afro-American (newspaper), 43, 53
Baltimore Circuit Court, 52
Banks, Manley E., 202n53
Barber Scotia College. *See* Scotia Seminary
Barnhill, M. V., 47
Baton Rouge, LA, 107, 140
Bay, Mia, 143
Baylor, Ernestine, 116
Beech, Harvey, 167
Bennett College, 116
Berea College, 65
Berea College v. Kentucky, 65
Berlin, Germany, 75
Bessemer, AL, 139
Bethune-Cookman College. *See* Bethune-Cookman University
Bethune-Cookman University, 136
Biddle University. *See* Johnson C. Smith University
Biden, Joseph, 1
Birmingham, AL, 130, 141
Black, Hugo, 78
Black college presidents, 28, 40, 116, 120, 125–26, 136, 141, 169; and desegregation, 73, 88–89; position on segregation scholarships, 12, 73, 91–93, 129; and segregation, 46, 89, 98, 101–2, 107, 109
Black Dispatch, 145, 147
Black public school teachers, 40; demands of segregation scholarships, 62, 64, 128; and desegregation, 172–73; as segregation scholarship recipients, 36, 94, 120–22, 129, 170; and superior credentials, 173; and Teachers College, Columbia University, 121
Blakely, GA, 134
Bluefield Colored Institute. *See* Bluefield State University
Bluefield State University, 24

Bluford, Ferdinand D., 109, 113, 125, 164
Bluford, Guion, 30–34, 38
Bluford, Guion, Jr., 33
Bluford, John Henry, Jr., 30, 31
Bluford, John Henry, Sr., 30
Bluford, Lucile, 38; early life and education of, 30–32; legal fight to enter Mizzou of, 84–87
Bluford, Viola Harris, 30, 31
Bond, Horace Mann, 27, 129
Bonner, Charles, 116
Bonner, Frances Jones, 116
Booker T. Washington High School (GA), 132
Boone, Elwood, 33
Boone County, MO, 76, 85
Boston, MA, 134
Boston University, 116, 118; School of Medicine, 116, 132, 134
Bowie State University, 49, 175
Bowling Green, KY, 94
Boyd, John A., 75
Boyd, Laurence Eugene, 39
Boynton, Bruce Carver, 142–43
Boynton, Samuel William, 143
Boynton v. Virginia, 143
Brandeis, Louis, 78
Brawley, Sumter, 48
Bright, William Milton, 67–68, 172
Briscoe, Mineola Isabella, 36–38, 39
Brooklyn Law School, 43
Brookwood College, 108
Brown, Aaron, 129
Brown, Annie Louise, 129–30
Brown, Charlotte Hawkins, 107
Brown, Harry, 38
Brown, John, 23
Brown v. Board of Education, 8, 53, 61, 72, 82, 91, 129, 171; resistance to, 176–77; resistance to desegregation prior to, 10–11
Bryant, Paul "Bear," 13, 142
Bucket and Dipper, 27
Bullock, W. A. J., 146–47, 149
Bunche, Ralph J., 29

Butler, Philander, 202n53
Byrd, H. C., 57

Cabarrus County, NC, 116
California, 118
Call, The (newspaper), 31, 85, 86
Cambridge, MA, 48
Canada, Silas, 73, 85
Cape Girardeau, MO, 36
Cardona, Miguel, 175
Cardoza, Benjamin, 191n28
Carnegie Foundation, 118
Carney, Mabel, 121
Carolina Times, 104, 106
Carroll, Alfred, 69, 91–92
Carroll, Charles, 119
Carter, Jimmy, 142
Carter, Robert, 148
Carver, George Washington, 143
Case Western Reserve University, 110, 131–33; Law School, 1–2
Caswell County Training School (NC), 121
Central High School (KY), 68, 95, 99
Central Tennessee College, 160
Chamberlain, Leo, 95, 96
Chandler, Albert Benjamin, 91–92
Chapel Hill, NC, 46, 125, 167
Charlotte, NC, 117
Chicago, IL, 19, 35, 81, 140
Chicago Defender, 108
Chicago State University, 140
Chickasha, OK, 146
Church of God in Christ, 146
Cincinnati, OH, 131
citizenship rights: Black fight for, 72, 83, 103, 109, 171; denied to Black people, 7, 25, 52, 54, 86, 87, 123, 157, 161. *See also* Fourteenth Amendment
Civil War, 20, 21, 23
Clark College, 170
class, socioeconomic, and segregation scholarship recipients, 14, 34, 111, 116
Clawson, M. Don, 163

Clayton, Dewey M., III, 123
Clemon, U. W., 13, 141–42
Cleveland, OH, 1, 2, 110, 131
Cleveland County, OK, 148
Cole, I. Willis, 92
College Park, MD, 48
Collier White Lead and Oil Works, 19
Colored Agricultural and Normal University. *See* Langston University
Colored Normal, Industrial, Agricultural and Mechanical College of South Carolina. *See* South Carolina State University
Colored Teachers Associations, 120. *See also* Arkansas Teachers Association; Black public school teachers; Kentucky Negro Educational Association (KNEA)
Columbia, MO, 75, 76, 87
Columbia University, 6, 9, 36, 40, 56, 58, 60, 67, 68–69, 83, 119, 130, 138; Law School, 141; racism at, 130–31; School of Social Work, 25; Teachers College, 121
Columbus, OH, 61
Colvin, Claudette, 1
Conference of Presidents of Land Grant Colleges, 162
Congress of Industrial Organizations, and Committee Against Discrimination, 162
Coppin State University, 49, 175
Cook, Samuel DuBois, 128
Cooper, Anna Julia, 6
Cornell University, 26, 29, 60, 93, 94, 121
Courier-Journal, 98
Crisis, The, 27, 33, 85, 97, 112
Crockett, Almeta Virginia, 35–36
Cross, George, 145–48, 152, 156
Crozer Theological Seminary, 130
Culberson, Carl, 38
Culberson, Frances, 38
Cummings, Henry, 49

Daily Tar Heel, 104
Daniel, Victor, 51
Davis, Allison, 127–28, 140

Davis, John W., 88–90, *89*, 93, 109, 141. *See also* Black college presidents
Davis, Nancy Randolph, 155
Day, Carl, 65
Day Law, 65, 69, 96, 97, 98
Daytona Beach, F.L., 136
Dean, William H., 28
Deboe, Adell, 40
Delany, Henry, 108
Delany, Logan, 108
Delaware, 3, 152, 173
Delaware Conference Academy. *See* University of Maryland Eastern Shore
Delaware State University, 152
Delta Sigma Theta Sorority, 32
Demopolis, AL, 140
Dennis, Herman, 51
Detroit, MI, 19
Dillard, N. Longworth, 121
Dinwiddie, W. M., 76, 86
diploma privilege, 137, 142
Donovan, Herman Lee, 96
Dorman, J.R., 98
double taxation, 7, 131
Douglass, Aaron, 39
Douglass, William O., 150
Dreer, Herman, 39
Dreer, Vivian, 39
Du Bois, W. E. B., 6, 10, 28, 33–34, 112
Dubra, Charles, 202n40
Duggan, B. O., 161
Duke University, 47, 101, 105, 123; Black faculty at, 128
Dunbar High School (WV), 90
Dunjee, Roscoe, 145, 147, 148
Durham, NC, 43, 45, 46, 101, 104, 105, 118, 124, 144
Durham County Superior Court, 47–48
Dykes, Eva Beatrice, 181n36

Early, Mary Frances, 170
Eason, Charles Reginald, 110–11
Eaton, Hubert, 117–18
Edmonds, Helen G., 12–13, 61; *The Negro and Fusion Politics in North Carolina*, 13
Elder, Alphonso, 119, 125
Elizabeth, NJ, 110
Elizabeth City, NC, 107, 121
Elizabeth City State Teachers College. *See* Elizabeth City State University
Elizabeth City State University, 107, 121, 169
Ellington, Duke, 36
Emma Ransom House YWCA, 130
equal protection. *See* Fourteenth Amendment
Epps, Harold Thomas, 101, 123
Espy, Henry, 74
Eubanks, Charles, 95–98
Evers, Medgar, 139
Evers, Myrlie Beasley, 120
Executive Order 8802, 33

Fairfield, AL, 140
Fairmont, WV, 90
Fayette Circuit Court (KY), 96
Fayetteville, NC, 117
Fayetteville State Teachers College. *See* Fayetteville State University
Fayetteville State University, 110
Federal District Court for the Western District of Oklahoma, 154
Fellows, J.E., *151*
Fisher, Warren, 147
Fisk University, 5, 26, 39, 60, 67, 91, 93, 94, 99, 113, 120, 160, 179n8; creation of graduate programs, 27
flagship institutions: admission of Black students at, 9, 89–90, 98–99, 152, 167–70; Black history makers at, 13, 49, 169, 170; desegregation of, 73, 82, 88–91, 95, 98–99, 152–53, 154, 156, 159, 165, 167–71; and distance education for Black students, 93; nonwhite, non-Black students at, 8, 54, 86, 90, 105; racial discrimination at, 31–34, 39, 68, 90, 111, 153, 169
Flexner, Abraham, 118

Index

Florence, Charles, 74
Florida, 3, 135, 176; creation of a public Black law school in, 137; creation of segregation scholarships in, 128
Florida A&M College for Negroes. *See* Florida A&M University
Florida A&M University, 135, 136, 176; graduate courses at, 136–37
Florida Board of Control, 137
Florida Legislature, 136
Florida State College for Women, 135
Folsom, James, 138
Ford, H. Church, 97, 99
Ford Foundation, 171–72
Fort Monmouth, 111
Fort Valley State College. *See* Fort Valley State University
Fort Valley State University, 129
Fourteenth Amendment: alleged compliance of states with, 4, 18, 56; Black fight for state compliance with, 52, 60, 78, 129, 148, 150, 156; violation of, 18, 72, 74, 76, 77, 79, 83, 96, 150, 159
Fourth US Circuit Court of Appeals, 176
Fraenkel, Osmond, 77
Frankfort, KY, 62, 63, 64, 93, 94
Franklin, Chester, 31
Franklin, John Hope, 10, 59; *From Slavery to Freedom*, 10
Franklin, TN, 82, 84
fraternities, 32, 48, 49, 53, 56, 73, 81–82, 139. *See also names of individual organizations*
Freedom Rides, 143
Friday, William, 174
Friedman, Milton, 114
From Slavery to Freedom (Franklin), 10

Gaines, Callie, 73
Gaines, Henry, 73
Gaines, Lloyd Lionel, 72–85, 87, 95, 101, 143, 148, 165, 169
Gaines decision. See *Missouri ex rel. Gaines v. Canada*

Gammon Theological Seminary, 5
Gellhorn, Walter, 141
gender: impact of, on interstate travel, 35, 102; and segregation scholarship recipients, 14, 94
General Education Board, 6
Georgia, 3, 13, 28, 39, 131, 134, 159, 170, 173; creation of segregation scholarships in, 128, 129
Georgia Board of Regents, 129
GI Bill. *See* Servicemen's Readjustment Act of 1944
Gleason, Eliza Atkins, 111, 112–13, *113*, 116
Gleason, Maurice, 112
Glen Allan, MS, 174
Gosnell, William, 48–49, 52
Graham, Frank Porter, 103–4
Grambling State University, 116
Gray, Fred, 1, 2, 3, 4, 6, 9
Gray, William, 136
Great Depression, 25, 29, 46, 91
Great Migration, 6, 10, 19. *See also* migration
Green, Victor H., 35; *Negro Motorist Green Book*, 35
Greene, Ruth, 40
Greensboro, NC, 31, 105, 107, 112, 115, 174
Greensboro Daily News, 46
Gregory, Dick, 181n8
Greyhound buses, 131

Haines Normal Institute, 131
Hall, Amos T., 127, 148, 148, 150, *151*
Hall, Woodland, 107
Hampton Institute. *See* Hampton University
Hampton University, 4, 51, 58, 68, 93, 95, 99
Hanson, Fred, 149, 150
Harkins, William, 95
Harlem, 25, 36, 121, 130
Harper, Ebeneezer Howard, 26
Harpers Ferry, WV, 23
Harrison, Abram L., 29

Harrison, Gwendolyn, 167–68; campus housing application of, *168*
Harris-Stowe State University. *See* Stowe Teachers College
Harvard University, 6, 56, 58, 59, 67, 128, 134; Law School, 47, 48, 71, 152; Medical School, 116; racism at, 10
Hastie, William, 47
HBCUs. *See* historically Black colleges and universities
Henderson, Bodie, 96
Hidden Figures (film), 90
Hill, T. Edward, 24
Hillside High School (NC), 45
historically Black colleges and universities, 3, 11, 24, 49–54, 82–83, 129, 131, 157, 169; and academic preparation of graduates, 134–36; and accreditation, 28, 48, 75, 88, 91–92, 123, 136–37, 141, 145, 147, 151, 158, 183n40; and administration of segregation scholarships, 93–94, 109, 125; faculty at, 13, 27, 28, 29, 33, 36, 38–39, 110, 116, 118, 131, 132, 136, 140, 154, 157, 169; and graduate programs, 27–29, 84, 86–87, 99, 102, 119, 136–37, 138, 175; lack of state investment in, 8–9, 22–23, 30, 49–50, 54, 61, 62–63, 65, 67, 75, 77, 88–89, 91–92, 96–97, 106, 122–24, 126, 145, 159, 173–76; and professional schools, 9, 46, 48, 61, 80, 91, 108, 117–18, 123–24, 126, 136–37, 141, 151–52, 158, 160, 173; and redress for discrimination, 177; and regional education, 161, 163–65; second curriculum at, 11. *See also* Black college presidents
historically white institutions: Black faculty at, 127–28, 141; explanation of, 180n15; refusal of, to hire Black faculty, 39, 128, 171–72, 206n17
Hitch, Minnie, 94
Hocutt, Thomas Raymond, 45–47, 48, 69, 102, 104, 107, 109, 168
Hocutt case, 47–48
Hoey, Clyde, 106
Hogsett, William, 75, 76, 77, 78, 85

Holden, Missouri, 37
Holmes, Hamilton, 170
Holt, Homer A., 88
Hope, John, 28
House, Robert, 168
House of Representatives, US, and regional education, 163
Houston, Charles Hamilton, 23, *58*, 108, 117, 137; criticism of segregation scholarships by, 66; as dean of Howard Law, 63; death of, 159; early life and career of, 48; and legal efforts to dismantle school desegregation, 5, 7, 72, 80–82, 83, 85, 86; *Missouri ex rel. Gaines v. Canada*, 74–78; and *Murray v. Pearson*, 52, 53–58, 127; NAACP work of, 5, 7, 8; work with Marshall, 48–49, 96
Houston, TX, 157, 158
Houston College for Negroes, 158
Howard University, 4, 20, 26, 30, 31, 34, 54, 58, 60, 67, 83, 93, 99, 138, 139, 179n8; College of Medicine, 9, 61, 118, 132, 153; graduate study at, 29; School of Law, 9, 26, 27, 40, 41, 43, 47–50, 52, 56, 61, 63, 66, 69, 74, 80, 91, 95, 105, 129, 142, 146, 169
Howell, Monticello J., 116
Howell, Roger, 55
Hubert, Benjamin, 129
Hunt, Silas, 152–53
Hunter, Charlayne, 170
Hunter College, 104

Illinois, 22
Independence, Missouri, 37
Indiana University, 67, 172
intellectual warfare, 2, 5, 7, 11, 13, 61, 95, 136, 142
Interstate Commerce Act, 143
interstate travel, 7, 9–10, 130, 131, 135; impact of gender on, 35, 102; racial discrimination during, 34–35, 117, 143–44
Iowa, 222, 37–38, 74
Iowa City, IA, 38

Index

Iowa Federation of Colored Women's Clubs, 38
Iowa State University, 91
Irby, Edith, 153–54
Ireland, Leila Beatrice, 107

Jackson, Alice Carlotta, 59–61, 69
Jackson, Luther, 162
Jackson State University, 120, 174
James, Kenneth, 90
Jefferson City, MO, 17, 31, 72, 73, 76, 80, 87; segregation in, 20
Jessamine County, KY, 98
Johns Hopkins University, 58, 153
Johnson, Caroline E., 68–69
Johnson, Charles, 49
Johnson, James Weldon, 39
Johnson, Katherine, 90
Johnson, Lyman T., 99
Johnson, Mordecai, 88
Johnson C. Smith University, 107, 111, 116, 117, 123, 167
Jones, David Dallas, 116
Jones, John W., 97
Jones, Paul R., 138–39
Jones, Thomas Elsa, 160
Jones, Vertna Sneed, 59
Journal of Negro Education, 29, 172
Journal of Negro History, 172

Kansas, 19, 22
Kansas City, MO, 30, 31, 39, 84
Kappa Alpha Psi Fraternity, 32
Kenan Stadium, 167
Kennedy, Harold, Jr., 130
Kennedy, Wadaran, 59
Kentucky, 3, 14, 62–69, 91–99, 112, 172, 173; creation of segregation scholarships in, 62, 65
Kentucky General Assembly, 64, 65
Kentucky Negro Educational Association (KNEA), 62–63, 64, 95. *See also* Black public school teachers; Colored Teachers Associations

Kentucky State College. *See* Kentucky State University
Kentucky State University, 62–65, 68, 91, 94–98, 170; and graduate courses, 93
Kimball, WV, 25
King, Christine, 130
King, Martin Luther, Jr., 1, 130
Kinston, NC, 167, 168
KNEA. *See* Kentucky Negro Educational Association (KNEA)
Knox College, 39
Knoxville College, 107
Ku Klux Klan, 167

L&N Railroad, 35
Laffoon, Ruby, 64
Lamar, Willarena, *131*, 132–33, 140
Langston, John Mercer, 145
Langston, OK, 144
Langston University, 59, 144–45, 146, 147, 150, 153, 154, 155, 157; School of Law, 151–52, 156
Lassiter, James, 167
Lathen, John, 36
Lawrence, KS, 31
Lawrenceville, VA, 61
lawsuits. *See* legal challenges
Leathers, Robert, 124
Lee, J. Kenneth, 167
legal challenges: and *Brown*, 8, 61; and creation of academic programs at Black colleges, 9; to desegregate historically white institutions, 7, 43–59, 66–67, 69, 71–87, 95–99, 124, 129, 148–50, 154, 156–59, 165, 167, 168, 169; and desegregation of recreational facilities, 130; and desegregation of the University of Alabama football program, 142–43; and Hubert Eaton, 117; for more funding at Black colleges, 23, 174–75; NAACP refusal to take on, 108; resistance to school desegregation and, 10–11. *See also names of individual court cases*
LeViness, Charles T., III, 53, 56

Lewis, John, 1
Lewis, Julien H., 200n3
Lexington, KY, 65, 93, 97, 99
Lincoln High School (KS), 31
Lincoln High School (OK), 146
Lincoln Institute. *See* Lincoln University (MO)
Lincoln University (MO), 35–37, 40, 72–82; Black efforts to upgrade, 22–23, 30; Board of Curators, 22–23, 30, 76; creation of journalism program at, 86–87; lack of journalism program at, 31, 85; origins of, 20–21; School of Law, 80–82, *81*, 142; underfunding of, 18, 22, 30, 75, 76, 77, 85, 176
Lincoln University (PA), 27, 49, 110
Lindley, Ernest, 32, 33–34
Lindsay, Arnett G., 75
Livingston College, 39
Locke, Alain, 29
Logan, Rayford W.
Looby, Z. Alexander, 83
Los Angeles, CA, 19
Louisiana, 3, 38, 140, 141, 173; creation of a public Black law school in, 137; creation of segregation scholarships in, 128
Louisiana State University, 13, 141
Louistall-Monroe, Victorine, 90
Louisville, KY, 62, 63, 64, 66, 68, 69, 91, 95, 97
Louisville Leader, 92
Louisville Municipal College, 63, 65, 66, 67, 68, 93, 95; closing of, 171–72
Lyle, Ethel Hedgemon, 181n8

Madison, Wisconsin, 114–15
Madisonville, KY, 94
Madry, Lucille, 94
Malone, Annie, 80
March on Washington, 141
Marshall, Thurgood, 63; and *Boynton v. Virginia*, 143; and *Brown v. Board of Education*, 61; education and early career of, 48–49; and legal work to desegregate historically white institutions, 92, 96, 127, 145, 148, 150, *151*, 154, 156, 158, 165; and Pauli Murray, 108; and *Murray v. Pearson*, 52, 53, 55, 56, 58, *58*; and opposition to regional education, 162
Martin, Frank, 86
Martin, Sarah, 110–11
Maryland, 3, 48–59, 60, 66, 69, 75, 79, 119, 149; creation of segregation scholarships in, 52–53
Maryland Agricultural College. *See* University of Maryland
Maryland Court of Appeals, 165
Maryland Department of Education, 50
Maryland State College. *See* University of Maryland
Massachusetts, 54
Massachusetts General Hospital, 116
Massachusetts Institute of Technology, 67
Mayer, Stanley, 65
McAlester, OK, 145
McClinton, Hortense, 128
McCoy, Cecil, 43–47
McCready, Esther, 58, 165
McDaniel, J. H., 106
McDowell, Cleve, 171
McDowell County, WV, 25
McGill University, 58
McKissick, Floyd, 167
McLaurin, George, 154–55, *155*, 165
McLaurin v. Oklahoma State Regents, 156–57, 159, 169
McMillan, Lewis, 93, 101
McRae, James, 110
McReynolds, James, 78
Medical College of Georgia, 132, 134
Medical College of Virginia, and regional education, 161
Meharry, Samuel, 160
Meharry Medical College, 5, 9, 26, 61, 67, 83, 110, 112, 118, 123, 132, 138, 153; financial problems at, 160; proposed selling of, 160; and regional education, 162–63, 165; and Tennessee partnership, 84, 160–61; and Virginia partnership, 163–65

Index

Meek, Harold, 136
Memphis, TN, 83
Meredith, James, 170–71
Merrill, Maurice, 150
Methodist Episcopal Church, and Delaware Conference, 50
Miami, FL, 136
Miami Dade College, 136
Miami-Dade Community College, 136
Michigan, 117
Michigan State University, 116
Middlebush, Frederick, 77
Middlesboro, KY, 94
migration, 6, 19, 73, 112, 140. *See also* Great Migration
Miles College, 141
Milledgeville, GA, 88
Miller, Lucille, 114, 115
Milton, NC, 121
Minnesota, 68, 132, 168
Mississippi, 3, 8, 19, 73, 135, 139, 170–71, 173, 174; creation of segregation scholarships in, 120, 128
Mississippi Bar, 171
Mississippi Institutions of Higher Learning, 120
Mississippi Supreme Court, 171
Mississippi Valley State University, 174–75
Missouri, 3, 13, 17–23, 29, 33, 35, 36, 39–40, 44, 60, 66, 69, 71–81, 83, 96, 105, 110, 176; creation of public Black law school in, 79–80; creation of segregation scholarships in, 29–30; segregated schools in, 19
Missouri ex rel. Gaines v. Canada, 71–79, 85, 86, 88, 91, 95, 99, 103, 105, 106, 108, 123, 128, 149, 150; impact of, 9, 88, 96, 102, 104, 105, 127, 136, 152, 161; overview of, 7–8
Missouri General Assembly, 17, 20, 29, 40, 77
Mitchell, Parren, 58
Mizzou. *See* University of Missouri
Mobile, AL, 140
Montgomery, AL, 1, 2, 141

Moore, John, 19
Moore, Sarah, 19
Moore, Walthall, *21*, 40–41, 92, 176; and creation of segregation scholarships, 18, 20–21, 29–30; early life and education of, 19–20; historic election of, 17; support of Lincoln University, 18, 22
Morehouse College, 28, 88, 132, 134, 170
Morehouse School of Medicine, 13, 134
Morgan College. *See* Morgan State University
Morgan State University, 50, 52, 61, 175; state affiliation with, 58
Morgantown, WV, 90
Morgan v. Virginia, 148
Morrill Land Grant Act (1862), 21, 50, 51
Morrill Land Grant Act (1890), 21, 51
Morris Brown College, 39
Morse, Wayne, 163
Morton, Fred, 60
Moses, Clarence E., 202n53
Moss, Henry C., 202n53
Mount Olive, NC, 116
Mowbray, Geraldine, 34
Murphy, Carl, 53, 187n46
Murphy, Frances, 53
Murphy, Walter, 48
Murray, Donald Gaines, 48, 51–54, *58*, 59, 61, 69, 74, 79, 127, 149, 165; matriculation at University of Maryland School of Law of, 55–58
Murray, Pauli, 101–5, 108
Murray v. Pearson, 53–58

NAACP, 132, 143, 158, 162; and Black plaintiffs, 5, 45, 48, 56, 72, 82, 92, 108, 143–44, 146; and desegregation of public universities, 5, 43–45, 48–58, 60, 69, 72–85, 95–99, 127–28, 146–50, 152, 162, 165; Durham chapter of, 47; Louisville chapter of, 66, 91; National Legal Committee of, 47; St. Louis chapter of, 72, 74
NAACP Legal Defense Fund, 142
Nabrit, James, 162

Index

Nashville, TN, 82, 83, 84, 110, 112, 160
National Aeronautics and Space Administration, 33
National Alliance of Postal Employees, 144
National Association for Colored Women, 38
National Association for the Advancement of Colored People. *See* NAACP
National Association of Colored Graduate Nurses, 162
National Dental Association, 162
National Medical Association, 162
National Negro Insurance Association, 162
National Negro Publishers Association, 162
National Urban League, 94
Nebraska, 22, 74
Negro and Fusion Politics in North Carolina, The (Edmonds), 13
Negro Motorist Green Book (Green), 35
Newbold, Nathan, 106
New Jersey, 35
Newport News, VA, 169
New York, 25, 43, 47, 69, 104, 139
New York Amsterdam News, 108
New York City, 19, 25, 40, 101, 121, 130, 139
New York Law School, 123
New York School of Social Work. *See* Columbia University: School of Social Work
New York University, 83, 110, 116, 121, 124, 138
Noell, J. W., 106
Norman, OK, 145, 147, 149, 152
North (region), 131, 134; racial discrimination in, 10, 25, 31–34
North Central Association of Colleges and Secondary Schools, 75, 88
North Carolina, 3, 6, 14, 39, 43–48, 69, 101–26, 169, 173, 176; creation of public Black law school in, 105, 108; creation of segregation scholarships in, 105; and regional education, 164
North Carolina Agricultural and Technical State University, 31, 59, 107, 109, 112–14, 122, 125, 164, 168, 174, 176; creation of graduate program at, 105–6

North Carolina Central University, 13, 45–46, 61, 90, 101–7, 116, 118, 119, 123–26, 168, 179n8; creation of graduate programs at, 105–6; School of Law, 105, 108, 123
North Carolina College. *See* North Carolina Central University
North Carolina General Assembly, 46, 105–6, 125; first Black woman in, 130
North Carolina Mutual Life Insurance Company, 43
North Carolina State University, 174, 176
Northwestern University, 26, 93, 140, 141, 153

Oberlin College, 27, 30
O'Dunne, Eugene, 55
Ohio, 68, 91, 131
Ohio State University, 12, 26, 61, 67, 104, 110, 121, 172, 174; racism at, 27, 110–11
Oklahoma, 3, 10, 33, 37, 59, 60, 62, 66, 129, 144–57, 169; creation of public Black law school in, 137; creation of segregation scholarships in, 59
Oklahoma A&M College/University. *See* Oklahoma State University
Oklahoma Board of Regents for Higher Education, 149–51, 156
Oklahoma City, OK, 151, 154
Oklahoma Department of Public Welfare, 59
Oklahoma Legislature, 144
Oklahoma State University, 145; desegregation of, 156; and regional education, 164
Old Dominion Delta Society, 60
Orangeburg, SC, 173
Oregon, 163
out-of-state tuition aid. *See* segregation scholarships
Owens, Jesse, 27, 75
Owl, Henry, 186n5

Paducah, KY, 64
Painter, Theophilus, 150
Page, Esther, 25–26

Palmer Memorial Institute, 107
Panama, 131
Parks, Rosa, 1, 2
Parrish, Charles H., 172
Paul Robeson Dramatic Club, 32
Pearson, Conrad, 43–47, 48, 168
Pearson, Raymond, 49, 51–52, 54
Penn Station, 130
Pennsylvania, 130
Pennsylvania State University, 59, 121–22
People's Finance Building, 71, 76
Permanent University Fund, 157, 158
Perry, Matthew, Jr., 173
Person, Henry L., 202n53
Petersburg, VA, 59
Phi Beta Kappa, 48, 110
Phillips, Theodore D., 26–27
Phylon (academic journal), 28
Pierson, William Whatley, 103
Pittman, Carrie, 135; election to US Congress, 136
Pitts, Lucius, 141
Pittsburgh Courier, 80, 123, 163
Plessy v. Ferguson, 22, 55, 57, 69, 72, 78, 79
Poland, 131
Poplar Bluff, MO, 169
Poro Beauty College, 80
postbaccalaureate education: Black demand for, 5, 59, 61, 84, 101–3, 123, 136, 154; at Black institutions, 4–5, 8, 9, 27–29, 39, 48, 59, 60, 69, 80, 84, 86–87, 93, 94, 99, 105–6, 108, 119, 123–24, 128, 136–37, 138, 141, 151–52; and Black pioneers, 6, 49, 55–56, 61, 101–2, 105, 112, 116, 119, 152–53, 171; and desegregation, 73, 88–90, 152–52, 167–71; and funding sources, 6; and *Gaines*, 7–8, 74; as lawsuit priority, 44
Powell, Adam Clayton, 36
Prairie View A&M College. *See* Prairie View A&M University
Prairie View A&M University, 13, 157, 159, 176; law school at, 157–58
Prestage, James, 38
Prestage, Jewel Limar, 13, 38–39, 140

Prince Edward Academy, 176
Prince Edward County (VA), 10, 176–77
Princess Anne Academy. *See* University of Maryland Eastern Shore
Princeton University, 134
professional schools: and dearth of Black attorneys, 9, 108; and dearth of Black physicians, 9, 61–62, 116–18
Public Black colleges. *See* historically Black colleges and universities
Public Works Administration, 104

racism, in historically white universities, 10, 19, 27, 31–34, 37, 38, 39, 130–32, 153–56, 155, 167, 169–72, 206n17
Radcliffe College, 110
Raleigh, NC, 118, 130, 174
Ransom, Leon, 96
Rasmussen, Don, 140
Rasmussen, Lore, 140
Ray, Charles, 118–19
Reason, Charles, 200n3
Reddix, Jacob, 120
Redmond, Sidney, 71–72, 74, 76, 85
Redmond, William, Jr., 82–84
Reed, Leon, 60
regional education, 127, 163–65; Black opposition to, 162–63; and Meharry Medical College, 128, 160; origins of, 161–62; overview of, 128
resistance to education discrimination, 7, 33. *See also* legal challenges; *and names of individual court cases*
Revels, Hiram, 71
Rice, Mertye, 122
Richmond, VA, 59, 60, 61, 130, 143
Ridgel, Gus, 169–70
Ridley, Walter Nathaniel, 169
Robinson, Amelia Boynton, 143
Robinson, Spottswood William, III, 61
Rogers, Gwendolyn DuBose, 140
Roosevelt, Franklin, D., 33
Rosenwald Fund, 6
Royston, John Eric, 39–40

Russell, Bessie T., 68
Russell, Harvey C., Sr., 68
Russell, Roger, 119–20
Rutgers University, 60, 110

Saint Augustine's College, 108
Saint Augustine's University. *See* Augustine's College
Salisbury, NC, 30
Savannah, GA, 6
Savannah State College. *See* Savannah State University
Savannah State University, 129
Schomburg, Arturo, 36
school choice, 177
school desegregation, and negative consequences, 171–73
Scotia Seminary, 107
Scott, Rex, 63
Scottsboro Boys, 77
Scruggs, Sherman, 40
Seaboard Air Line Railroad, 130
segregation: and bus transportation, 2, 143–44, *144*; and the Day Law, 65, 91; and land-grant institutions, 22; and law schools, 1, 2, 9, 91; and medical schools, 9, 34; and pharmacy schools, 45–47, 83; and railroad cars, 2
segregation scholarship recipients, 1, 10, 12, 13, 14, 19, 32, 33, 35–40, 59, 60–61, 67–69, 91, 94, 110–24, 129–36, 140–42, 169, 170, 172; and Black institutions, 39–40, 59, 122–24; and family separation, 121–22; and housing challenges, 37–38, 111, 114, 124–25; and transportation challenges, 117, 118–19
segregation scholarships, 4, 6, 51, 54, 56, 77, 78, 79, 83, 86, 90, 93, 109–10, 153, 157, 173; administration of, 3, 30, 53, 66, 109, 125, 138; Black resistance to, 26, 60, 66; in defiance of court orders, 8, 73, 93, 99, 105; and EdD vs. PhD, 119; emotional and psychological costs of, 9, 10, 25–26, 114;
failed attempt to create, 48, 64; as form of Black resistance, 5, 11, 53, 171; as form of racism, 14–15, 52; and GI Bill, 124; and HBCU appropriations, 9, 62–63, 83, 126, 128, 135–36, 152, 176; inadequacy of, 4, 26, 29–30, 37, 40, 53, 55, 57, 59, 60–61, 67, 69, 74, 75, 95, 113, 116, 118, 119, 122, 125, 131–32, 137–39, 141; as model for white resistance to *Brown*, 11, 176–77; origins of, 17–18, 22; professional disadvantages of, 40, 55, 57, 68, 76, 94–95, 118, 132, 137, 142; as unconstitutional, 7–8, 72, 79
Sellers, Grover, 157
Sellers, Juanita, 130
Selma, AL, 142
Senate, US, and regional education, 163
separate but equal doctrine, 1, 22, 52, 55, 57, 59, 78, 79, 80, 93, 129, 145; *Gaines* decision and, 7, 8, 72; impossibility of, 5, 44, 69, 98, 102, 122–23, 150
Servicemen's Readjustment Act of 1944, 115, 124, 143
Shaffer, Albert, 33
Shaffer, Minnie, 33
Shaw University, 110; Leonard Medical School, 117–18; Leonard School of Pharmacy, 107
Shepard, James, 46, 90, 101–2, 107, 109–11, 118, 125, 126. *See also* Black college presidents
Shobe, Benjamin, 94–95
Siddle, Helen Beasley, 121–22
Siddle, Theodore, 122
Sigma Xi Scientific Honor Society, 38, 132
Silver Comet train, 130
Simmons College, 65
Simpkins v. City of Greensboro, 130
Simpson, Georgiana Rose, 181n36
Sipuel, Ada Lois, 144–53, 154, 156–57, 160, 165
Sipuel, Helen, 146
Sipuel, Lemuel, 146, 147
Sipuel, Martha Belle, 146

Index

Sipuel, Travis, 146, 149
Sipuel v. Board of Regents of the University of Oklahoma, 150; impact of, 152, 154, 169
Slater Industrial Academy. *See* Winston-Salem State University
slavery, and antiliteracy laws, 20; and West Virginia, 23–24
Smith, James McCune, 6
Smith College, 59
Snowden, Frank M., 28
Social Science Research Council, 6
sororities, 32, 34, 35. *See also names of individual organizations*
South Carolina, 3, 89, 137, 159, 173; creation of public Black law school in, 137; creation of segregation scholarships in, 128
South Carolina State College. *See* South Carolina State University
South Carolina State University, 93, 126; Law School, 137, 173
Southern Association of Colleges and Schools, 28, 91
Southern Governors' Conference, 162
Southern Regional Education Board, 163–65
Southern Regional Education Compact, 162, 163
Southern University of Baton Rouge, 13, 38, 107, 140; Law School, 141
Sparks, Chauncey, 162
Spaulding, Charles Clinton, 43
Spelman College, 28, 129, 130, 131, 132, 167
Spevack, Samuel, 64
Spradling, Mary Macy, 94
SS *Manhattan*, 75
State University of Iowa. *See* University of Iowa
Stiles, Lindley, 169
Stillwater, OK, 145, 156
St. John, Vernon, 138
St. Louis, Missouri, 17, 19, 31, 35, 39, 69–85 passim
St. Louis Globe-Democrat, 71
St. Mary's County, MD, 51

Storer College, 24
Stowe Teachers College, 35, 73
Sugar Hill, 36
Sullivan, Louis, 13, 132, 134–35
Sumner High School (MO), 19–20
Supreme Court, Alabama, 142
Supreme Court, Missouri, 77–78, 82, 86, 191n19
Supreme Court, Oklahoma, 149–50
Supreme Court, US, 44, 57, 65, 92, 99, 101, 103, 129, 131, 143, 148, 150, 156, 157, 158–59, 160, 163, 169, 174, 177; and *Gaines*, 7–8, 71–72, 77–79, 85, 96, 104, 105, 127, 191n28
Swanson, Gregory, 169
Sweatt, Heman, 144, 157–59
Sweatt v. Painter, 159, 169
Sweets, Nathaniel A., 75

Talladega College, 103, 104, 131, 140
Tallahassee, FL, 135
Talmadge, Herman, 159
Tate, Merze, 181n35
Taylor, William, 80
Teague, Helen Noel, 94
Teaneck, NJ, 36
Tennessee, 3, 19, 68, 105, 107, 110, 117, 175; creation of segregation scholarships in, 83; partnership with Meharry, 84, 161
Tennessee Agricultural and Industrial College. *See* Tennessee State University
Tennessee Coal, Iron and Railroad Company, 139
Tennessee Office of Legislative Budget Analysis, 175
Tennessee State University, 82, 84, 175–76; and graduate programs, 84; and Meharry partnership, 161; and segregation scholarship appropriation, 83
Texas, 3, 4, 19, 33, 105, 129, 143, 144, 159, 169, 176; creation of public Black law school in, 137; creation of segregation scholarships in, 157

Texas A&M University, 157, 158
Texas Legislature, 157, 158, 159
Texas Southern University, 158, 159; law school at, 158
Texas State University for Negroes. *See* Texas Southern University
Thirteenth Amendment, 24
Thomas, Edwina, 102–4
Thomas, Prentice, 95–96
Thompson, Charles H., 29
Thurmond, Strom, 159
Times Square, 130
Tinsley, J. M., 60
Todd, Thomas, 140–41
Tokyo, Japan, 8
Toney, Charles, 36
Toney, Lillian, 36
Trailways buses, 143
Travis County, TX, 157
tuition assistance program. *See* segregation scholarships
Tucker, Charles Ewbank, 64
Tulsa, OK, 148
Tulsa Race Massacre, 146
Turner, Roy, 155
Turner, Tina, 181n8
Tuskegee Institute. *See* Tuskegee University
Tuskegee Syphilis Study, 2
Tuskegee University, 40; graduate courses at, 138; and regional education, 163–64

University of Alabama, 1, 2, 137, 138; desegregation of football program at, 13, 142; Law School, 139, 140, 141, 142; nonwhite students at, 8
University of Arkansas, 152; desegregation of law school at, 152; desegregation of medical school at, 9, 153; internal segregation at, 153
University of Arkansas at Pine Bluff, 28, 146, 152
University of California Berkeley, 112, 167

University of Chicago, 9, 60, 88, 91, 94, 112, 128, 140, 153, 172; Black faculty at, 127; Law School, 49
University of Cincinnati, 94
University of Delaware, 152; desegregation of medical school, 9
University of Denver, 58
University of Florida, 135; Black students apply to, 136
University of Georgia, 129, 131; desegregation of, 170; and regional education, 164
University of Glasgow, 6
University of Havana, 122
University of Heidelberg, 6
University of Illinois, 67–68, 112
University of Iowa, 13, 39, 140; racial climate at, 37–38
University of Kansas, 31, 85, 86, 154; racism at, 31–33; School of Medicine, 34
University of Kentucky, 62, 64, 65, 68, 69, 91, 92, 93; desegregation of, 95–99
University of Louisville, 63, 64, 66, 93, 95, 98, 171, 172
University of Maryland, 53, 54; desegregation of, 55–56, 58–59, 127, 165; funding in comparison to Black college, 50, 54; School of Law, 48–49, 51, 52, 53, 55–57; School of Nursing, 165; segregation at, 57–58
University of Maryland Eastern Shore, 49, 51, 52, 107, 175; origins of, 50; state affiliation with, 52; state neglect of, 54
University of Michigan, 26, 30, 32, 60, 77, 99, 107, 110, 121, 135, 136; Law School, 94; Medical School, 117, 132
University of Minnesota, 68, 169; Medical School, 132
University of Mississippi, 120, 139; desegregation of, 170–71
University of Missouri, 21, 29, 30, 36, 75–82, 176; admission of Black students, 82, 169; in contrast to Lincoln, 18, 22; and *Gaines*,

Index

72–82, 85; journalism program of, 8, 31, 84, 86–87; nonwhite, non-Black students at, 86; School of Law, 72–73, 76, 80, 104
University of North Carolina, 110, 118, 119, 125; Black efforts to attend, 101–5, 123; Black faculty at, 128; desegregation of, 43–48, 167–68; Law School, 123; School of Medicine, 117; nonwhite, non-Black students at, 8; racism at, 104
University of North Carolina System, 173; Board of Governors, 174
University of Notre Dame, 139
University of Oklahoma, 59, 145–46; Board of Regents, 147–48, 157; College of Law, 144, 147, 150–52, 156; desegregation of, 147–48, 154–55, 157, 159; internal segregation at, 154–55, 156
University of Paris, 6
University of Pennsylvania, 27, 58, 60, 67, 119, 122, 152
University of Pittsburgh, 67
University of South Carolina, 173, 206n19
University of Southern California, 118
University of Tennessee, 82–84, 161, 175–76
University of Texas, 158; desegregation of, 159; Law School, 129, 144, 157; Medical School, 127; School of Dentistry, 4
University of the District of Columbia, 111
University of Virginia, 59–61, 69, 169; Curry School of Education, 169; desegregation of, 169
University of Wisconsin, 9, 26, 93, 99, 113–15, 170
US Agency for International Development, 115
US Court of Appeals for the District of Columbia Circuit, 61
US Department of Health, Education and Welfare, Civil Rights Office of, 173
US Department of Health and Human Services, 134
US Foreign Service, 115

US District Court for the Eastern District of Kentucky, 96–97, 99
US District Court for the Eastern District of Virginia, 177
US District Court for the Northern District of Alabama, 142
US House of Representatives, and regional education, 163
US Olympic Committee, 116
US Steel Corporation, 139
US Supreme Court. *See* Supreme Court, US

Vashon High School (MO), 73
Vessels, Alma, 162
Vicksburg, MS, 120, 171
Vilsack, Thomas, 175
Vinson, Fred, 159
Virginia, 3, 6, 10, 11, 12, 23, 59, 61, 62, 117, 119, 143, 161, 176–77; creation of segregation scholarships in, 60; partnership with Meharry Medical College, 161, 163
Virginia General Assembly, 176
Virginia State College. *See* Virginia State University
Virginia State University, 26, 33, 51, 59, 61, 119, 162, 169, 188n70; creation of graduate programs at, 60
Virginia Union University, 59, 61, 99
vouchers, 176–77

Wagoner County, OK, 37
Walden University, 160
Walker, James Robert, 123, 167
Walker, LeRoy T., 116
Walker, Madame C. J., 80
Walker, Maggie Laura, 117
Walker, Maggie Lena, 117
Walker, Robert, 171
Walker, Vanessa Siddle, 122
Washington, DC, 65, 67, 75, 99, 130, 139, 150
Washington Duke Hotel, 45
Washington University (MO), 35
Wayne State University, 170

Websters Grove, MO, 35
Wells, Ira James Kohath, 26–27
Wentz Memorial Congregational Church, 103
Wesley, Charles H., 29
West Charlotte High School (NC), 122
Western Kentucky Industrial School, 64, 68
Western Reserve University. *See* Case Western Reserve University
West Virginia, 3, 23–27, 44, 60, 66, 88–90, 161; creation of segregation scholarships in, 24; desegregation of public postbaccalaureate programs, 73–88
West Virginia Colored Institute. *See* West Virginia State University
West Virginia Legislature, 88; and regional education, 161; and segregation scholarships, 24, 26
West Virginia State College. *See* West Virginia State University
West Virginia State University, 24, 25, 26, 36, 39, 73, 88–89, 93, 109, 141
West Virginia University: and desegregation of graduate education, 88–90, 93, 127; and regional education, 161; graduate programs at, 24, 26, 88; racism at, 90
White, Walter, 43–44, 93, 108
white hostility, to Black education, 7, 8, 10, 19, 49, 163, 176–77; and discontinuation of academic program, 87; and poor treatment in classroom, 10, 131; and paltry funding to Black colleges, 18, 22, 29–30, 49–50, 54, 55, 60–61, 136, 145, 159, 167–68; and threats of violence, 55, 104, 170–71, 175–77

white supremacy: and Black educational choices, 18–19; segregation scholarships as tool of, 14–15
Wilberforce University, 63, 91–92, 111
Wilkie, Harold, 87
Wilkins, Roy, 85
Williams, Allen, 82
Williams, Ben T., 149
Williams, Georg W., 26–27
Williams College, 128
Wilmington, NC, 117
Wilson, George D., 172
Wilson, Henry S., 172
Wilson, NC, 106–7
Winston-Salem, NC, 102, 103, 116
Winston-Salem State University, 39
Wisconsin, 114
Withers, John, 112–15
Woodson, Carter G., 6
World War I, 39, 48, 91
World War II, 5, 38, 83, 91, 119, 129, 137, 138, 146, 147, 152, 160, 163; impact of, on academic programs, 87; impact of, on Black workforce, 33; segregated army during, 115; and tuition benefits for veterans, 115, 124, 143, 162
Wright, Milton S. J., 6
Wrighten, John Howard, 201n34

Xavier University, 5, 99

Yale University, Law School, 105
Yancey, D'Arcey, 107
Yancey, Maude J., 106–7
Young, Whitney, Jr., 93
Young, Whitney, Sr., 94